Introducing
More Books

Introducing More Books
A Guide for the Middle Grades

by
Diana L. Spirt

R. R. Bowker Company
New York & London, 1978

To JARRON

Published by R. R. Bowker Company
1180 Avenue of the Americas, New York, N.Y. 10036
Copyright © 1978 by Diana L. Spirt
All rights reserved
Printed and bound in the United States of America

Library of Congress Cataloging in Publication Data
Spirt, Diana L
  Introducing more books.
  Includes indexes.
  1. Children's literature—Bibliography.
2. Books and reading for children. I. Title.
Z1037.S758 [PN1009.A1] 028.52 78-13490 ✓
ISBN 0-8352-0988-1

Contents

Foreword

PROVIDING READING guidance to children in the middle grades is satisfying hard work. It is at this stage that young readers not only expect you to give good advice, they will accept it and act on it and report back to you on exactly how well your readers' advisory skills met their needs.

Those needs are seldom precisely expressed. Most often, the request for help comes in the form of a vague statement along the lines of, "I need another good book like this one. . . ." "This" may refer to plot, subject, genre, or theme and because the request for guidance is quite personal, it calls on all the skills in personal service as well as all the reading background of the guiding adult to arrive at an answer that will prove to be really helpful and fully satisfactory to questing young readers.

Physicians, when faced with a similarly vague request for diagnosis from their patients, are not expected to deliver an instant response. While their patients haul themselves off the examination tables and fumble back into their clothes, the doctors retreat to their reference shelves and prepare to reappear as the founts of all wisdom. Lawyers are also prone to doing their research out of sight.

In making the best use of *Introducing More Books*, I would urge librarians and teachers not to hide the fact from youngsters that they are turning to a helpful book in order to be of help to them. Although the young may attribute heroic stature and encyclopedic knowledge to those who can stand still and instantly reel off a string of titles easily associated with their "just-like-this-one's," a silent lesson is taught and reinforced by openly consulting a source such as this—it demonstrates that there really are books at every age and stage that can help you on your way. It is the most important lesson that *Introducing More Books* has to teach.

The easy association of related titles on similar topics and themes comes with long experience, a constant effort at remembering, and close attention to the reactions of young readers. It is the suggested related materials appended to the description and discussion of the books included here that I value the most in the author's carefully organized approach to introducing children to books.

Special notice should be taken of this approach for the aid it can give to adults trying to individualize reading guidance from what are, after all, general collections of books. At the beginning of each group of titles reflecting the developmental goals of middle childhood, there is a brief, nondirective, gently uninsistent reminder of what factors go into these goals, how they relate to other ages and stages of development, and the ways in which children respond to books and indicate their reading preferences. These are short and stout supports for inexperienced librarians or teachers and quick refreshers for warriors grown weary in long battles against unpracticed or habitually unused reading skills.

Within each developmental goal group, there is a wide range of suggested titles—wide ranging in terms of the reading skills to be encountered among 8 to 14-year-olds as well as in terms of levels of complexity in content. This book cannot supply the assessment of reading skills or the developmental profiles of the youngsters who require some guidance, but after you have supplied that, it can help you to some recent books that have a good track record among other young readers whose reported reactions played a part in the selection of the titles included. It is this aspect of *Introducing More Books* that has made its predecessor successful among librarians and teachers, and earned it a reputation for reliability as an aid to the preparation of book talks that work with audiences of young readers.

The preparation and presentation of effective book talks is in the same rank of difficulty as clear writing and coherent public speaking. No matter how often you do these things, no matter how successful your past efforts may have been, each successive attempt requires study, preparation, and rehearsal. As complete and straightforward as the plot descriptions of the titles suggested here are, as acute as the analyses of content and theme are, and as shrewd as the suggested titles for related materials are, book talk presenters would be ill-advised to lift these in toto and offer them as is to a young audience. But, after you have selected the titles you will present, and after reading and rereading the titles you select, *Introducing More Books* offers a handy guide to the basic elements that go into the necessarily personal mix that helps produce the sort of talk that spurs young people to want to read what you have talked about.

The last chapter of *Introducing More Books* is called "Appreciating Books." What comes through with strength from the first chapter to the last is that we are fortunate in our field to have in the author one of the effective energetic appreciators, helping to identify the books that start— and keep—youngsters reading.

Much is made, and justifiably so, of the necessity for librarians and teachers working with children and books to sharpen their critical book evaluation skills. Too often, in delineating the factors essential to evaluation and the degrees of skill that measure critical capacity, it is forgotten or de-emphasized that the ability to appreciate a book for what it is worth is the highest level to which book selectors can or should aspire. The author has a long record of achievement at this, which she has carried the extra, hard step further; she shares what she has learned and knows with her fellow teachers and librarians in the conviction that children and young people will ultimately benefit from the continuum of effort involved. It is the unmeasurable leap of faith that keeps us all going—it is what *Introducing More Books* is all about: helping young people to help themselves through books.

LILLIAN N. GERHARDT
Editor-in-Chief
School Library Journal

June 21, 1978

Preface

USING THE WORDS of *Introducing Books* (Bowker, 1970) is tempting, but I shall not because this companion volume makes its own unique contribution as a reading guide for the middle grades. Since introducing books to young people from the ages of 8 to 15 is as vital as it has always been, it is comforting to note that anywhere you go people seem to be reading—paperbacks on conveyances, hardcovers in homes. We must be doing something right. Let's keep it up!

There can be little doubt that our electric environment tugs at a youngster's time. However, there is the saving grace that "the golden hours of childhood" are long hours (longer than most adults can even remember). That together with a youngster's strong interest in reading about and working through the difficulties of childhood give adults an opportunity to encourage reading. We are too often concerned with the doomsayer's gloomy predictions about reading—and everything else. Helpful adults— parents, teachers, librarians—can continue to deflect some of our youngsters' time toward reading by introducing deserving books that will appeal to them. Hopefully, *Introducing More Books* will help the person who is working in a junior high school, an elementary school, or a public library to give book talks and other types of reading guidance. Although each title in this volume will speak directly to some, they all reflect the wide range of conceptualization, readability, and interest levels that exists among young people. The majority are for ages 9 to 14.

In this volume, there are plot summaries of 72 books, which together with the 6 or 7 related materials suggested for reading, viewing, or listening make a listing of almost 500 titles. The titles have been carefully read and put under an appropriate developmental goal for middle childhood. These goals are based on the previous work plus added research in the field. For example, Lawrence Kohlberg's book on moral character growth and David Elkind's work on reading have been incorporated. In the process, there has been some rewording and condensation, primarily by including thought abstraction in the goal of appreciating books and the goal of reading for fun. That goal has assumed its rightful place within each goal. The goals also serve as chapter headings: (1) Getting Along in the Family, (2) Making Friends, (3) Developing Values, (4) Understanding Physical and Emotional Problems, (5) Forming a View of the World, (6) Respecting Living Creatures, (7) Understanding Social Problems, (8) Identifying Adult Roles, and (9) Appreciating Books.

Each of the main titles is divided into these sections:

1. *Plot Summary.*   The story is summarized emphasizing the important characters and situations and hopefully retaining some of the author's flavor. Brief references to the author and illustrator, as well as age appeal, are given in the beginning paragraphs.

2. *Thematic Analysis.*   Both main and subthemes are stated to encourage multiple uses in presenting the title.

3. *Discussion Materials.*   Various ways of introducing the book are suggested. Pages and illustrations that are suitable for reading aloud, describing or displaying, book talking, or discussing are also given.

4. *Related Materials.*   Included are books and audiovisual titles on similar themes or topics that may interest the same readers.

As a first step in the selection process, a poll was made of the reading preferences of children and their teachers and librarians. The results were compared with bibliographies and selection aids. A heavy reliance on reviewing magazines kept the content as current as possible. Relating the theme of the book to the appropriate developmental goal, however, was the ultimate criterion. Throughout the process, "Many were named, but few were chosen." The process was long and hard and finally subjective, although based on sage advice—"No book is worth reading at age 10 that isn't worth reading at age 50." The final choices represent an amalgam of the most popular books of the finest literary quality, as well as a sample of different reading levels, in children's literature since the early 1970s.

Also included in this book are: an index of biographical information on the authors and illustrators; a title-author-illustrator index of all the titles; and a subject index that lists the main titles under conventional topics, such as Animal Stories. The subject index also contains an Easy Reading category.

This volume is meant, as was the first, to help librarians and teachers to recall the books they know and encourage them to read these titles and many others. It is also meant to suggest titles and encourage their use by adults to stimulate youngsters' reading and enjoyment.

This book is dedicated to my older daughter. All my own children are too busy with their own adult lives to help with more than their sustaining love: Deirdre graduated from college during the writing; Stephen finished his first year in private psychiatric practice as this goes to the printer; and Jarron and Jim got married while the final selections were being made.

For faith Pat Schuman who inaugurated the work and Judy Garodnick who saw it to completion deserve the "Patient Griselda" award for bearing with me. To production editor Iris Topel and others who saw the book from manuscript to pages, my thanks. My thanks also to my several research assistants through the lengthy preparation: Ilene Baker, Roy Vitters, Leslie Tobias, and Garrett Farr. To my strong right arm and typist, Dorothy Dowd, my deep appreciation.

Finally, however, it is to all of you and your millions of children that I owe a debt of gratitude. Let this be an installment payment.

DIANA L. SPIRT, Professor
Children's Books and Materials
Palmer Graduate Library School
C. W. Post College/Long Island University
Greenvale, New York

June 20, 1978

1

Getting Along in the Family

THE MIDDLE YEARS of childhood provide the youngster with an opportunity to integrate biological changes and social experiences. Spanning the turbulence of infancy and puberty, the years can be deceptively quiescent. Nonetheless, a youngster in the middle grades is undergoing continual internal development for which a special sort of guidance and understanding is needed.

Although adults expect children to be fairly self-sufficient by school age, the age at which independence is reached fluctuates widely. Some children may be dependent on a mother or surrogate mother long beyond infancy, while others may resolve this problem with dispatch. The majority, however, will continue to need the reassurance that being a valued member of a family unit gives. Successful venturing outside the home, whether in school, city, or world, has its genesis in the child's developmental growth in an environment in which the children can explore their own worth.

Because of this, family stories have always been valuable for this age group. In today's society with its many different types of families, the stories assume even greater importance in order to allow the child to reflect on her or his place in the broad range of humanity.

The books in this chapter show youngsters in a variety of family situations from traditional to modern to alternate. They also explore the range of needs of children who are striving to be adequate.

Vera Cleaver and Bill Cleaver, *Dust of the Earth*
Lippincott, 1975, $7.95; pap., New Am. Lib., 1977, $1.25

From the desk of two well-known authors comes this title about growing up, one in their long procession of popular children's books. Narrated by 14-year-old Fern who is opinionated, argumentative, and a mite philosophical, the story covers the year that Jenny and North Drawn move

1

their family to Chokecherry, South Dakota. Although Grandfather Bacon long ago had sent the young Jenny to live with his divorced wife in Kansas City and subsequently called Jenny's husband and family the dust of the earth, he bequeathed Jenny his house and sheep ranch. The book explores the family, its members, and crises in the fateful year during which Fern's view of her family changes from that of a child to that of an adult, with the recognition that the bonds and love in a family grow stronger as each member's understanding deepens. Together with the information about sheep raising, the characterizations of the central characters are especially noteworthy. The book is written in the Cleavers' unique and readable style. Young people between the ages of 11 and 14 will find the story and background absorbing.

Fern had spent the earlier part of her 14 years accepting the lonesomeness of being human and the mandate to either hide the loneliness or get rid of it. She recognizes the peculiarities of her family members: father, North Drawn, a quiet accountant; mother, Jenny, who despite being a grown woman longs to dwell again in her remembered father's house; brother, Hobson, 16-year-old living replica of Grandpa Bacon; sister, Madge, an 8-year-old who wants to make a marriage-match for Fern; and the 3-year-old baby, Georgie, who eats from a high chair and likes to play a piano. Fern is convinced that Grandfather Bacon's estimate of the Drawns is right.

Some of Fern's fondest memories come from her friendship with the sheepherder Ash Puck Joe, who is also a Native American. It is he and his family whom she will miss most as they prepare to leave for Jenny's inheritance—her father's house in Chokecherry, South Dakota. The Drawns head east through the Black Hills in an old Ford. After getting lost in a canyon and passing for 4 days through tumbleweed country, they receive the greatest shock when they see their house and rundown ranch. Nell Parrott, a temporary caretaker, shows them around the house, barn, sheds and corral, shows them the small flock, and introduces them to the horse, Ned, and Clyde, the collie sheep dog. She tells Fern that in spite of what they see, they have the beginnings of a good flock.

However, an influenza epidemic lays low everyone but Fern. Once they recover, Hobson says he is going to school to be somebody. Fern decides that she is going to tend the sheep and build up the flock. While Hob and Madge ride Ned 6 miles to the town of Chokecherry to go to school, Fern learns the techniques of herding sheep. As autumn passes, Fern dreams of marrying a rich old man to escape the drudgery, while Madge tries to help out by making a match for the 14-year-old with a retired new neighbor,

Colonel Harbuck. Meanwhile, Hobson, who both fears his father may lose his precariously held job at the Chokecherry bank and feels uneasy because Fern is doing the hard work, quits school to help build a money-making flock.

The holidays arrive with all the expected cold weather problems. Around Thanksgiving, Hobson convinces Fern that they should take the sheep wagon to the grazing countryside to stay put for a few days at a time. Unfortunately, a sudden tornado destroys the wagon and forces them to drive the sheep back and forth to pasture once again. At Christmas time, Clyde is savagely attacked by marauding grass wolves who raid the sheds at night and kill ewes. The thaw from the February chinook temporarily brings hope. Even the late blizzard fury brings joy with the birth of a new sister, Ruth Patience. The problems culminate, however, when Papa loses his job.

In a family "pow-wow," the Drawns strengthen their determination to make their ranch a successful business. With Colonel Harbuck who arranges to sell the wool at a good price, the Drawns start shearing the lambs. Everyone contributes to the effort. Jenny helps with a difficult birth when spring lambing follows. Fern looks back on their first year and realizes something new about her family. "We will persist because we are the heritors of this land and its spirit" (p. 158). As the second fall arrives, Hobson goes off to Kansas City to fulfill his dream of schooling; Fern looks at the family's valley saturated with sunlight and sees the members clearly through adult eyes.

Thematic Analysis

A change in the way children learn to look at their childhood and family as they become more mature is the theme that is well stated: "Why must kids, always before sunk in·self, but now done with childhood affairs, always phrase themselves as prophets." Implicit in this is learning to understand yourself and other members of the family. The theme of survival is also an important secondary theme, made vital by the forceful scenes of nature. The background of eastern South Dakota—one of the less populous states—gives the young reader a good understanding of the landscape of the country.

Discussion Materials

The story can be introduced and the title explained by reading about the Drawns (p. 18). Amplify it by adding Fern's final verdict, "Take the dust of the earth away and much of our rain and sun would go. And clouds and fog and mists . . . it is dust that . . . scatter's the earth's and sky's color rays" (pp. 155–156). Describe the humorous "dog stew" scene that opens the book (pp. 14–16). Bridge to life on the sheep ranch which can be dramatically described in the following episodes: sheep in distress (pp. 72–75); shearing (pp. 140–142); lambing (pp. 147–156). Some of the scenes of Fern and the dog, Clyde, on the range with the sheep also instructive and full of adventure.

Related Materials

Many of the Cleavers' earlier titles will also be enjoyed: *Me Too* (Lippincott, 1973; pap., New Am. Lib., 1975); *Delpha Green and Company* (Lippincott, 1972; pap., Lippincott, 1972 and New Am. Lib., 1976); *I Would Rather Be a Turnip* (Lippincott, 1971; pap., New Am. Lib., 1976); and others. Three filmstrips can also be used. Two of them are about females: one historically set, *Women in the American Revolution* (Multi-Media, 1975) and one contemporary, *Veronica Ganz* (from the Famous Fiction Multimedia series, Insight Media Programs, 1976). The third, about the outdoors, is *Camping* (from Outdoor Education, The Great American Film Factory, 1975). Chester Aaron's book *Spill* (Atheneum, 1977) follows a California ranch family as they struggle to keep an oil spill from ruining their water supply. *The Freewheeling of Joshua Cobb* (Farrar, 1974) by Margaret Hodges tells about a summer bicycle trip of young adults and will appeal to older readers. Younger readers will enjoy Norma Klein's *Confessions of an Only Child* (Pantheon, 1974; pap., Dell, 1975), which describes 9-year-old Antonia's acceptance of a new baby brother.

Ellen Conford, *Felicia the Critic*
Illus. by Arvis Stewart. Little, 1973, $5.95

This popular children's author tells an amusing school and family life story about a brash heroine who is a talented, but tactless, critic. With the same sure powers of observation and understanding that her earlier titles show, Ellen Conford draws real youngsters in action. The story indicates that difficulty in getting along at home may well carry over to school and other spheres in life. The resolution is realistic for the age portrayed and the present state of our knowledge about human behavior.

The 5 illustrations and jacket design of Felicia and her girl friends are reminiscent of Nonny Hogrogian's drawings in *Sam, Bangs and*

Moonshine. Youngsters from the age of 8 to 13 will relate to or remember being like the characters in this easy-to-read book. Less able readers will be propelled by the humor.

Felicia, who lives in Plainville with her mother, father, and 13-year-old sister Marilyn, is wholly absorbed in her family and girl friends and in correcting everyone's deficiencies. Although she is only about 8, Felicia, a smart and outspoken youngster, finds the morning radio weather reports consistently inaccurate and tells everyone so. Each chapter opens with a radio weather report.

After her opening salvo about the radio report, Felicia meets her best friend, Cheryl, to go to school and immediately bawls her out for being late. Later over lunch, Felicia, Cheryl, and 3 other friends discuss forming a club. It is obvious to Felicia, however, that she is being excluded. At home she tells her appearance-conscious older sister that her "Concord grape" nail polish reminds her of Dracula. Mrs. Kirshenbaum tells Marilyn to remove the polish; she informs Felicia that she should recognize the difference between truth and opinion and use only constructive criticism.

An extremely well-organized person, Felicia decides to make lists of constructive suggestions to offer when the occasion demands. Nevertheless, she walks a tightrope because she has not yet learned how to offer suggestions. Felicia goes from bad to worse as she: tells a school crossing guard what to do, thereby causing a traffic jam; takes a pot roast about which her mother complained back to Shopwise, forcing Arnold Kirshenbaum to take the family out to supper; "reviews" aunt Celeste's latest juvenile book casting a deadly silence on the family dinner; calls the radio to announce over the air that they have made a two-degree mistake in Plainville's temperature and receives the label "Pest of the Year" from Marilyn. The delayed good results—five other phone calls verifying her temperature claim and a letter of apology containing $4.00 for her mother—come too slowly. To help make amends to Marilyn, Felicia gives her a list of desirable new first names to help Marilyn in her quest for glamor. When Marilyn announces at the dinner table that henceforth she is Desiree Kirshenbaum, her father is nonplussed. Felicia is happy because the name is from her list. Meanwhile, Cheryl proves herself a staunch friend by promising not to join a club unless Felicia is also asked.

Nothing is really changed, however, as cousin Josh's wedding proves. Felicia unhappily tells the bride's mother how to correct the dissatisfactions of Table 14, the children's table, for another time: use a microphone in the chapel; serve cake for the children; and do not put the children's table directly next to the band.

Felicia finally takes to heart one of the stipulations of her new club membership and decides not to give any more recommendations unless asked. This new resolve carries her through the first meeting of the Five F's (Friendly, Fabulous, Funny, Fearless, and Frank) when everyone else is elected to an office. Cheryl objects and Felicia becomes the elected sergeant at arms. Withholding suggestions is hard, especially when the Five F's decide to hold a fund-raising outdoor carnival in the winter which Felicia realizes dooms it. Nevertheless she keeps her own counsel. The total profit from the affair is $2.25 because of a heavy snowstorm and the resulting mayhem. Adding insult to injury, the girls are annoyed because Felicia didn't tell them what might go wrong. Her growing awareness is evident in her only comment, ". . . a good idea, only maybe in the summer." Her final act, however, shows she has far to go. Felicia writes a couple of suggestions to the President, "to help you run the country a little better."

Thematic Analysis

The relationship between freely giving your opinions and upsetting others' feelings is explored here as a vital part of getting along well in your family. The need for a degree of tact in treating others as well as the emotional peril to oneself if tact is not exhibited is shown concretely. This familial dependence is extended to close friends as well. As a corollary, the book suggests that truth generally prevails, but that the personal cost must be borne if that is what one pursues.

Discussion Materials

Introduce Felicia and the nature of her problem by using the illustration on the jacket. Tell how, because of her critical nature, her family problems culminate in the wedding scene (picture p. 106; ch. 7). Some of the background and material on the Club can also be used (p. 112; ch. 8) singly or together with the final catastrophe, Carnival (p. 135; ch. 9). A conversation on people's feelings might also be useful.

Related Materials

Any of the author's earlier books will be enjoyed: *Impossible Possum* (Little, 1971); *Why Can't I Be William?* (Little, 1972); *Dreams of Victory* (Little, 1973; pap., Dell, 1974). *Truth and Consequences* (Scholastic Bk. Services, 1975; pap., 1976) by Miriam Young is a good companion volume. For readers of the same age group both *Naomi in the Middle* (Dial, 1974) by Norma Klein and *Isabelle the Itch* (Viking, 1973; pap., Dell, 1974) by Constance Greene are suggested. Audiovisual titles related to the theme are the 16mm films *Is It Always Right to Be Right?* (Bosustow) and *Learning Values with Fat Albert and the Cosby Kids* (4 films distributed by McGraw-Hill), particularly *What Is a Friend?*

Constance C. Greene, *Beat the Turtle Drum*
Illus. by Donna Diamond. Viking, 1976, $5.95

> O'dance along the silver sand
> And beat the turtle drum
> That youth may last forever
> And sorrow never come

This profilic author has fashioned a moving tale from the tragedy of a younger sister's death and set it to a stanza from a poem by Ian Serraillier (Oxford Univ. Press, 1968). Well known for her perceptive stories about preadolescent concerns, Constance Greene, in a spare style that becomes lyrical at times, recreates the summer when Joss dies and her older sister, Kate, learns to cope with the loss.

The illustrator captures the heightened essence of memories that accompany grief in the pencil drawings that precede the 4 chapters bearing the names of the fateful summer months. Each chapter is drawn from the perspective of Kate looking out the window at the shed (May), the horse (June), the empty yard (July), and the apple tree (August). The latter signifies the acceptance of death and the passing of grief. The book jacket in pastel shades of apple green and lavender has a cameo insert of the two sisters in the tree on the front and Joss smiling in the center of a medallion of leaves on the back. The stipling and shading techniques used in the illustrations underscore the indefinable quality of grief. Youngsters from 8 to 14 will appreciate this poignant story.

In a small Connecticut town near Westport, Joss, who is usually calm and collected, spends the entire month of May daydreaming about renting a horse for her eleventh birthday in June. Thirteen-year-old Kate, a dreamer and budding poet, can't get over the obsessive quality of her younger sister's fervent hope for a horse. She watches as Joss rides her bike regularly to the Essig stable to make arrangements to bring Prince to the backyard for a week, makes friends with blowsy Mrs. Essig, tries unsuccessfully to build a horse shelter with the help of her young friends, and finally in desperation promises her father the first ride on Prince if he'll keep the automobile out of the garage for a week.

June arrives, and with it Joss's birthday and presents: a heart-shaped rock from 8-year-old Tootie, a slightly retarded and adoring neighbor; a pin with a horse on it from Mrs. Essig; the hoped-for check from grandma; and Prince. The horse's arrival in the backyard for a week precedes the family's birthday supper and more presents for the equestrienne. Joss is up early the next few mornings riding and giving rides, polishing and currying, and shoveling a pile of manure for next year's garden. Even the complaint of Miss Pemberthy, a neighbor, cannot dim this supreme adventure.

As a treat during this week, Kate packs a picnic lunch for the two to share up in the apple tree. Before climbing up, Joss ties Prince to a nearby tree and kisses him on the nose. The next thing Kate remembers is a branch cracking, Joss falling, and Kate calling to the crumpled figure on the ground, "There, there, it's going to be all right." But, Joss is dead. Kate thinks sadly later that Joss had once told her matter-of-factly that when her imaginery childhood playmate, Jean-Pierre, left, Joss couldn't get him back, and he didn't even say goodbye.

The rest of June and the month of July become a painful blur of scenes of the police coming, Prince being taken back to the stable, Tootie hovering forlornly about, her parents mourning, and going to the funeral. Although Joss seemed to be smiling in death, Kate continues to feel guilty about the picnic and has vain regrets at not saying goodbye. Kate and her family are griefstricken.

The rest of the summer is a jumble of events and memories: Joss's empty bed; a letter from her teacher, Mrs. Mahoney; a condolence visit from Miss Pemberthy. By the end of August, however, she realizes that her two most treasured memories of Joss are her sister's eyes and lovely odor. Finally, after rereading Mrs. Mahoney's letter, Kate can say, "Yes if I have a daughter, I'll name her Joss. Right now it hurts."

Thematic Analysis

The recognition that the death of a close family member is painful but that the grief can be surmounted is important in this unsentimental story about two sisters. A secondary theme of sharing and appreciation of differences among family members is also stressed. The fondness that many youngsters, especially preadolescent girls, exhibit toward horses is also central in developmental growth.

Discussion Materials

An introduction to the story can be woven by displaying the drawings that precede each of the 4 chapters and explaining how each relates to

Kate's remembrance of the death of her younger sister, Joss. The Serraillier verse or Kate's own poem of loss (end of book) can also serve as an introduction or conclusion to the preceding introduction. Joss's birthday morning will describe some of her excitement and anticipation (p. 56). Her thoughts on death can also be used to demonstrate her healthy 11-year-old nature (pp. 11–15). An episode that will explain some of what Kate learns about people and facing death is covered in her delivery of a package to Miss Pemberthy (pp. 27–30).

Related Materials

Another book by the same author, *I Know You, Al* (Viking, 1975; pap., Dell, 1977)—a sequel to *A Girl Called Al*—has a heroine of about the same age. Elizabeth Winthrop's *A Little Demonstration of Affection* (Harper, 1975; pap., Dell, 1977) deals with an older brother and sister who turn to each other for comfort and affection; this suits better and sophisticated readers. For younger readers the conflict caused by a little girl's birthday, an unexpected visitor, and the unhappiness of finding a dead sparrow is gently resolved in picture book format in *The Birthday Visitor* (Scribner, 1975) by Yoshiko Uchida. The filmstrips in the series *Death and Dying: Closing the Circle* (Guidance Association, 3 strips and 3 cassettes) can be used if the youngsters are prepared to view the material individually or with a group leader. Another filmstrip, *The Velveteen Rabbit* (Miller-Brody Productions), with illustrations augmented from the original book by Margery Sharp, gives expression to the theme of renewed life sustained by love. The recording (Miller-Brody L512) read by Eva Le Gallienne is also effective alone.

Virginia Hamilton, *Arilla Sun Down*
Greenwillow, 1976, $7.95

This award-winning author is noted for her sensitive perceptions and lyrical prose style that both conveys a mood and message and demands the reader's involvement. In return, there is an unstated guarantee that the book will be long remembered. This book opens with a remembered dream fragment and retains that dream quality interspersed with vibrant scenes of action. The story concerns a Native American-Black family of four who struggle to come to terms with their interracial ethnic heritage in this society. Each has a personal solution; however, 12-year-old Arilla's development as a family member and individual is uppermost.

The full-color jacket painting that shows the profile of the dark-haired Arilla in a collage with an Indian pony emphasizes one of the conflicts of this interracial child. The book will be appreciated by good readers of ages 10 to 14. It can be read aloud a chapter at a time to the intermediate age for units on minorities in social studies or in the language arts and literature classes.

Arilla is perplexed by the members of her family and the society around her. "The People" as they have traditionally named themselves are now known as Native Americans to the white majority in the United States, and called Amerinds by each other. Although this situation is confusing to the thoughtful girl, it doesn't seem to bother her handsome older brother, Jack Sun Run Adams, who considers himself a Native American. Sun Run wears his Amerind name as proudly and well as he rides his magnificent horse. Unfortunately, Arilla mistakes Sun Run's stoicism toward his mixed heritage for personal dislike and silently hates him in retaliation. She also regrets not having an Amerind name as her father and Jack do.

Her Black mother, Lilly Perry Adams, former dancer and owner of a dancing school, is well respected in the community and obviously able to accommodate to the practical affairs of her family. Although Lilly tries to instill confidence and an acceptance of her mixed blood in her daughter, Arilla identifies with remembered scenes of sledding when she was very young with her father and of his deep need to sustain his heritage through occasional visits to his old haunts.

The family throw a fourth of July birthday party for Arilla and give her a Palouse mare (for pictures of an Indian pony, see *Lone Bull's Horse Raid* in "Related Materials"). The gift of the pony, Running Moon, triggers another dream memory of a time when her brother left her and an elderly shaman, James False Face, found her and took her to the Shy Woman, his old wife, Suzanne. The memory is both painful and pleasant because James False Face, in the secret tradition of The People whispered in her ear so that none might know her real name, Wordkeeper. She feels truly Amerind.

After James's traditional and moving funeral, Arilla begins to realize that many of her imaginings exhibit prescience or some of the traditional mysticism of The People. Nevertheless, she also realizes that she cherishes many of the fine ethnic traditions of her mother. Arilla will do her best to fulfill James False Face's prophecy, "One day you will keep my stories, and you will truly be the name I have given you" (p. 6), as well as trying to fulfill the expectations of her mother.

In a venturesome escapade, Arilla goes to the Skateland Rink after dark with Jack and his girl friend, Angel. After an exciting forbidden evening of fun, Arilla begins to feel that Jack is not at all the way she believed him to be and that he is her friend. She is certain of it when they are caught in a dangerous ice storm as they are horseback riding and he manages to get help. Arilla in her newly gained maturity sees that Jack loves her and that they are truly brother and sister. She is finally able to be proud of her interracial heritage and her family in a way that helps to make her a whole person.

Thematic Analysis

Growing up and getting along in a family can be more difficult for some than for others. The theme of this book shows the added difficulty for a sensitive child when the family is interracial and, further, when neither heritage is in the mainstream traditionally. The story demonstrates that the strength of one's heritage can be a powerful influence in bringing one to maturity. The story also stresses individuality and acceptance and that each person has to arrive at a personal decision.

Discussion Materials

Use the jacket cover to set the mood of conflict between two heritages for this interracial child. Emphasize the strength of her Indian heritage and its effect upon Arilla, especially her desire for an Amerind name (pp. 6, 99, 179-180). After introducing Lilly Perry Adams, Sun Stone Adams, and the brother, Sun Run, describe Sun Run's skill in horseback riding and tell about Running Moon, "The Birthday Pony" (pp. 72-98). Make sure the listeners understand Arilla's doubts about her brother's love; describe the ice storm (pp. 189-203) and Arilla's final realization of the mixed blood and deep bond they share (pp. 216-218).

Related Materials

The documentary film *Tomorrow's Yesterday* (Brigham Young, 1971) realistically portrays the Native American in the past and present. The stylized film *Arrow to the Sun* (Texture, 1973) graphically displays the trials of an Indian youth in the search for his father. An 88-page illustrated book, *A Clash of Cultures: Fort Bowie and the Chiricahua Apaches* (Supt. of Docs. S/N 024-005-00661-3, 1977) retells an episode in the tribe's relocation to Florida in 1886 and describes their life-style before the invasion of the white man. *Lone Bull's Horse Raid* (Bradbury, 1973) by Paul and Dorothy Goble is a book about horse raiding among the Plains Indians. There is an excellent bibliography and exceptional, colorful drawings. *Spotted Flower and the Ponokomita* (Westminster, 1977) by K. Folles Cheatham is the authentic story of a Blackfoot girl who introduces her tribe to horses in the eighteenth century; this book will appeal to younger readers.

Norma Klein, *Taking Sides*
Pantheon, 1974, $5.99; pap., Avon, 1976, 95¢

Known for her straightforward expression of the perceptions of childhood, this author has again crafted a story about 2 young children who are forced into the whirlpool of choosing allegiances between divorced parents. The book jacket portrays the theme well: mom and daddy face in opposite directions with thoughtful 12-year-old Nell between them and 5-year-old brother Hugo set in a pale torn fragment beside her. The story, which covers a year of change and growth in the heroine, is a simple one but rich in the understanding the author brings to a problem that is not always restricted to children of divorce. Children, especially girls from 9 to 13, will find the book absorbing and truthful in its descriptive episodes of family living in two-family situations.

Practical and intelligent, Nelda (Nell) Landau faces her twelfth year with some apprehension. She remembers that once long ago before Hugo was born she and mom, a highly paid computer programmer, lived with grandma Rose in Boston because mom and daddy had separated. Now, however, they are divorced and both she and Hugo are to live with daddy. Jake Landau, a free-lance science writer, has moved from his original apartment in New York City into another so that Nell will be nearer to St. Agatha's, a fashionable girl's school, where she is a scholarship student. Although Nell has enjoyed living in the family country home of Greta, her mother's college friend, with Hugo and mom, she likes her daddy best and is secretly pleased to be going to stay with him. After enjoying a glorious summer, she will miss Greta's cat, Tangiers; Mom and Greta's piano–flute duets; and their advice about saying what you think. She will particularly miss writing replies for Rebecca Ingersoll, the pseudonymous Gothic author that is the team of mom and Greta.

On the bus ride to New York City, Nell tries to pacify Hugo, a typical 5-year-old, who misses his adored mommy and lets everyone know it with his cries. Hugo, upset by the trip and the rupture of leaving, resumes his screaming in the new apartment bedroom he and Nell are to share. Although Nell is delighted to see Jake and be called D.D. (Darling Daughter), she is distressed at sharing a room with her baby brother. After a while, the screaming does subside. Noticing the silence, Jake and Nell search and find Hugo asleep in the bathtub with his pillow. Although Willi, Daddy's friend, builds a partition to divide the room as promised, the wall doesn't keep the odor from Hugo's bed-wetting from permeating the room. Nell is further upset to find that Jake doesn't always put on fresh sheets.

Once school starts Nell loses no time in going to see her friends, the McCormmachs. The 5 beautiful girls are models, except for Nell's best friend Heather, who is no longer interested in modeling as a career. During one of Nell's frequent visits Deirdre, the oldest, tells her that she can recommend a fine doctor to fix her nose. Surprised, Nell comments on the remark when she goes to New Jersey the following weekend. Mom points out that Greta has a large nose and talks to Nell who begins to see that large or small the size of one's nose doesn't really matter.

The children spend Thanksgiving in Boston with grandmother Rose. While there Nell visits the Lipkowitz's and renews her friendship with 15-year-old Arlo. When they return to New York City and school, Heather meets Arden Kassoss, a frequent visitor. Over the Christmas holiday which they spend in the country, mom tells Nell that Arden is Jake's girl friend and is insanely rich. As she tries to piece this all together, Nell also observes how comfortable Hugo is with his mommy and with Greta, who seems to manage him better than anyone else. Nell begins to understand that Hugo may also have difficulty taking sides.

Once back in New York City with daddy, Nell goes with Heather on an expedition to a large store and they carefully cut out the fancy labels to put on their own clothes. Both families are horrified and explain that it is wrong to do something like that. Meanwhile, daddy plans a spring vacation in Jamaica for the children and Arden. Nell enjoys it until daddy gets sick and Arden leaves precipitously. Nell packs for their emergency trip home and goes with Hugo to New Jersey while daddy goes to the hospital. Mom tries to comfort Nell by telling her that Jake's brother also had a heart attack in his forties. Mom and Nell travel to New York City together each day and Nell goes from St. Agatha's to her mother's office to wait for the return drive. In May just before Nell's thirteenth birthday, Jake gets out of the hospital and they buy two bikes; one is her birthday present and one is for his new exercise program. He tells Nell that he intends to rent a house for them on Long Island for the month of July, after which she and Hugo can spend August in New Jersey with their vacationing mother.

School ends and Nell, substituting as a favor for Heather, takes a baby-sitting job in a hotel for an evening. Since Arlo comes to town that night, he and Nell both spend the evening baby-sitting. Nell realizes how much she has always liked Arlo when he kisses her. She later confides about it to Heather and they giggle together over their distortion of the old stereotype, "Will I still respect him?" Another stereotype dies when she sees Arden while shopping and realizes that in a few years she won't even recognize her.

Nell's 12-year-old vision of liking daddy better than mom has grown into a more mature affection for both her parents and friends. Nell tries to encourage Hugo to reach a similar understanding by telling him that he would be a bigamist if, as he stoutly maintains, he were to marry mommy and Greta. Hugo thinks about it and with flawless 5-year-old logic intones, "Two a me."

Thematic Analysis

Preferring one parent to the other is a common, if misunderstood, feeling in childhood; it is made more obvious in the case of a divorce where a choice or an accommodation must be made. Treating the situation sympathetically without blaming either the parents or the child is a healthy approach toward helping a child realize that choosing one or the other is unnecessary, as well as unhealthy. Another theme in this contemporary story is the completely natural acceptance of people and life styles and repugnance for the cultural and sexual stereotypes.

Discussion Materials

Use the cover portrait while setting the theme of the story, including liking daddy best (pp. 8-20). Also use the first day with daddy in the new apartment to describe Nell's mixture of elation and disappointment (pp. 23-32). In a lighter vein introduce the McCormmachs (pp. 33-40). If the "big nose" story is emphasized, follow up with mom's explanation to Nell (pp. 51-53). The Boston Thanksgiving visit to Arlo's family relates well (pp. 61-67), as does mom's best Christmas ever (pp. 89-98). Any of these will appeal to youngsters: the labels incident (pp. 100-102); baby-sitting and Arlo (pp. 129-140); the report to Heather (pp. 145-149).

Related Materials

The author's earlier titles, *Confessions of an Only Child* (Pantheon, 1974; pap., Dell, 1975) and *Mom, the Wolfman and Me* (Pantheon, 1972 and Hall, 1973; pap., Avon, 1974, 1977), are suggested. Three other books will please the same audience: *Wings* (Lippincott, 1974; pap., Dell, 1977) by Adrienne Richard; *Me and Mr. Stenner* (Lippincott, 1976) by Evan Hunter; and *The Driftway* (Dutton, 1973) by Penelope Lively. The latter has a young boy as hero. Three 16mm films are also appropriate: *The Fable of He and She* (LCA); *Separated Parents* (Current Affairs Films); and *First It Seemed Kinda Strange* (Films, Inc.). The latter has a male hero.

Peggy Mann, *There Are Two Kinds of Terrible*
Doubleday, 1977, $5.95

In two of her earlier books for children, this award-winning author whose work has been shown on television wrote about improving the environment of an urban street and adjusting to divorce between parents. Here she tells simply about a mother's unexpected death and the reaction of the bereaved husband and the young son. The writing is as sharp as the feelings of grief that it describes. With her unusual insight and economical style, the author builds an irrevocable loss into a positive statement of life.

The jacket design by Mike McIver graphically delineates the young protagonist's sense of aloneness. Many 8- to 13-year-olds will find this easy-to-read story poignant.

In just about the same time that it takes the earth to make one revolution around the sun, 12-year-old Robert Farley learns firsthand that there are two kinds of terrible. The first, which he calls "regular terrible" because it has an end, happens to Robbie when he falls off his bike while riding with his best friend Tom Judson. Robbie spends the next 8 days in the hospital in pain after the operation to fit a metal plate into the bone in his right arm. Although Susan, his adoring mother, visits regularly and his father, a busy CPA, comes when he can, it was a terrible time. Not even receiving aunt Emily's package from Muncie, Indiana, helps. Robbie, encased in a cast, spends the summer longing desperately to play the snare drum which Susan gave him for his birthday in April, even though dad hates noise.

Fall finally arrives and with it renewed hopes for founding a band called "The Robs." Robbie notices, however, that his mother and father are arguing behind closed doors. Suddenly, Susan tells Robbie to take his house key to school because she is going to be in the hospital overnight for tests. Upset, Robbie cooks dad's supper and talks to his mom over the phone. When he finds out later that she has had an operation and keeps calling him "pumpkin"—his baby name—Robbie knows something serious is happening. To make matters worse, father and son are like two strangers. Finally, breaking down, Reginald Farley tells his son that Susan faces imminent death from a virulent form of cancer. He warns Robbie to prepare for the worst during the visit he arranges. When Susan sends Robbie from the hospital room because of her great pain, both Farleys cry on the ride home.

Aunt Emily arrives to help a few days before Susan dies. When Robbie is told of her death, he becomes hysterical in hopeless frustration and cries out to his father, "Why did you let her die?" Robbie's anger at losing his mother directs all his actions; he goes resentfully through the wake at the funeral parlor and flees the graveside wondering why he is being punished.

Aunt Emily goes home after telling Robbie that his father and mother argued because she wouldn't go to the doctor when she first felt pain. It occurs finally to Robbie that his father also adored Susan. Eventually, the father and son talk. Robbie feels so relieved that he goes to the father's bedroom to continue and discovers him asleep with a lighted cigarette. Scared, Robbie yells at him; stunned Mr. Farley slaps him. Robbie retaliates by punching his father in the stomach.

Under the father's pillow in the forlorn house, Robbie finds Susan's wedding picture album. He finally realizes how selfish he has been; he lost the dearest mother any 12-year-old could have, his father a lifetime mate. That evening Robbie expresses his love to his father in a note. The next morning he finds a poignant thank you and the following evening a surprise set of drums that Susan had earmarked in a catalog for Robbie. Although an important person in their life is gone forever, the father and son because of their shared grief have established a new and vital bond.

Thematic Analysis

The difficulty of grieving for a parent and relating well to the one who remains is deftly treated as the unifying theme. Within the plot the author has shown concretely that in order to accomplish this herculean task there is need for an understanding of the vulnerability of others. Other strands, such as the comfort of friends in times of sorrow and the ability to be less egocentric, are also well stated.

Discussion Materials

A retelling of the idea behind the title as expressed by Robbie gives an overview (p. 61). "There are two kinds of terrible . . . the second kind has no end." Paraphrase the episode of Robbie's accident and broken arm (pp. 2–6). Also discuss youngsters' personal experiences with hospitals. A description of the school-yard fight with a tenth-grader may interest some (p. 57); the at-home callers and condolences of friends after the mother's burial (p. 99) may also be of interest. Finally, the establishment of Robbie's relationship with his father provides a high point (pp. 122–129).

Related Materials

The Edge of Next Year (Harper, 1974) by Mary Stolz is a book about a 13-year-old boy who loses his mother in a car accident. *The Garden of Broken Glass* (Delacorte, 1975) by Newbery Award author (now attorney) Emily Cheney Neville deals with the family problems of a white youth in a St. Louis slum from the perspective of a black family. Arthur Roth's novel *The Secret Lover of Elmtree* (Scholastic Bk. Services, 1976) is an easy-to-read story about a 17-year-old adopted boy who feels rejected. For music lovers try *How to Make Electronic Music* (EAV, 1975), 4 filmstrips with sound. All youngsters will enjoy the symbolic film story of love between people, *A Fuzzy Tale* (Mass Media Ministries, 1976); and *Dad and Me* (BFA), a film about a Black boy and his father in New York City.

Harry Mazer, *The Dollar Man*
Delacorte, 1975, $5.95; pap., Dell, 1975, 95¢

The author writes simply and with understanding about a young adolescent who searches for the father he has never known in this modern retelling of a classical "search." Markey's trials and tribulations with school chums and situations are compounded by the acute sense of deprivation the boy feels. A child's right to know about his parents and to make up his own mind about them is skillfully highlighted. Youngsters from 9 to 14 years old will find that this story about a child in a one-parent family rings true.

Fat and fatherless, 13-year-old Marcus Rosenbloom makes up stories about his father to bolster his courage and make himself feel better about not having one. Although he loves his pretty, independent young mother, Sally, she cannot make up for his longing to know his real father. Sally has always taken good care of him, and he has other supportive people around him in the city: grandma May, Bill Brenner, who lives with them when he is not on tour as a trumpet player, and school chum, Bernie McNulty. Nothing, however, helps to restore his slim reservoir of confidence, except his fantasy about "the dollar man" (p. 49). All avenues seem closed to this boy just entering adolescence.

Marcus even asks futilely if Bill Brenner knows his father. Finally, while visiting grandma May he learns something. Grandma May shows Markey a picture of his father, George Renfrew, and tells him that the family used to own a variety store in lower Manhattan. Marcus is overwhelmed with his unexpected richness of information.

In his pursuit of acceptance at school, Marcus goes out for football because his idol, Dorritty, has done so. Bernie meanwhile is avoided by Marcus and becomes angry because he understands that Dorritty and his crowd are unsavory characters who are liable to lead the nonathletic Marcus into trouble at school.

As Bernie suspects, Marcus gets into trouble trying to act "big" and "brave" in front of Dorritty and his group by sharing beer—the first he has ever tasted—and cigarettes with them. Mr. Firstman, the vice-principal, finally catches Marcus with a "roach" that Dorritty and Phillips force on him. Although Family Court to which the school sends his case drops it, there is a separate school hearing before the Superintendent. At the hearing Marcus refuses to implicate Dorritty and Phillips. Although Sally is proud of the way Marcus handles himself, the Superintendent's recommendation to send him to another junior high school makes Marcus ache even more to see his father.

Marcus sets out to locate him. He finds the variety store and from the present owners he learns that George Renfrew moved to New Jersey and owns a construction and equipment company in Latham. Feeling both elated and determined, Marcus takes a bus to Latham. Marcus telephones his father who picks him up in a large station wagon and drives him past his house. Mr. Renfrew is surprised that Marcus is his son, but no more than Marcus is by the unpleasant reality of his male parent. He is not at all the way the boy expected. Far from being pleased to find Marcus, George Renfrew explains that he has a busy well-ordered life with a family in which there is no room for the boy. Marcus confronts the real image with the fantasy image that has kept him from having confidence in himself and determines to accept the reality. He considers himself fortunate to have Sally, Bill, and grandma May as a warm loving family and a fine person like Bernie for a friend. But most of all he realizes that building confidence is his own chore in his new school.

Thematic Analysis

The terrible burden of not knowing a parent and feeling the loss is well explained here. The effects of this type of one-parent family on a preadolescent youngster's image of himself is explored with honesty and accuracy. A secondary theme of the problems of school life for the unwary and insecure is pointed up. The resolution is hopeful but realistic because it shows the young person facing up to helping himself while expecting that it will take time.

Discussion Materials

"The Dollar Man" fantasy that dominates Marcus's young life will paint the picture well for youngsters (p. 49). A few sentences stressing the trouble at school or the search for his father will intrigue listeners. For discussion purposes, the realization that his father is not really the way Marcus imagined him will serve as an interesting and useful point of departure (pp. 188–190).

Related Materials

Two books suggested for younger audiences are *She Come Bringing Me That Little Baby Girl* (Lippincott, 1974) by Eloise Greenfield and *The Ogre Downstairs* (Dutton, 1975) by Diana Wynne Jones. The first tells about a young boy's reticent acceptance of a baby sister, the second tells about a youngster's accommodation to a stepparent. For older readers try Louise Fitzhugh's *Nobody's Family Is Going to Change* (Farrar, 1974; pap., Dell, 1975), the story of a professional upper middle-class black family that has typical social prejudices and stereotypes. Their intellectual 11-year-old daughter finally realizes that nobody's family changes and that she must stop worrying about it—a profound lesson in the task of getting along in a family. Also useful are a 1976 Hans Christian Andersen Honor List title *The Ghost of Thomas Kempe* (Dutton, 1973) by Penelope Lively, and Arnold Adoff's book of poetry *Make a Circle Keep Us In: Poems for a Good Day* (Delacorte, 1975) which illuminates family strength and security with verse and illustrations.

Marietta Moskin, *Waiting for Mama*
Illus. by Richard Lebenson. Coward, 1975, $5.95

The author's own experience lends dignity and warmth to this portrayal of the struggles of an immigrant family in New York City in 1901. A Jewish family of 6 leaves the rural landscape of Senjiki, Russia, to escape increasingly harsh measures. After weeks of difficult travel to the Bremen seaport and the ship for America, the mother and baby Leah are forced to go back to wait for the baby's recovery and passage money from papa. The story which is told in flashbacks takes place during the last few months of waiting.

Detailed pencil and ink drawings convey both the charm and the reality of life on the lower side of East New York at the turn of the century. The compelling double-page child eye's view of the street life that surrounds the immigrants is a notable example (pp. 24–25). There is also a fine multi-image portrayal of the 3 young immigrants at work (p. 39). Children of ages 8 to 10, especially girls, will enjoy this easy-to-read family story.

Papa and 10-year-old Jake, who share cramped quarters in the ship's hold, together with 12-year-old Rachel and 8-year-old Becky, who try to comfort each other in the women's hold, are met at the Ellis Island immigrant station by cousin Louis who has been in New York for a year. Together with their guide and new boarder, they go to their fifth-floor rooms in a walk-up on Cherry Street in downtown New York. The place, which is dilapidated and dirty with a communal toilet one flight down, depresses this farm family. However, as their father tells them, life in America may be hard, but it is free from the whims of a Czar.

Although Rachel tries to console her, Becky misses their mother as fiercely as any little girl can. They all work hard to accomplish their dream of bringing mama and baby Leah to America. Papa works as a pants presser on Lafayette Street, Jake runs errands for a nickel and goes to night school, Rachel does the chores and sews skirt and shirt parts in the daytime; only Becky, who is sent to regular school, is spared from earning money for living expenses and mama's passage. As the second year passes, Becky decides that she must join Rachel in sewing at night to make extra money in order to welcome mama with a warm wool coat. At the end of their second summer in New York City, papa sends the passage money to Russia and the family waits impatiently for mama's arrival.

Papa, escorted by Becky who, in fluent English, asks directions to Ellis Island, greets his wife in her familiar green shawl and their youngest daughter who is now walking beside her. Mama is delighted to be reunited with her industrious family. She is proud of them all, especially happy about Becky's newly acquired ability to speak English and the solicitude of her two older daughters so tangibly expressed in the warm coat on her shoulders.

Thematic Analysis

The willingness to do one's best as a family member, even under difficult circumstances, to show respect and love to parents and siblings is the main theme. Everyone in this family displays the fortitude and love that are the necessary ingredients of happiness. The idea of working and waiting for satisfaction and pleasure is also presented. This is an old-fashioned story with verities about family life that are as current as the human race.

Discussion Materials

An excellent book-talk device for this brief story is the prologue, "About the Book." Read and illustrate it by showing Richard Lebenson's sensitive, but strong, drawings culled from historical photographs of the lower East side and his own family pictures of his paternal grandparents who came from Russia to America at the turn of the century. A retelling of Chapter One will set the scene for the story and describe the family's journey to America and Becky's sadness at the separation from her mother. A brief description of the rooms on Cherry Street will give children a look at the lodgings of earlier immigrants (pp. 34-37). Mama's pride on hearing Becky speak English explains the feelings of immigrants in the early part of this century (p. 90).

Related Materials

Martin Scorsese's interview of his parents in the film *Italian American* (Macmillan Films, 26 min., color) will enhance the picture of immigrant life on the lower East Side of New York through the eyes of another ethnic group who settled in this area. Three books with contemporary settings are also suggested: for younger children, *The Quitting Deal* (Viking, 1975) by Tobi Tobias; for readers of the same age group, *Think About It, You Might Learn Something* (Houghton, 1973) by Robyn Suproner; and *Ramona and Her Father* (Morrow, 1977) by Beverly Cleary. The film *Charlie Needs a Cloak* (Weston Woods, 1977) is based on the traditional story of making a coat from sheep to stitching. Another Weston Woods film, *This Is New York*, gives a pictorial history of the city from tepees to skyscrapers.

2

Making Friends

As YOUNG CHILDREN try to establish friendships and lay a foundation for later sexual bonding, their prior experience with family members plays a significant part. The level of trust that has been developed will help determine how successful they will be at that time and in the future. Acceptance in some sort of group and cooperation within the group become important sources of satisfaction and give a youngster a sense of individual worth.

Since few are able to complete fully the necessary inner growth, making friends often involves trying to get along in a family, or substitute family situation, as well as taking this step outside a protective environment. Children experiment by taking one step away from home and family and rushing back for reassurance. It is not always a smooth progression, especially when being a secure member of some type of family is not possible.

In this chapter, the books discussed range widely over a variety of situations and experiences that will give boys and girls a chance to discover vicariously how to respond in different social situations. The stories show how the characters extend and receive offers of friendship, play and work with other youngsters, and build self-confident attitudes.

Patricia Beatty, *How Many Miles to Sundown*
> Frontispiece by Robert Quackenbush. Morrow, 1974, lib. bdg. $6.43

In a rousing tale of an adventure-packed trip from Texas through the New Mexico and Arizona territories in the 1880s, the author skillfully pits the vitality of three youngsters in search of the missing father of one of the children against the rugged terrain and the frontier personalities. Outstanding is the faithfulness with which Patricia Beatty recreates the time and place. The flavor of the Texas lingo from "bogged down in carpets" for housework to "dropping tallow" for losing weight adds luster to the impeccable research. One could make a map of the journey using historical atlases to find likely locations. Both boys and girls from 9 to 14 will find the story exciting.

Robert Quackenbush has done the frontispiece and book jacket illustration. The heroine, Beeler, in trousers, appears in a bold black-and-white woodcut. The jacket cover painting of cactus and with Beeler astride her longhorn steer, Travis, against a color-drenched background of purples, oranges, and pinks suggests the Southwest.

A family of orphans being raised by their older brother, Earl, and his wife, Nerissa, in Santa Rosa County, Texas, is visited by Jonathon (Nate) Graber, a sodbuster friend of 15-year-old Parker, to enlist his aid in Nate's search for his father, Wilberforce. With Earl away selling cattle and Parker laid up at the doctor's house, red-haired 13-year-old Beulah Land Quiney (Beeler) and 11-year-old Leo are the next oldest at home. Three girls, Elnora, Lucy, and Polly and a dog, J. E. B. Stuart (for the Confederates still favored in Texas), complete the family which Nerissa, a city girl from Fort Worth, finds such a trial. Beeler, whom everyone always calls "he," lives up to the volunteering; however, Leo sneaks off with Nate on Beeler's horse, Jinglebob. Independent Beeler follows on Leo's horse, Two-Cents, with her pet steer, Travis, in tow.

She catches up with Nate and Leo. After Beeler bawls out Leo and reclaims Jinglebob, they all agree to continue to search for Mr. Graber, a "wisdom bringer" (teacher) turned miner last seen with three other men heading for Sunset or Sundown.

The three youngsters come first to a new town, Over-the-River, which is full of "Bluebellies" because Camp Concha is nearby. They pass fields in gorgeous bloom before they reach Comanche Springs which is busy with the laying of railroad track. They inquire everywhere without luck about the four men. In Lovelock's post office there is no listing of Sunset or Sundown. Finally they arrive at Deadahead on the Texas border.

Here they meet the Bellywhiskers. The wife, Elfie, takes a liking to Leo and accepts his lie that Beeler is his cousin, the notorious insane child murderess, Bertha Mae Muller. Also because she is narrow-minded and dislikes Beeler's appearance and independence, Elfie doesn't think twice about trapping Beeler in her root cellar. With Travis's help, Beeler escapes and follows Nate, Leo, and her horse. When she finally catches up with them, she discovers that Leo had convinced Nate that she stayed behind because she was ill. Beeler is again furious, but curiously still "tender" toward Nate whom she fancies. She also discovers that they have acquired a traveling companion with a derringer and telltale wrist markings, Henry McCarty (one alias for Billy the Kid). Luckily she advertised her arrival by whistling "Evalina" as she led Travis in to join them.

Determined to keep on searching, they cross into the lawless territory of New Mexico that harbors many desperadoes. Beeler, however, is glad to go for two good reasons; she has never been far from the ranch and figures they could all, including Travis, "drop tallow." As they go forward, McCarty parts company peacefully with the stalwart youngsters.

Soon they pass through Apache country. Traveling ahead of them to Silverado is the Clayton Circus with the bicyclienne Marvelous Melinda (Holcomb), and the owner who is also the lion tamer and Melinda's love-light. When the youngsters catch up, they ask to join the circus for safe escort through the dangerous countryside. One evening after passing over the Ramada Hill, they notice that the Apaches have silently surrounded them on the towering rocks. Quietly and earnestly they perform in the starlight for their silent audience. Everyone performs, even the youngsters take part by turning somersaults when Marvelous Melinda is slow in appearing with her unicycle. When she finishes, the Chief comes down and unceremoniously takes the shiny unicycle. Melinda and Clayton collapse in each other's arms. When they all reach the mining town of Silverado, the two are married.

Nate's father and his companions have not been in Silverado. Inquiries send the youngsters toward the Southwest and the town of Sunrise Flats. There, Travis is scared by a pack of dogs into breaking up the local saloon where everyone has a good laugh when they learn his name. "Big Missy" Travis, the mayor's wife, gives Beeler $20 to take her steer and leave town.

The children press on to the Arizona Territory as Beeler laments, "How many more miles do you suppose it's going to be to Sundown?" She notices the desert scenery, as well as the sunlight they are losing at a rapid rate. Unexpectedly their campsite is visited by the dreaded skunk, soon followed by small Marie Lopez who is trying to find her pet, Señorita Mofeta (Miss Moffett). The child leads them to her grandma's shack beside a silver mine. Señora Mary Rose Seton de Lopez, originally from Galveston, Texas, is a colorful figure who is trying to raise Marie and her older brother, Matias, who helps work the small vein. While the youngsters are there, a letter is delivered by a man on horseback who tries unsuccessfully to steal from the mine.

Taking the Señora's advice, Beeler and the boys travel at night across the desert to Hard Rock near the goldfields. This town is a surprise with its adobe houses, post office, theater, church, boardinghouse-hotel, and newspaper, *The Nugget*. Major Ella Gordon, a feisty transplanted Scot, who believes in cleanliness and helps orphans and strays, is particularly impressed by Beeler and her independent ways. She introduces her to Mr. Hays, the newspaper editor, who publishes the trio's story with a request for the whereabouts of Sundown. They soon find, from a couple, that Sundown is a California town just over the Colorado River border. While they are getting ready to go there, Nate, who is beginning to feel tender toward Beeler, is stepped on by Travis. On advice from Major Gordon, Beeler and Leo alone take the train to Gilaville and cross the Colorado on a ferry. Finally arriving in Sundown, they learn from the two remaining miners who struck it rich in a Mexican silver mine and lost it to desperadoes that Wilberforce Graber died thinking his son was dead. However, they give Beeler Graber's Bible and watch to give to Nate. When the watch plays "Evalina," Beeler is reminded that she still hopes that Nate may someday be one of the Quineys. Although it is the hardest thing of all for her to do, she comes to an understanding with Leo.

Thematic Analysis

Several themes are explored. Friendship and trust between siblings and acquaintances is tested to its limits under the harshest circumstances. A sense of independence and a feeling for equality of the sexes are graphically portrayed. The latter theme assumes a special importance because it shows children that some females have long tried to assume an equal place in the family of man. Survival in a hostile environment is clearly shown to be directly traceable to determination and aspirations. The portrayal of several historical figures and folklore incidents is worthy of note: McCarty (Billy the Kid); Major Gordon (Ella Gordon); and Señorita Mofeta (the fear of skunks in the old Southwest).

Discussion Materials

After introducing the locale and the Quiney family, briefly outline the long search (pp. 1-31). Trace the saga on a historical map relating some of the highlights. Describe: how Beeler is trapped in the root cellar (pp. 69-70); Henry McCarty (pp. 79-91); the silent Clayton Circus performance (pp. 115-135); Travis in the Travis Saloon (pp. 136-155). To explain Señorita Mofeta's appearance use (pp. 156-175) and introduce the intrepid Major Gordon (pp. 176-194). The author's note (pp. 216-222) should be read.

Related Materials

Patricia Beatty's earlier titles *A Long Way to Whiskey Creek* (Morrow, 1971), about 13-year-old Parker Quiney and his friend Nate, and *By Crumbs, It's Mine* (Morrow, 1976) can be suggested to the same readers. Another title is *Naomi* (Nelson, 1975; pap., Bantam, 1976) by Berniece Rabe. Bruce Clement's story of a 14-year-old boy's adventure-filled journey down the Mississippi, *I Tell a Lie Every So Often* (Farrar, 1974), will be enjoyed as will Betsy Byars's story *The Eighteenth Emergency* (Viking, 1973; pap., Avon, 1974). For younger readers and viewers try two films, *Sam, Bangs and Moonshine* (BFA, 15 min., color) and *Lightning* (Tyman Films, 20 min., color). Marlo Thomas's *Free to Be Me* (McGraw-Hill, 1974) can be used in any of its formats—book, film, or record.

Bette Greene, *Philip Hall Likes Me: I Reckon Maybe*
Pictures by Charles Lilly. Dial, 1974, $5.95; pap., Dell, 1975, $1.25

Over the period of a year, an intelligent, spunky young Arkansas farm girl assumes her rightful place as the best in her class, in the 4H Club contest, and in the eyes of her proud family and of the boy on the next farm—her only competition and her first crush. The reader is expertly drawn into the feelings of the characters by an author who grew up in Arkansas. The descriptions of the locale and the characterizations of the people are sharply drawn by an author who proved herself a master storyteller in her earlier ALA Honor book, *Summer of My German Soldier*.

The 8 pictures by Charles Lilly, who also illustrated the earlier title, are in pencil and charcoal. They portray the different shades of the Black characters simply and with grandeur; 3 illustrations are double pages. The jacket cover superimposes the heroine on the scene of the turkey farm outside of Pocahantas, Arkansas, in soft autumnal tones ranging from the newly painted green farmhouse and red barns to the neat furrows and fall-tipped leaves. Girls and boys from 8 to 13, and good readers at a younger age, will find the story interesting. The jacket illustration of the heroine, pigtailed Beth, may tend to deter boys. However, they should be encouraged to read the book because the story is a nonsexist one and equally the tale of how difficult it is for Philip Hall to accept Beth as an equal and in some ways a superior, and yet say at the end of the story, "Sometimes, I reckon I likes you, Beth Lambert."

Eleven-year-old Elizabeth Lorraine Lambert (portrait frontispiece) lives with her loving family—an older brother Luther and sister Anne, as well as her mother, who is pregnant, and her father, Eugene. Beth has a crush on Philip Hall who lives on the next farm and is the president of a small group of boys called The Tiger Hunter's Club. Although she privately calls him a "dumb bum" when he avoids her and breaks his promises, she knowingly takes second place to him in school and tells her momma that she likes doing Philip's chores in his barn because he plays the guitar while she works. Mom just explodes with the comment, "When are you going to get some sense."

Around the holidays, worried because he continues to lose turkeys, Mr. Lambert goes into town for a change of scene and to do some shopping at Calvin's Meat Market. He continues to report that turkeys are missing each morning. Finally Mr. Lambert writes to his trade magazine, *Turkey World*, asking what animal could be causing this loss. Meanwhile, Beth and Philip meet late one night to try to catch the marauder. Armed with flashlight and BB gun, they catch the Calvins in their panel truck stuffing turkeys into sacks. While Philip runs for help, Beth makes the Calvins pay for all the turkeys and release those in the sacks.

Beth is unfortunate later in the winter when she discovers that she is allergic to dogs after receiving and naming, Friendly, a collie pup given to her by her parents. Following the advice given by the teacher, Miss Johnson, and information found in a book, they once again exchange him for a short-haired Chihuahua (Tippietoes) and then for a poodle (Puffy). Beth is quick and clever at bestowing good names on her pets but she has a difficult time accepting her allergic reaction to all dogs. As her mom patiently explains, in life you have to be ". . . happy about the good, . . . brave about the bad" (p. 52). Beth gets a reward when the new baby, whom she immediately calls Benjamin, to her parent's pleasure, is placed in her arms. She finally has someone she can help care for.

Spring arrives with more excitement. Doc Brenner says he will help pay for Beth's college education to be a veterinarian. In order to earn money to help herself, Beth persuades her father to plant vegetables for her to sell. Philip objects to the wording of the sign on the roadside stand, "The Elizabeth Lorraine Lambert and Friend Vegetable Stand," until Beth, who has given up subservience as a way of gaining his affection, points out that he didn't do the planting, weeding, picking, or other work. After she makes her first sale to Mr. Putterham, the local variety store owner, she goes to replenish the stock. On her return she discovers that Philip has eaten the one remaining melon, and watches in horror as his dairy cows cross the road and knock down the stand. She faces the bad situation bravely and begins to reconstruct her business.

By July her girl friends, Susan, Esther, Bernice, and Ginny, known as The Pretty Pennies, hold another club meeting, elect Beth president, and decide to have a relay race, in their new uniforms, with The Tiger Hunters. They purchase T-shirts for 89¢ and embroidery thread from Mr. Putterham at the Busy Bee Bargain Store and spend a long time finishing the work on the shirts. When the embroidered T-shirts shrink in the first wash, the girls, led by Beth, decide to picket the store (picture p. 87). They get their money back.

At the end of the summer at the old Rugged Cross Church picnic Philip gets lost on a nearby mountain. While everyone is looking for him in the lake, Beth finds Philip on the mountain with a painfully injured leg. She half carries him to a field where they find a tractor. Since Philip can drive it, they rejoin the picnic, to everyone's delight.

When the 4H Club of Pocahantas holds its annual September fair, Philip and Beth both enter the calf-raising contest; he with Leonard, she with Madeleine. Both have worked hard preparing the calves for this event. However, for the calf and her handling of it (Beth keeps the calf's head up with a soft whistle), Mr. Paulson awards Beth the blue ribbon and $5.00 and Philip the red ribbon and $3.00. Later when the square dancing begins, Beth is without a partner. Realizing that Philip has no partner either, but is too humiliated to ask her, Beth goes to the cow barns and finds him sitting beside Leonard. She tells him that not winning first prize is nothing to be ashamed of; he tells her she has forgotten how it feels to lose. Finally recognizing that square dancing is doing things together, they join the merriment.

Thematic Analysis

Carefully shown is the artificial and corrosive "double standard" for young boys and girls that denies females a right of expression and males a sense of adequacy and carries with it the threat of being called a "sissy" for playing with a girl or "fraidy cat" for having a girl as a friend. The theme is friendship and what it means to middle-grade-age children in a society that exhibits sexist discrimination. The unpretentious and dignified exposition of a loving Black family promotes better racial understanding. The descriptions of farm life will broaden the experience of many city children.

Discussion Materials

Any of the preceding themes can be used with the following pictures and talks. Simply put them in a sequence appropriate to the theme or topic. If for some reason Black English is a barrier, the chapters should be read aloud. The pictures can also be used as a device around which to introduce or tell the story.

Pictures: Beth (frontispiece); Philip's barn (p. 13); Eugene Lambert tells ma more turkeys are missing (p. 24); Friendly, the collie pup (pp. 40–41); the vegetable stand (p. 61); shrunken T-shirt (p. 87); kids on tractor (pp. 110–111); blue and red ribbons (pp. 126–127).

Talks: Philip and Beth catch turkey thieves (pp. 33–35); Mr. Putterham buys vegetables and cows knock down stand (pp. 62–67); church picnic (pp. 96–99); Philip is rescued (pp. 102–112); calf-raising contest (pp. 119–125).

Related Materials

Other titles to suggest are: Richard Peck's *Patooie* (Knopf, 1977), about two boys in rural America; Mildred Taylor's *Roll of Thunder, Hear My Cry* (Dial, 1976), a story of an earlier era in Mississippi; Bette Greene's *Summer of My German Soldier* (Dial, 1973; pap., Bantam, 1974), for older readers; and Sheila Greenwald's *The Mariah Delany Lending Library* (Houghton, 1977). Also suggested is the film *Be My Friend: A Visit to Four American Families* (Ramsgate Films, 12 min., color).

Constance C. Greene, *The Unmaking of Rabbit*
Viking, 1972, $6.95; pap., Dell, 1974, 95¢

An accomplished author of contemporary stories for young adolescents, Mrs. Greene writes knowingly about a fatherless boy who lives with his grandmother while waiting for his mother to make a home for him. Buffeted by the taunts of his classmates because of his small size, stutter, and protruding ears, Paul is made even more miserable by his loneliness for a family and friends. The author, who has 5 children, shows keen insight in the plotting of the story—a skill she undoubtedly refined while working for the Associated Press.

There are no illustrations, save the one on the jacket done in bright colors, that displays a group of boys talking together and laughing at "Rabbit" who is outside the circle. It is a poster-type painting with the facial features flattened and made slightly grotesque to lend a cruel effect. It is obvious from looking at Paul's ears why he received the nickname. Boys and girls from 10 to 13 will find the story satisfying.

Eleven-year-old Paul lives with his 66-year-old grandmother and her cat—old, fat Flora. Paul, who stutters and dreams forlornly of going to live with his beautiful young mother, Anne, is a fine boy with few weaknesses. He does not like Flora, especially when she sleeps in his bed, and he often yells at her. He would much rather have a dog. He does his school work cheerfully and treats Gran well, often fetching her long black cigarette holder for her after-dinner smoke. Gran tells Paul that it is foolish to think that he will ever live with her daughter because Anne is selfish and willful, very much a child herself. Paul looks up the word "ne'er-do-well," which Gran calls his father, and discovers that it means no good, whereupon Paul begins to think less often about his father and to admit to himself that there is no use pretending his life is like that of other kids.

At school, Miss Olah the teacher tries to comfort Gran who objects to the pencil drawings the other kids put in his lunch pail, knowing that there is little she can do to the three who taunt him: Freddy Gibson, Pete Todd, and Scott Detmer.

Paul and Gran each have a good friend. Bess Tuttle is Gran's friend, in spite of her continual boastfulness about her grandson whom Paul dubs Gordon the Genius. Mr. Barker, the corner grocery store owner, is Paul's friend. Gran frequently sends Paul to the store, always carefully explaining the care one must excercise in checking quality and price. On an errand, Paul, seeing a "Boy Wanted" sign, gets up his courage to ask for the job. Mr. Barker cannot hire him because he is under 16. Dejected Paul leaves and bumps into Freddy and his gang who continue to taunt him. However, a call from his mother announcing her impending visit with a special beau quickly restores him.

The day they are to arrive, Gran sends him to the store for eggs and he meets the new hired helper, Eugene, a 17-year-old with pimples. Upon Paul's return he sees a bright yellow car with wire wheels at the curb and runs in to see his mother and meet Art Bogovich. Art tells Gran he is a free-lance photographer and graphics artist while mom tells Paulie (a name he dislikes almost as much as Rabbit) they are getting married and will send for him when they get a bigger apartment. Gran comments after the brief visit that "there isn't an apartment big enough in the entire world" (p. 47). Paul, however, thinks Art looks nice, like Lincoln, and hopes they will send for him soon. Meanwhile, Eugene advises Paul to be a gigolo in Miami Beach. After Anne calls to say that she and Art have been married, Gran gives Paul a special pie and ice cream for supper.

And life goes on as usual. At school Miss Olah gives the class an assignment to write a story with a moral. While Paul is thinking about it, Freddy stops him to outline a plan for stealing valuables from a house whose owners are away. He wants Paul to be one of the gang and promises that they will have a big sleep-out party in the spring in his backyard. Thoroughly upset, Paul faces a difficult weekend with Gordon, Mrs. Tuttle's grandson, coming to visit, supper with his friends the Barkers on Friday night, going to visit Art and his mom in New York City on Sunday, and now this mandatory caper with the gang on Saturday. Eugene who continues to dispense advice tells Paul that he's going to "hitch" all over because you can always get out of a bad situation if you threaten to puke.

Gordon proves to be a regular guy, the same size as Paul and friendly. Paul gets Mrs. Barker to invite Gordon to Friday night supper, too. The Barkers and the boys have a marvelous dinner and night out. Saturday dawns, however, as Paul knew it must. Freddy hoists Paul to his shoulders to crawl through a small open window in the empty house. At the last moment, Paul remembers Eugene's advice about getting out of unsavory situations and manages to get home safely.

The train takes him to New York City where he once more waits for his mother who arrives alone. After a disappointing trip to the automat, Anne calls Art, a late riser, who joins them. Although Paul wants to go to the museum, they wind up at Paddy's bar where Art and Anne's friends gather. Disgusted and determined to live his life as it actually is, Paul goes back to Gran on an early train.

He writes his composition for Miss Olah about the gang and himself, sharply outlining the moral: "A clear conscience is worth more than friends. . . . But, it would be nice to have both" (p. 121). Miss Olah calls on him to read it which he does without stuttering. Freddy and the others start to call him Paul after he tells them to stop calling him Rabbit. When his Mom calls to ask him to visit, he replies, "maybe." The final transformation occurs when he calls out to Gran, "I love you."

Thematic Analysis

There are several concurrent themes that run throughout the story. Each concerns emotional maturation. A positive attitude toward living based on an acceptance of one's lot is stressed. Also emphasized is the point that a child must try to discriminate among the adults around him to emulate and honor whose who act responsibly on his behalf, not necessarily on his wishes. The story shows forcefully that a youngster can have like-minded friends and a clear conscience.

Discussion Materials

Introduce the story by describing the main characters and Paul's yearning to live with his mother (pp. 1–17). The episode describing Mr.

Barker the grocer and Paul's desire for the "Boy Wanted" job will further set the scene (pp. 25-33). Eugene, the new grocer's boy, and the advice he gives can be related: be a gigolo (pp. 48-50) or travel with impunity (pp. 61-66). Freddy outlines the plans to steal (pp. 56-60) and tries to carry it out with Rabbit as bait (pp. 93-101). Another dramatic incident is Paul's New York City trip (pp. 102-118). The writing of a composition is assigned (pp. 54-60) and Paul, not "Rabbit," wins an accolade from Miss Olah (pp. 120-124).

Related Materials

Scott Corbett's *Run for the Money* (Little-Atlantic, 1973; pap., Archway, 1976) will appeal to the same readers as *The Unmaking of Rabbit*. Also suggested are *The Bongleweed* (Macmillan, 1973), a fantasy by Helen Creswell, and Judy Blume's *Otherwise Known as Sheila the Great* (Dutton, 1972; pap., Dell, 1976), about an insecure girl. Other titles to suggest are *A Year in the Life of Rosie Bernard* (Harper, 1971; pap., Avon, 1974) by Barbara Brenner, which tells about a motherless girl growing up in the Depression, and *Johnny May* (Doubleday, 1975; pap., Avon, 1976) by Robbie Branscum, the story of a lonely Arkansas girl who lives with her grandparents. *The House of Sixty Fathers* (Miller-Brody Productions) is an exciting filmstrip that adapts Meindert de Jong's Newbery Honor book about a Chinese orphan boy.

Jean Little, *Stand in the Wind*
Pictures by Emily Arnold McCully. Harper, 1975, $5.50

This Canadian author of many a "good read" for youngsters has again written a warm story about two sets of sisters who discover how to be better friends to each other and to others. The setting is a lake cottage that the author knew as a child, and the story is based on personal experience. The 19 episodic chapters cover a 2-week vacation period at a lake near Toronto. Little's style exemplifies the childhood of the North American matrix with its unique American and distinctive Canadian similarities and differences. It is honest and appealing and will entertain girl readers from the age of 8 to 12.

Emily McCully's 4 pictures and book jacket painting are tailor-made for this family story of friendship among young girls. The sketches portray in pencil-and-ink line the sawed-off hair and angular movements typical of real children on vacation. The jacket shows a solid Martha in the middle of the beach grass with her arm in a sling standing in the wind with her petrified looking friend, Kit, behind her. The colors are summer yellows, blues, and white. Emily McCully, a well-known illustrator, is responsible for the Children's Book Council poster, "Book Power," as well as Meindert de Jong's *Journey from Peppermint Street* and Emily Nevelle's *The 17th St. Gang.*

After a pleasant vacation at their lakeside cottage, the Winstons pack to return to Toronto to welcome mother's college classmate Mrs. Swann and her two daughters, Rosemary and Christine. Eleven-year-old Martha Winston, the protagonist, is joyously packing for camp to make more room at home for the visitors who are joining her 13-year-old sister, Ellen, and two adopted Indian brothers, 7-year-old Bruce and 5-year-old Toby. Before they can leave the cottage, however, Martha, who is admittedly fat, falls and breaks her arm after carefully packing her two best practical jokes: Henrietta, a hairy spider, and Herman, a rubber snake. Dr. Hill, who lives nearby, sets the arm and recommends that Martha stay home. In spite of the pain, Martha, who has been looking forward to her 2 weeks in camp, pleads to go. The camp, however, won't accept her. In a last-minute decision, Mrs. Winston agrees to leave the 4 girls in the cottage, which is promptly named, "Camp Better Than Nothing."

When the red-haired Mrs. Swann, an American travel agent, arrives, she coos, "You poor, poor baby" to the insulted Martha. Red-haired Rosemary, who is only 13, although she appears much older, is very bored because she wants to visit a rich chum in Maine. When she discovers that there is no TV in the cottage, she is devastated. Only Christine who is 10 and dresses like a baby is quiet and happy to be there to escape 2 weeks at camp. Marth, as Ellen calls her, is disgusted with the guests.

Kit, as Christine prefers to be called, begins to reread many of the children's books in the cottage, such as *A Little Princess* and *Julie of the Wolves.* Eventually, the long first day during which the mothers announce that they are going to visit college friends for a week comes to an end with the appearance of a bat in Marth and Kit's room. Ellen and Rosemary come in to help with a broom and towel. Marth finally traps the bat in a wastepaper basket and, covering it with a copy of *Where the Wild Things Are,* releases it outdoors. By the time they fall asleep, Marth and Kit are friends.

It is the beginning of an adventure-filled week. The girls discuss their different heritages and use of language, e.g., Chesterfield or sofa? Ellen does the cooking and they all shop at Mr. Doyle's grocery where Marth is once more delighted by his batches of homemade peanut brittle. Meanwhile, Marth tries to teach Kit how to be a free spirit and throw bread to sea gulls, play gin rummy, and most of all stand up to Rosemary instead of acting like a mouse when Rosemary nags her. Marth knows Kit is capable—she swims so well Marth wishes she could teach her—and Marth feels sorry for her until she realizes that her sulking and crying make Rosemary pick on her.

With a "Big Blow" a day away, Marth decides she will help Kit to stand up to Rosemary by teaching her the self-reliance of standing in the wind (p. 137). Armed with peanut brittle, they practice outside saying into the wind, "I stand in the wind and eat peanut brittle."

Ellen and Rosemary serve a supper one night of solid pork chops and raw vegetables fit only for pigs. Marth and Kit take over and make pancakes which Rosemary, who has started to become sociable, drowns in syrup and eats with gusto. Marth, however, as a practical joke has put a little burn ointment on them instead of butter. They rush Rosemary across the windy fields to Dr. Hill who says no harm has been done.

The storm subsides as they recapitulate their week's adventures. Suddenly they realize their mothers are due and the kitchen is a mess. They clean it in the nick of time. Mrs. Swann picks up her transformed daughters. Ellen and Marth, who miss their new friends, call Toronto to ask them to come back. There is no answer, but the next morning Mr. Winston arrives with the Swann girls and the Winston boys who chant, "We can be part of the camp."

Everyone joins in the spirit of playing camp by orienteering (hiking), building a campfire, obeying rising and lights-out whistles, and keeping to a camp schedule. "Camp Better Than Nothing" is fun and a real success even to a tinfoil dinner disaster and a sing-a-long over the campfire. As a special event for Martha who has felt so deprived of her longed-for 2 weeks at camp, a sleep-out under the stars is arranged. Although it is rained on, Martha is thrilled. As the Swanns leave, Rosemary is telling her mother that Christine is Kit and no baby. Kit responds to Marth's final comment, "Stand in the wind," with "And eat peanut brittle."

Thematic Analysis

Learning to make friends under difficult circumstances with youngsters of different ages and cultural values, however slight, is a development that the majority of youngsters should try to understand. A secondary theme of getting along in one's own family and with the families of friends is well developed. The idea of understanding differences between children of different ages and countries is also well delineated. As a family story, it is packed with honest, exciting incidents that youngsters will find familiar.

Discussion Materials

Introduce the chief characters (pp. 1–14) and briefly outline the plot. Illustrate the primary theme by showing the book jacket. Use the pictures to relate some of the incidents: Marth and Kit in the "Big Blow" (p. 136); Rosemary is poisoned by pancakes (p. 152); four girls near the fire (p. 229); Kit packs (p. 241). Other episodes to talk about are: entertainment at the cottage (pp. 57–68); bat in the bedroom (pp. 72–84); feeding the gulls (pp. 100–111); standing in the wind (pp. 132–139; picture p. 137); orienteering (pp. 180–194); singing around the campfire (pp. 225–232; picture p. 228).

Related Materials

Two books that relate well are *The Sign on Rosie's Door* (Harper, 1960) by Maurice Sendak and *Getting Something on Maggie Marmelstein* (Harper, 1971; pap., 1971) by Marjorie Sharmat. Another title that older readers will enjoy is *Louly* (Macmillan, 1974) by Carol Ryrie Brink, about a group of children in a small town in 1908. Four films that will appeal to everyone are: *Hugo and Josefin* (Macmillan), about two Swedish children on vacation; *Really Rosie* (Weston Woods), based on Maurice Sendak's *The Sign on Rosie's Door* and his Nutshell Library; *The Owl Who Married a Goose* (NFBC), an animated film based on a Canadian Eskimo legend; and *Cockaboody* (Pyramid), an animated film with the voice-over of two young girls.

Betty Miles, *All It Takes Is Practice*
Knopf, 1976, $5.95

In another of her many books for children, the author constructs a story about a fifth-grader in Kansas who has two abiding wishes: a long-range one to be a Kansas City Kings basketball player and an immediate one to have a best friend. For our contemporary society, the author adds the realistic ingredients of interracial prejudice and sexual discrimination. There are no illustrations. However, the book jacket shows the young hero dribbling a basketball with his black-and-white spaniel following, surrounded by facial cameos of two friends and the Black mother of one of them. Young people from 9 to 14 will find the story honest and appealing.

Although 10-year-old Stuart Wilson, who is an only child, daydreams that a scout will see him playing ball expertly in his Clayton, Kansas, driveway, he tries to get a classmate Robert to come over to play with him. Robert, however, always has an excuse. Stuart's parents' advice to extend himself and be friendly isn't helpful because he knows that just having your parents tell you to have friends does not help. Another classmate and neighbor, Alison Henning, is also a good basketball player and always acts friendly toward Stuart. Stuart has warm parents, Mark Wilson an architect and Mrs. Wilson a home teacher, who provide a stable home. Their dog, Rover, welcomes Stuart home from school every day with several frantic turns around the house and much tail-wagging. However, it is not until the family of the new aeronautical engineer at the local manufacturing company settles in Clayton that Stuart finds a friend of the same sex.

Miss Hansen, the fifth-grade teacher, asks Stuart to show the new boy, Peter Baker, around. The boys hit it off right away; Peter invites Stuart to come swimming in his pool when Peter finishes his afternoon dental work.

In the meantime, Stuart discovers that Robert isn't really avoiding him, but is embarrassed to explain that he has to help his mother after school. Stuart begins to realize that Alison suffers because of her father's refusal to recognize her skill at playing basketball. Stuart also becomes aware that Alison has always been his friend and likes him. Alison and Stuart dress up as a lady and a hobo to go trick-or-treating on Halloween and they have a great time. Before they go out, Stuart shows Alison his large bedroom and accepts her friendship.

Eventually Stuart accompanies Peter to his beautiful home on Woodburn Street, one of the swankiest addresses in Clayton. Stuart is shocked to discover that the Black maid with the Afro-styled hair, who is holding Diane, Peter's 3-year-old sister, is really Peter's mother. He has seen the white Mr. Baker in school and never thought about Peter's racial background. Stuart adjusts to the interracial aspect of the family, but wonders if Clayton will do so because of the people like Mr. Henning who continually say "You can do anything you want, all it takes is practice." Moreover, Stuart finally realizes that he, too, may be prejudiced about some things when his mother announces that the basketball period at school may be for both boys and girls, and he gasps when she adds that he may have to take home economics.

Peter goes to visit Stuart and tells him how uncoordinated he is at basketball and how lucky Stuart is to have a dog. They talk about Peter's older brother, Geoffrey, a ninth-grader, who is an excellent football player. Stuart begins to see that stereotypes can be false and dangerous. As the two friends cross a town park, several tough youths who have been threatening his brother Geoffrey pick a fight with the boys. Although Stuart and Peter fight bravely, they are seriously hurt. Afterward, when the Bakers come to the Wilsons to get Peter, Stuart tells him, we're blood brothers now.

As Stuart and Alison talk about the fight and prejudice, she admits her father's feelings and hopes that "maybe he'll come around someday. Maybe all he needs is practice." The feeling of inadequacy that his stereotypical, albeit well-meaning, thinking has instilled in her floats near the surface. Stuart has accomplished his immediate goal twice over by recognizing Alison as a friend and discovering Peter as a friend-brother. The career goal does not seem impossible. Nevertheless, as Stuart finishes writing all the good news to a pen pal, Mrs. Wilson calls upstairs, "Did you finish your homework?" reminding him that there is more growing up to come.

Thematic Analysis

The longing for a best friend by youngsters in the middle grades is a primary theme. The growing awareness of the hero that he may already have a best friend of the opposite sex is another theme that becomes clearer as he also forms a deep friendship with the new boy in school. Throughout the story is threaded an important secondary theme about the destructive nature of prejudice, whether it is racial or sexist.

Discussion Materials

This book lends itself to many different book introductions: the inner problem "You can't make a friend just because your parents want you to" (pp. 8-9); school elections (pp. 10-12); the metric project (pp. 14-16); Rover's antics (pp. 5-6, 73, 76-77); and swimming (pp. 40-42). Some episodes deal with prejudice: antifeminine (pp. 17-18); meeting Peter's mom (pp. 36-38); interracial (pp. 43-45, 46-48); Mr. Henning (pp. 67-70, 73-74). Alison and Stuart's Halloween tells well (pp. 54-63). A good discussion could also be stimulated by describing the beating (pp. 79-88).

Related Materials

Some titles to suggest are: *The Real Me* (Knopf, 1974; pap., Avon, 1975) by Betty Miles, a story of an 11-year-old's fight for female equality; *The Hockey Girls* (Dutton, 1976) by Scott Corbett; Ellen Conford's *Dreams of Victory* (Little, 1973; pap., Dell, 1974), about a developing self-awareness; *After the Goat Man* (Viking, 1974; pap., Avon, 1975) by Betsy Byars, which deals with gaining strength to overcome problems; and *Ludell* (Harper, 1975) by Brenda Wilkinson, about a young girl's year to be special. For younger readers use Natalie Babbitt's rhyming story about an 8-year-old feminist, *Phoebe's Revolt* (Farrar, 1968). Two related films are *Joey* (Institutional Cinema, Inc., 54 min., color), about a Puerto Rican boy who is beaten by toughs, and *The Flashettes* (New Day Films, 28 min.), the story of an all Black girls' track team in Brooklyn, New York.

Katherine Paterson, *Bridge to Terabithia*
T. Y. Crowell, 1977, $7.95

Mrs. Paterson, who writes historical Japanese stories for children with such authority and grace, turns her talent here to the story of a farm boy who loses his new friend in a tragic accident, but not before she introduces him to a new way to find satisfaction by expanding his imagination. The author who writes with such style about gaining confidence has fashioned a story of childhood that boys and girls will like. It is an uncommon book and a compelling one that many can appreciate. There are no illustrations, but child readers may visualize some in their own minds. Youngsters from 9 to 13 will appreciate the book.

Ten-year-old Jesse Olmers Aarons, Jr., lives on a farm in Lark Creek, an unfashionable rural area near Washington, D.C. He has four sisters: Brenda, Ellie, 4-year-old Joyce Ann, and his favorite, 7-year-old May Belle. His dad commutes and shares the outdoor chores with him. He has two special talents: he draws well and is a good runner who practices every day. He also has special aspirations: he wants to be the fastest runner in the fifth grade and longs to have a friend. When Leslie Burke, the new girl in school, enters his class, Jesse never dreams that she will be that friend.

Leslie who is the same age as Jesse is the intelligent only daughter of Judy and Bill Burke, both writers, who have moved to the farm next to the Aarons to escape many of the features of city life they do not share. Leslie wears blue jeans and sneakers without socks, and is unlike any girl Jesse knows. She is also a runner, and scuba diving is her hobby. When she asks to run a race with three boys after school, the other two protest until Jesse sticks up for her. She dashes one of his aspirations by proving that she is the fastest runner in the fifth grade.

However, she makes it up to Jesse by establishing a secret hiding place for just the two of them behind the old Perkins place across the fields and creek. In this secret place Leslie shares with Jesse all of her imagination and knowledge of literature. "Leslie was more than his friend. She was his other, more exciting self—his way to Terabithia and all the worlds beyond" (Chapter 4). The bridge of tree branches thrown across the creek leading to the made-up name place Terabithia actually became a road toward confidence for the shy intelligent boy.

Jesse, nonetheless, remains May Belle's companion in school when she comes crying to him because Janice Avery, a big seventh-grader, has taken the child's lunch "Twinkie." He contemplates writing a letter to Willard, her supposed boyfriend, that would expose that false claim. He takes pity, however, when he learns that Janice's father beats her and that her feckless girl friends tell everyone about this. As Christmas approaches he decides to give Leslie a puppy which she promptly names Prince Terrien for his place in the kingdom.

Meanwhile, Jesse begins to like Bill Burke as he helps him fix up his house. He realizes that Leslie has understanding parents. Jesse reciprocates by inviting Leslie to Easter service with the Aarons. The two friends anticipate the Easter vacation and make plans to spend a good deal of it in Terabithia. When Easter Monday dawns, the creek, swollen almost to flood stage, continues to fill from the continuing rain. Jesse, who knows the area well, is afraid to cross the bridge to meet Leslie. He is uncomfortable because he has no "guts."

Instead of going to meet Leslie he accepts an invitation from his music teacher, Miss Edmunds, to go into Washington to tour the National Gallery of Art. They have a wonderful time, visiting the Smithsonian Institution, which Jesse has never seen, as well as the National Gallery. When he gets home, Jesse is told that Leslie is dead.

He feels guilty because he was in the galleries rather than on the dangerous bridge where he might have helped Leslie. When his family discusses how the Burke girl was found in the creek, Jesse runs away with his father in pursuit. Jesse finds it hard to understand her death and blames himself. Nevertheless, he goes with his parents to pay his respects to the bereaved family.

In the somber Burke house, Leslie's grandmother tells him that she knows he must be *the* Jesse whom Leslie told her all about. In an angry act, he flings the Christmas present Leslie gave him as he stares at the branches from which she fell. Finally, Jesse accepts her death by silently saying, "I am now the fastest runner in the fifth grade."

When spring arrives and the creek subsides, Jesse crosses the bridge to Terabithia thinking again that he didn't come on the fateful day because he didn't want to die. May Belle, who follows him and gets stuck in crossing, is rescued in an act of bravery by her brother.

At school their teacher, Mrs. Meyers, tells Jesse how sorry she is about Leslie's death, and inwardly she realizes that Leslie was someone special in his life who turned him into a king. When the Burkes move and leave Jesse their extra lumber, he makes a real bridge and leads May Belle to Terabithia to give her some of the magic Leslie gave him, saying to himself, ". . . beautiful girl arriving today might be the queen they've [inhabitants of Terabithia] been waiting for."

Thematic Analysis

Gaining confidence through the use of imaginative play and literature that expands awareness together with the nourishing friendship of an age mate are the main themes of this story. Another important thread is the tortuous path a youngster must travel to the realization and acceptance of a young friend's death.

Discussion Materials

For an introduction to the characters, use parts of the first three chapters. A visit to the magic Narnia-like country of Terabithia can be reconstructed from the pages of Chapter 4. Jesse's dilemma over what to purchase for Leslie for Christmas is found in the last pages of Chapter 5; a description of the item in Chapter 6. Each of the 13 chapters is filled with tellable or discussable material. Particularly suitable for discussion is Jesse's discovery of the pragmatic announcement in Chapter 12 that Leslie is to be cremated.

Related Materials

If youngsters have not read them, suggest the titles in the "Narnia" series by C. S. Lewis (*The Lion, the Witch, and the Wardrobe*, etc.). There are several other books for the same readers: *In the Time of the Bells* (Delacorte, 1976) by Maria Gripe, the story of two half-brothers; *Wild Boy* (Harper, 1973) by Joan Tate, the story of a runaway orphan and a young friend; and *To Tame a Sister* (Viking, 1973), the story of a girl who conforms rather than be isolated. Rosa Guy's *The Friends* (Holt, 1973) is about a girl's growing awareness that the gulf between her and her best friend is due to her own actions. Two films are suggested: *Little Pig* (LCA, 27 min., color) is about a young Chinese girl desperately trying to care for her infant brother and *Kites Aloft* (Acorn, 15 min., color) is about the pleasures of kit flying. Instructions for some imaginative play are available in Marcia Lynn Cox's *Make-Up Monsters* (Grosset, 1977).

Doris Buchanan Smith, *A Taste of Blackberries*

> Illus. by Charles Robinson. T. Y. Crowell, 1973, $5.50; pap., Scholastic Bk. Services, 1976, 95¢

Here is a touching story about the death of a young boy and the grief it brings to his young playmate. The author writes sympathetically, drawing from a reservoir of personal knowledge about children. Although the subject of death is a difficult one to handle for any age, the author's understanding of young children's feelings and thoughts keeps the book from being maudlin. It is lavishly illustrated with 16 charming soft wash pen-and-ink drawings by Charles Robinson whose work has won him the recognition of a gold medal from the Society of Illustrators. The book jacket is a lush watercolor drawing that portrays the first episode in the book. It shows two boys in the midst of blackberry bushes and three shadowy figures walking away in the distance.

Youngsters from 8 to 11 will appreciate the tale. Because the book is an easy-to-read one, it can be suggested to 7-year-olds as well as to slower 13-year-old readers.

Jamie is facile, with a quick tongue and ready answers. He also exaggerates situations in a humorous manner carrying each to a fare-thee-well. In spite of this, everyone considers him someone special because he has a knack for making things pleasant. He is the oldest child in his family and has a 4-year-old sister, Martha, and a baby brother. The boy who lives next door to Jamie is the youngest in his family, and the narrator of the story. Although the neighbor boy is also friendly with another classmate, Heather, and others, Jamie and he are best friends. The best friend tells the story as he remembers it.

He remembers vividly overhearing comments, while picking black-berries before they were ripe, from the other youngsters about Jamie's funny behavior and he silently condemned Jamie. He was sick of always being less than Jamie in everything. He also recalls "snitching" apples from an orchard on the walk home from berrying only to find the taste terribly bitter. Although he tosses his uneaten apple in the nearby pond, Jamie, in his fashion, doggedly eats his down to the core.

He recalls the day Jamie took him and Martha down to show her their school. He remembers how embarrassed and scared he was to "hitch" a ride when he and Jamie and Martha were caught in a sudden rainstorm. Jamie enjoyed the experience. Even the driver who picked them up told them not to do it again because the next time the driver might not be a classmate's father.

Although it turned out to be a tragic day, he remembers his elation at old Mrs. Houser's offer to pay him and his friends 25¢ a jar to take the Japanese beetles off her grapevine leaves. He gets everyone together armed with a screw-cap to scrape the Japanese beetles off the leaves. Suddenly, Jamie, who has been clowning around with a stick in a bee's nest, falls to the ground screaming and gasping. His friend who silently calls Jamie a "faker" stands fast among the swarming bees while they trail the children who run away. However, soon on the scene is a screeching ambulance called by Mrs. Houser who has seen that something is wrong with Jamie. Heather confirms this as the ambulance takes him away.

The friend soon learns from his mother at home that Jamie is dead from an allergic reaction to the bee sting. The young boy is shocked; looking out of his bedroom window he thinks of the times when they beamed light signals to each other's rooms. Although numbed by grief, at the last minute he joins his mother and father to go to the funeral parlor. Later he goes over to a neighbor's garden and listens to Mrs. Mullins talk about friendship. He finds it comforting. However, not until the day of Jamie's funeral when he saw his friend put in the grave did he begin to accept the finality of it. It isn't until he goes to pick the now ripe blackberries that he can accept it emotionally. He feels the presence of Jamie and realizes that the memory of his friend will always be with him. As if in celebration, he brings Jamie's mother a basket of blackberries.

Thematic Analysis

The shocking effect the death of a young playmate can have is thoroughly explored in the necessarily foreshortened normal sequence as it actually occurs. The disbelief, numbness, and guilt feelings that the protagonist experiences poignantly mimic the ones a live youngster would go through. At the same time, the theme of friendship is well delineated from its depths and heights to its lasting quality in memory.

Discussion Materials

To set the scene, describe the two friends picking blackberries and "snitching" apples (pp. 1-3); capturing Japanese beetles (pp. 8-9); and "hitching" a ride (pp. 13-16). The tragedy can be briefly stated together with its consequences (pp. 17-24, 27-29). Material on friendship and on the meaning of death to young people exists in Mrs. Mullins's talk with the bereaved friend (pp. 39-44; picture of neighbor lady p. 43) and the lasting meaning of real friendship is found in the resolution (pp. 52-57). Good discussions will follow under a competent leader.

Related Materials

Another book on ambivalent feelings toward family and friends occasioned by the death of a loved one is Honor Arundel's *The Blanket Word* (Nelson, 1973; pap., Dell, 1975). Ellen Conford's *Me and the Terrible Two* (Little, 1974; pap., Archway, 1977) is about a girl's feelings for her twin brothers and Beverly Cleary's *Ramona the Brave* (Morrow, 1975; pap., Scholastic Bk. Services, 1977) is about two sisters. *The Rooster Who Understood Japanese* (Scribner, 1976) by Yoshika Uchida is illustrated by the same artist as *A Taste of Blackberries* and will appeal to the same readers. For a special treat show Maurice Sendak's *Really Rosie Starring the Nutshell Kids* (Weston Woods, 26 min., color).

Barbara Brooks Wallace, *Victoria*

> Jacket painting by Charles Liese. Follett, 1972, lib. bdg. $4.98; pap., Dell, 1974, $1.25

Barbara Wallace, whose previous books deal with boys or tomboys, writes here about the events during one fall in the lives of 2 girls new to boarding school: that faintly old-fashioned genre so popular with girls. This author writes with such perception about the thoughts and actions of the young heroines that a sense of timelessness suffuses this story of a privileged economic class. Her knowledge of private-school life enhances this poignant narrative of friends who uncover the deeper meaning of close friendship. Written without sentimentality, the book treats a subject that is common to a few, and of interest to many. Girls from the age of 8 to 13 will be captivated by both the theme and the setting.

The jacket painting, by Charles Liese, of Victoria in a white lawn party dress reminiscent of an earlier era conveys the loneliness that such "privileged" children can symbolize. It can be used to introduce the book to girls. Indeed, it will do this on an individual basis because of a haunting quality that surrounds it.

Victoria Corcoran, an 11-year-old motherless girl, and Dilys Rattenbury, her friend of the same age, both of whose fathers are in government service live in the same apartment house in Washington, D.C. Dilys relies on the seemingly independent Victoria even to the point of holding her hand when crossing busy streets. Dilys is surprised by Victoria's sudden announcement that she is being interviewed by Miss Lawrence, the Bennett School headmistress. Miss Lawrence is a school chum of Victoria's Aunt Cornelia Corcoran or "Smelly Nelly," a wealthy old lady who has recommended to Michael Corcoran that "Tory" be enrolled. Victoria tells Dilys, while seated on her favorite red hassock, that Miss Lawrence is out to marry her father. Dilys is quietly upset because she has a crush on Mr. Corcoran. Victoria, however, neglects to add that Dilys is also going because her little brother Gordy and her parents are going to be traveling. Mr. Corcoran drives both girls to Bennett which is between Washington and New York City.

There they join 20 junior boarders of grades 6 through 8. Together with two others, the friends and their new roommates, Eugenia Feldman, an owlish looking New York City girl, and Scarlett O. Harris, an angora kitten type, make up the entire sixth grade. Dilys is immediately lonesome, but Victoria, who never cries or expresses sadness, merely says that their roommates are freaks. Dilys objects to calling them freaks and points out that Scarlett, who wears old cut-down clothes, has no father.

Dilys and Victoria soon become involved in school activities. They meet deaf Mrs. Augustine who presides at their 14-place meal table, join the boy's school for chapel, and meet Joseph Vaughan the sixth-grade English teacher and Miss Andrea the teacher of sixth-grade science and girl's athletics. It is Miss Andrea who explains the intricacies of the traditional annual Halloween tree planting of the sixth-graders. From the endless introduction of "old-timers" or returning students, Victoria quickly grasps the importance of having had mothers or sisters at Bennett. She quickly labels this group "The Descendants" and, perched on the illegally transplanted red hassock, dubs her own group of four—the Victorians. This group that meets by flashlight after lights-out time takes its rules from Victoria's treasured Black Book, a gift from Mrs. O'Reilly, one of the many Corcoran housekeeper-governesses. Each girl has a code name (Vix, Dill, Scar, Jinn) and 18 rules to obey (number 13 is crossed out deliberately). The Black Book is supposedly responsible for curing Jinn's asthma by the use of a prescription of spider web pills which Victoria makes while on duty at "the woodpile."

Meanwhile, Victoria leaves her bed unmade each morning and unknown to her roommates serves her "pink slip" punishments by transporting logs from the woodpile to the school. Her friends discover her subterfuge when she leaves her bed unmade one day too long and each roommate gets a "pink slip." However, she goes to Miss Lawrence and arranges to accept the whole punishment and to make her bed in the future.

The Victorians decide, on the advice of the Black Book, to bury a dead animal under the apple tree that is chosen for planting in the churchyard. For the occasion Victoria provides a dead rat in a brown bag which each girl signs backwards before it goes under her bed. After several days, the smell alerts Miss Lawrence who finds the bag, rat, and girls' names. In a final attempt to follow the Black Book, the roommates plant the bony remains from a school chicken dinner under the tree after the school Halloween dance. When they are caught burying the bones in the churchyard by Miss Andrea and Mr. Foster, Miss Lawrence gives them a punishment to fit the crime. When Victoria, who lands in the infirmary, extracts a promise from the complacent, but resentful Dilys to crawl three times around the aisle in the chapel, she is discovered. In discussing this episode, Miss Lawrence explains that Dilys expects too much sympathy from Victoria and has a false dependence on someone who unfortunately has been forced too early into independence.

At Thanksgiving, most of the boarders go home, leaving Dilys, Scarlett, and Victoria, whose father is away. They meet Scarlett's mother, brother, and sisters and learn that she is a charity student complete with hand-me-down clothes. Dilys, who feels ashamed at the offhand treatment Victoria gives Scarlett, becomes increasingly angry with Victoria and begins to question her own dependence on her. When Eugenia returns with her asthma in full bloom because, as her physician father suggests, it may be an allergic reaction to a change of air rather than the Black Book pills, room number 7 becomes Coventry for Victoria. She is an outcast! Dilys suggests in her absence that they all look at the Black Book which turns out to be a compilation of superstitions.

Miss Lawrence finally broadens Dilys's understanding of Victoria and her private lonesomeness and alienation. She tells Dilys that as a small child Victoria used to sit on her hassock beside her sick mother's bed until the mother died. Miss Lawrence helps Dilys to appreciate how well Victoria has managed to cope and how much true friendship Victoria needs from Dilys. More aware now, Dilys thinks it would be a good idea if Miss Lawrence were to become Victoria's stepmother. Her own crush on Victoria's father vanishes, and a better quality of friendship with Victoria emerges.

Thematic Analysis

Sharing with friends and everyone's need for reliance on someone at times is the well-developed theme. That independent action may sometimes belie dependent emotional needs and that dependency can be an immature emotional ploy for attention serve as counterpoints in this story. The structure of life in a boarding school is explored for the uninitiated to grasp. Well developed also is an examination of facets of deprivation in a class priviliged with money.

Discussion Materials

There are many episodes that can be used as a basis for talks or for discussion, including an introduction of the main characters. Use any of the following: painful talk about boarding school (pp. 9–14); first day at school (pp. 62–65); Miss Andrea/tree planting/descendants (pp. 68–72); the Black Book (pp. 78–84); the Victorians (pp. 105–111); the rat smells (pp. 128–133); the chicken under the apple tree (pp. 148–153); Dilys crawls in the aisles (pp. 164–166); Thanksgiving at school (pp. 174–179).

Related Materials

Several books are suggested: Nancy Bond's *A String in the Harp* (Atheneum, 1976), about a widower and his three children who settle for a year in Wales; Frances A. Dunscombe's *Summer of the Burning* (Putnam, 1976), about 13-year-old motherless Hannah in 1779; Marilyn Sachs's *The Truth about Mary Rose* (Doubleday, 1973; pap., Dell, 1974), about a young girl who finds out that her namesake aunt is not exactly the way she thinks of her. Also recommended is a story about the negative aspects of human emotions, *The Forgotten Beasts of Eld* (Atheneum, 1974; pap., Avon, 1975) by Patricia McKillip. Two films are: *Sophie* (Films, Inc., 10 min., color) and *Friends or Foe* (LCA, 26 min., color).

3

Developing Values

CHILDREN BEGIN to develop a conscience and form a system of values at an early age. As they grow through the intermediate and adolescent years, youngsters demonstrate an increasing sense of responsibility to these values, which become an individual's deepest beliefs and the basis for making moral and ethical decisions.

Although achieving understanding of concepts is a long and difficult task, children are generally capable of beginning to understand the complexities of concepts, such as love and freedom. At no other stage of life will people be so desirous of learning useful ways for guiding their lives. Exposure to a range of sound principles through books can be a worthwhile venture in stimulating this awakening sense. Plots that show the fragile nature of value judgments and characters that portray the multifaceted quality of moral dilemmas provide youngsters with the welcome vicarious experience of testing their own values.

The books discussed in this chapter cover responsible and inspiring behavior toward a spectrum of situations ranging from establishing a properly balanced life perspective to appreciating the elderly and to understanding values of different cultures.

Robbie Branscum, *Toby, Granny, and George*
> Illus. by Glen Rounds. Doubleday, 1976, $5.95; pap., Avon, 1977, $1.25

The Ozarks that the author knows so well from childhood and youth serve as the setting here and in her earlier books, *Me and Jim Luke* and *Johnny May*. She spins a tale of everyday adventure, mystery, and romance around the young heroines that reverberates with honesty. This story of one summer in the life of a girl growing up in the hill country of Arkansas will appeal to girls from 8 to 13.

The pen-and-ink line drawings that begin the chapters and the frontispiece are from the drawing board of Glen Rounds, the well-known author-illustrator. Their scraggly, unfinished style which adds the sense of motion to the drawings captures well the flavor of the book. The characters fairly walk off the pages. The mountain cabin home, water well, and garden detail delineate the condition and character of the home.

Thirteen-year-old October (Toby), who remembers no other home but Granny's from the time she was put there as a baby, sometimes calls herself a bastard but publicly pushes schoolmate Marlene Smith for calling her that (picture p. 19). In the past, Toby has occasionally wondered if there are people in the city who look like her. She has looked at the few folks who live nearby and who worship in the one-room hill church with Granny and her, and has given up. Besides she loves the widowed Granny and would never leave her or George, their large, reddish hound dog. There are other more important things to do and consider.

For one thing, there is a disturbing split in the church since Minnie Jackson's drowning in the shallow baptizing hole. The folks like Toby and Granny, who believe Preacher Davis is guiltless, sit on one side of the church aisle, while those who believe he is guilty in sympathy with Deacon Treat sit on the other. Wearing their Sunday-best floral sack dresses instead of overalls for church service no longer seems special.

Both Davis and Treat are well known to Granny, the community's practical nurse who dispenses herbal medicine and attends to first aid, midwifery, and "laying out" of the dead. When Preacher Davis comes to call and talk about his unfortunate ministry and Deacon Treat's pulpit call for a new preacher, which Troyline (Granny) quickly stifles, Toby has to kill their last chicken and find a few ripe vegetables from the large garden they had planted to sustain them all year. Toby wishes they had a cow for milk and butter. But, as Granny says ". . . folks has to work for what they got instead of dreaming about it" (p. 12).

Meanwhile, Toby continues to observe the adults, work hard around the farm, gather wild herbs, and most of all to try to think of a way to get the farm to be better as it was when Troyline's husband and 10 children were around. She thinks that she might paint the schoolhouse in exchange for a cow if only rich fat Seth Treat did not have his skinny kids do it each year.

As a result of Toby's questioning about Deacon Treat and the whole affair, Granny takes Toby to his farm. There his wife, Opal, and 6 scrawny kids ranging in age from 15-year-old Johnny Joe, who has been almost mute since he and his mother became Treats, to the little baby, sit down with the visitors for a sumptuous meal from the prosperous farm. Toby is astonished to see Seth Treat ladle tiny portions to his family and a huge plate for himself. She realizes now that he is greedy, and that Granny, who has tended the family, wanted her to learn this for herself.

The following day Granny returns to "lay out" Deacon Treat, who has been shot with a .22-caliber rifle. The suspicion over Preacher Davis deepens. Meanwhile, Davis arranges for Toby to paint the schoolhouse for $50.00, which she trades for a cow. Johnny Joe, whose natural father was killed in an accident in the log woods, gives Toby a few chickens and a squirrel he has carved from a hickory nut. Toby rewards him with a kiss, and they both blush. With her fondest wishes coming true, Toby figures that she can get a calf if she drives her cow over to the bull in Clem Jackson's field. While she waits at the Treats, she first realizes that the baby is missing. Although Clem has to tell her when she returns that her cow is not "in heat," he promises to help her later.

Jolene, Granny's youngest daughter, who lives in the city with her 3 children, has come home unexpectedly after many years. Toby stares at her mirror image and knows instinctively that she is Jolene's daughter. Toby runs and hides at Johnny Joe's for 3 days because she is afraid she might be taken from Granny. While she is there, Johnny Joe gives Toby more chickens for her flock. Granny learns that Toby is her granddaughter. She and Toby both hear from Jolene, who left her baby (Toby) on Granny's porch one October, that a young man who was killed in the same accident in the log woods as Johnny Joe's father was Toby's natural father. Toby finally tells them that although she loves her mother, she loves Granny, who has been her mother for 13 years, more and she plans to stay and help the old lady. Jolene goes home. Soon afterward a dark brown mare arrives for Toby, who names her Honeysuckle. She now has a good beginning toward a farm.

Because Toby is shot at twice, once as she is coming from a glen where there is a little grave with a carved wooden cross, Granny and the Preacher form a group to hunt for the sniper. Toby soon tells the Preacher that Johnny Joe must have killed the Deacon in an effort to stop the Deacon from beating the baby who is buried under the cross carving in the glen. The Preacher talks gently with Johnny Joe and Opal, explaining that everyone is guilty for letting Seth Treat work his family so hard, practically starve them, and physically abuse his children. Granny, who has often been called to take care of them, wonders if she should not have told someone. As summer comes to an end, Toby realizes she has learned many lessons—about others and herself.

Thematic Analysis

The development of sound basic values is explored in this simple, easy-to-read story of complex human behaviors. The main theme is a young girl's slow realization of the many different shades of truth behind human behavior. Secondary themes of a youngster's sincere acceptance of a surrogate parent and the need for and satisfaction found in industriousness are honestly portrayed. The depiction of the way of life special to the Ozarks is well drawn and an extra bonus.

Discussion Materials

Introduce the main characters—Granny, Toby, George, Deacon Treat, Johnny Joe, and Preacher Davis—and briefly describe the main plot elements: the hard life on the farm; the church split; the mystery of the missing baby; Toby's parentage. Some episodes are especially good for "talking": dinner at the Treat's, before (pp. 38-40) and after the Deacon's death (pp. 58-59); Toby gets "Honeysuckle" (picture p. 73); the "hunting preacher" poem (p. 76); Toby finds a small grave (picture p. 85). The story can also be introduced by using the illustrations sequentially, perhaps on projected transparencies. A discussion about "heart-praying" (p. 14) or living with a grandparent will be worthwhile.

Related Titles

Two books that will appeal to the same readers are *My Grandson Lew* (Harper, 1974) by Charlotte Zolotow and *McBroom Tells a Lie* (Little, 1975) by Sid Fleischman. The first, illustrated by William Pene du Bois, is about a boy and his mother saddened by Grandpa's death. The second is a zany, humorous tale of an amazing farm. Also suggested are *Shoeshine Girl* (Crowell, 1975) by Clyde Robert Bulla and *Where the Lilies Bloom* (Lippincott, 1969; pap., New Am. Lib., 1974) by Vera and Bill Cleaver. The latter will also be enjoyed by older readers. Two films for this audience are *Katy* (BFA, 17 min., color), about a girl who takes over her brother's paper route, and *Rainshower* (Churchill, 16 min., color), about the utility and beauty of rain in the city and on the farm.

Ann Nolan Clark, *Year Walk*
Viking, 1975, $6.95

The author, who was born in New Mexico and now lives in Arizona, has many books to her credit, including the Newbery award winner, *The Secret of the Andes*. Because of her background, Ann Nolan Clark always wanted to write about the lone Basque shepherd who was constantly visible on the horizon of her childhood.

After 2 trips to Spain and several to Idaho where many American Basques live, she wrote this novel told in 5 parts that parallel the life of a sheepherder. It is the story of the despair and triumph of a Basque boy on his first year's walk with his band of sheep in a new land. Filled with the local color and fine characterizations for which the author is noted, as well as the adventures on the trail, this absorbing story will be read by youngsters from 9 to 14.

One of the scenes described—a lake in the wilderness and some of the animals of the area—serves as an attractive book jacket drawing. The boy in a typical Basque beret with his shepherd's crook and burro appears in the brightly colored painting together with tall evergreens reminiscent of the high country.

Kepa (Pedro), a 16-year-old from a small village in the Spanish Pyrenees, is the central figure in two meetings in his family's 3-story whitewashed caserio. His godfather, Pedro, has sent a letter asking Kepa to come to his sheep ranch in Boise, Idaho, as he had promised his namesake he would when he visited the family 4 years earlier. As is the custom among the Basques, whose motto is "seven is one" (referring to 4 Spanish and 3 French provinces), Kepa's family—father, little mother, 2 older brothers, and 3 older sisters—and the family of the first neighbor, Jose, godfather Pedro's older brother, meet in the sala (kitchen) on the second floor or living quarters of the caserio. Each is asked to vote. All agree that Kepa should go, except little mother, who doesn't want her youngest child to leave. At the second meeting, little mother agrees when the others explain that if he doesn't go, he must go away anyhow for service in the army. They feel secure in sending him to help on the sheep ranch because he has had the experience of training, under the "Old One" with his great Pyrenees dog Trinko, a flock of 20 sheep, using a hand-carved shepherd's crook (maleka).

Kepa and his friend Alejandro, who is on his way to California to become an automobile mechanic, arrive in Boise in 1910. Already aware of his impending loneliness, Kepa is driven by Pedro to the sheep ranch where they go over the financial considerations. Godfather Pedro, who loves his young namesake, knows the slim opportunities in the Spanish village for anyone other than the eldest son, and wants Kepa to have the same opportunity he has had. He secretly hopes that Kepa will stay long enough to save money for a ranch of his own. Nevertheless, he assures Kepa that he is free to return home with as much of his wages as he saves.

Pedro explains that his 3 bands of sheep are ready to take to the trail: a 2,500 band of twins with Juan; 3,000 with Carlos; and 2,500 with old Tio Marco, who is to be Kepa's teacher. The gift of a small black-and-white sheep dog raised by Pedro's daughter, 13-year-old Maria Cristina, is a second step in the preparations. Next, Kepa helps in the shearing pens as the skilled traveling Mexican shearers complete their job; he learns that there are 300 lbs. of wool in each sack. He is told that there is one black sheep among every 100 sheep so that when they are spread out on the trail a quick count can be made.

The morning after the dance at which Kepa sings Basque songs and accompanies himself on his guitar, Tio Marco and he pack their mules. Kepa names his young and frisky burro, Patto-Kak. Since they are the first to take to the trail, they can expect to find the best grass and water holes. Kepa soon learns other valuable things about sheepherding; (1) the band walks all morning behind the leader; (2) sheep rest and graze in the afternoon; (3) sheep graze uphill in the rain; (4) sheep are stupid and have a group mind; and (5) sheep obey only the dogs. Except for teaching, which he does well, Tio Marco doesn't talk. After all the years of solitude on the sheep trails with only his dog for a companion, he has lost the desire and ability to communicate. Kepa thinks about his father's teachings that in leaving home one leaves forever.

Kepa is never far from the trail in mind or body. He learns to shoot his new rifle well. It is not long before 3 cattle rustlers appear with 50 steers, and they argue with Tio Marco over the rights to a water hole. One of them cruelly shoots Tio Marco's dog on the spot, driving the old man into shock. Pedro arrives to send the broken old man back to the Spain of his lonely dreams. Meanwhile, Pedro takes over with Tio Marco's band. He feels confident, although he has yet to prove himself the boss to Patto-Kak. However, his young dog takes over keeping the sheep moving and lies down beside Kepa, who has made an important conquest. He shows the supply stringer, Alberto, the 10 rattles from the rattlesnake he shot. Alberto brings him supplies and news; letters from Alejandro and little mother. Kepa's loneliness is relieved only by the appearance of Hans, the gnomelike gold miner friend of Tio Marco. Hans takes Kepa to a lush hidden valley where the sheep graze while he teaches Kepa how to cook trail food properly. He also encourages Kepa to make carvings of the animals he sees around him.

After Hans leaves, carrying his treasured carved box, Pedro and Maria Cristina arrive with the supplies, letters, and news that Kepa will stay in their home while the lambs are sold and before he returns to the trail into the ranch. Kepa tells his godfather and Chris about Hans whom they know and like. Kepa also gives Chris his first carving of a bluejay and the privilege of naming his dog. She calls him "Keeper."

Kepa has finally realized that "being alone is standing by yourself . . . , but being lonely means despair at being alone" (p. 116). He has many adventures in the wilderness during the summer. The vastness of the surroundings and the strange animals which he sees and carves fascinate him: raccoons; deer; bears; and a mountain lion. Natural phenomena, such as a forest fire, a storm and lightning, and a torrential flood that swirls around his band draw upon his courage and resourcefulness. Through it all, however, he loses only a few lambs. Only Patto-Kak, his makela, and six tagalongs (sheep) are missing after the wall of water washes down behind him. As Kepa reaches the lookout point over the buying camp, Alberto compliments him on having his band in the best condition he has seen in a long time.

Three days later, after all the fat old ewes and three-quarters of the young lambs have been sold, the letters from home have been read, and the Basque songs and celebration have ended, Chris and her younger twin brothers leave on horseback with Kepa in charge on his first horse to find the missing tails for the count. They meet Hans who has the 6 tails and Kepa's makela. They are also delighted to see a bear and cub come to frolic at a pool (p. 160 and jacket).

In October Kepa's thinned-out band leaves the wilderness area to trail through the hills and desert to the home camp for the February lambing. Kepa has trouble finding the "hidden valley" on the way back until Patto-Kak leads them into the opening. As a respite on Kepa's seventeenth birthday, December 23, Pedro arrives with Kepa's Christmas presents including Chris's gift of a Spanish delicacy, "chorizos." In return, Kepa sends her the carving of the bear and cub.

Still undecided about whether to stay or not, Kepa continues his year's walk to the lambing sheds at the ranch. With only 2 days to go, he loses a young ewe, but saves the newborn twin lambs. Soon afterward Hans collapses in Kepa's arms. Kepa carries him until Pedro arrives. Hans tells Kepa that he lost the best thing in his life, Gretchen, who loved him. He knew she did because she was so good to him in the little things of the heart. Kepa loses another ewe, but saves the newborn lamb by wrapping it expertly in the skinned fleece of the dead mother. Pedro returns with the news that Hans is dead. Kepa proudly brings his band into the lambing sheds with a firm decision to stay as an American Basque and work to save for his own ranch while Chris finishes school. To seal his intention and carry out Hans's last request, Kepa and Chris go by horseback to the waterfall to open the carved box he left.

Thematic Analysis

This story has several important themes, none more important than the one that differentiates between being alone and being lonely (p. 116). Another is the emphasis on change and its consequences; as Kepa's father said you should never expect things to be the same when you return and as Kepa observed from Tio Marco's experience one should live and work where one's heart is. Many topics can be explored: sheepherding; Basque Americans; yesterday and today; the Idaho wilderness and the animals; signs of first love.

Discussion Materials

Any of the preceding topics can be discussed. A useful discussion under a leader can be developed around the values expressed about leaving home, changes, and being on one's own. For introducing Kepa and the other characters, use the frontispiece together with the plot outline and the flashback to Spain (pp. 1–23). Other episodes are: finances (pp. 24–30); the sheep ranch (pp. 31–38); Tio Marco and his teaching (pp. 41–53); the rustler (pp. 56–61); Kepa leads the band (pp. 62–65); loneliness (pp. 70–71; 116; jacket picture); rattlesnake (pp. 75–76); Hans and his carved box (pp. 84–99, 136–140); fire (pp. 126–135); wall of water (pp. 135–143); the rules (pp. 149–153); Patto-Kak, the hero (pp. 169–173); first love (pp. 154–160; 186); Kepa's birthday (p. 177); saving lambs (pp. 185, 186–192).

Related Materials

Try Harold Keeth's *The Obstinate Land* (T. Y. Crowell, 1977) for the same readers. Other suggested titles are: *This Is Espie Sanchez* (Dutton, 1976) by Terry Dunnahoo; *Phoebe's Family* (Nelson, 1974) by Pamela Sykes; and, for older or more sophisticated readers, Honor Arundel's *The Longest Weekend* (Nelson, 1970; pap., Grosset, 1973), which has a female protagonist. For information use two filmstrips: *Trails to the North West* and *Trails to the Rockies* from the BFA series *America's Frontier Trails West*. A 16mm film, *The Searching Eye* (Pyramid, 1970, 11 min., color), correlates with the intense nature of the observations in the story.

James Lincoln Collier and Christopher Collier, *The Bloody Country*
Scholastic Bk. Services, 1976, $6.95

This historical novel of a settler's life in Pennsylvania after the Revolution is written by brothers who are noted for their skill and popularity. James is recognized as a writer of juveniles and Christopher as a scholar and historian who has specialized in the history of Connecticut and the Revolutionary period. They collaborated on the ALA Honor book, *My Brother Sam Is Dead* (Four Winds), which questions the tensions and divided loyalties of a Connecticut family, and finally the war itself.

Based on documents and historical accounts, *The Bloody Country* is full of the harshness of frontier life and the ambiguities of people under stress. An exciting easy-to-read adventure story, it will be read avidly by youngsters from 9 to 14 years of age.

Ben Buck, who was born in 1770, and his age mate and family brother, Joe Mountain, the son of a Black man and a Mohegan mother who worked for the family, live in Windham, Connecticut. David Buck, and his family—wife, daughter Annie, her husband Isaac, and the boys decide to migrate to Wyoming Valley in Pennsylvania because Connecticut is becoming too crowded. A group of Connecticut people called the Susquehanna Company had bought the land in Pennsylvania in 1754 for the purpose of resettling.

After a week of traveling, the families arrive in the fertile valley beside the Susquehanna River. The Bucks settle on a mill on the river because David Buck had originally been a miller. They put it into shape, and soon build up a livelihood and a reputation as good millers. The boys help with the work but there is still time to play and enjoy the hunting, berry picking, and exploring.

They had been there about 4 years when what were formerly occasional uprisings by the Indians became more frequent. There were continual reports that the Indians were attacking. Once mother, Annie, Joe, and Ben had gone to the hill stockade to sit out some trouble. Life in the bustling and crowded fort was not to anyone's liking, and they soon returned to the mill. The Indians, however, were on the warpath and had increased their raids along the settlements. Although Father wanted everyone to go back to the stockade, both Annie, who was expecting her first child, and mother insisted upon staying.

One day soon after this decision was made, while Mr. Buck is out, an Indian war party arrives and scalps mother and Isaac, who elected to stay upstairs to protect the mill. Annie and the two boys are safe in the cellar. The baby, little Isaac, is soon born. Annie is disconsolate and keeps imploring her father to return to Connecticut. He, nonetheless, is adamant about staying. There is nothing for him in Connecticut and he wants to stay where they are for the sake of Ben's future.

Meanwhile, another situation develops. Alexander Patterson, a Justice of the Peace and a Pennsylvania ranger, demands the mill property in the name of the government, ordering Buck to vacate. In spite of Buck's legal certificates, Patterson charges that the Susquehanna Company's claim to the land is invalid. Mr. Buck investigates only to find that Patterson is working for land speculators. With steely determination, he decides to stay in spite of Annie's increasing importuning. Between the frequent Indian raids and this new bedevilment, some of the settlers head back: Annie and little Isaac among them.

During the time of this ferment, Joe learns from Colonel Patterson that he is legally a free man in Pennsylvania. Joe, who realizes that because he is Black he is considered a slave by Mr. Buck, is tempted to run away and free himself. Ben, who has always considered Joe one of the family and free, is astonished to discover that his father doesn't consider Joe an equal. Ben begins to learn what being free means.

Just before a spring downpour, the Bucks realize that the new settlers who have replaced the folks who have left under the threats of the Indians and Colonel Patterson have been chopping down many of the trees that line the river banks. The Bucks know that this portends serious flooding along the river. When it starts to rain and doesn't stop, Ben and Joe watch the swollen waters rise over the land, washing away possessions and whole barns and even carrying livestock down the roaring waterway. Ben tries to save the mill, and especially the huge waterwheel. Nevertheless, as the avalanche of water advances, the walls of the mill give way and the wheel slips its delicate mooring. In the midst of the havoc Ben and Joe argue about slavery and Joe leaves. When the waters finally subside, Ben and his father replace the waterwheel and try to reestablish a normal life in spite of the devastating flood. However, the remainder of the terrible winter and spring, the deprivations and the harassment by Colonel Patterson force the majority of the women and children to return to Connecticut.

Ben, now a young teenager, leads a 10-day march to Connecticut with more than 500 women and children who are being sent back to wait out the hard times. It is a painful journey with no transportation and little food. A 3-year-old drowns as they resolutely cross one river with the small children on their mother's shoulders. The trek finally completed, Ben visits Annie, who has recovered from her loss and is now married to a Connecticut farmer, before returning to the mill and his father. As the journey ends, he recalls his last brief meeting on the trail with Joe, and his own final realization of what freedom really means.

Thirty years later, Ben and his father and little Isaac, now full grown, have become respected tradesmen near the present town of Wilkes-Barre. They, like Joe Mountain, have with determination and pride faced the new wilderness and carved out a free life.

Thematic Analysis

As in any well-crafted story, there are several parallel themes. Each concerns the development of values: understanding another's point of view (being a slave); overcoming hardships to build a better future (rebuilding after scalpings, flood, terror); having pragmatic compassion for others (leading women and children). Also of interest are the exciting historical backgrounds of two states during the Revolutionary period. The economic perfidy of Patterson in the name of government and the mixed heritage of Joe Mountain unite the past with contemporary events that are famliar to the young.

Discussion Materials

This title lends itself to numerous types of discussions. For topical ideas see the preceding paragraph and the epilogue that describes the three generations of Bucks in Pennsylvania. Introduce the Bucks, Joe Mountain, and Colonel Patterson together with the plot outline to interest youngsters in reading the book. Several episodes can also be used to indicate the hardships and themes: the flood (pp. 99, 107, 129); how to make a waterwheel (p. 139); the march back to Connecticut (pp. 153–166); freedom—Joe and Ben (pp. 64–65, 90–94, 121–124, 173–175, 181).

Related Materials

Consider these titles for the same readers: *Snow Shoe Trek* (Dial, 1975) by David Budhill, about 12-year-old Dan, his friend, and the lure of the wilderness; and *Willie Jasper's Golden Eagle* (Doubleday, 1976) by F. N. Monjo, about 10-year-old Willie who takes a trip down the Mississippi and learns to be a good loser. Jay Williams's *The Burglar Next Door* (Scholastic Bk. Services, 1976) tells of the adventures of 13-year-old Penny and her friend Amos, who is accused of stealing. Patricia Gauch's *This Time, Tempe Wick?* (Coward, 1974) is the true story of a young New Jersey girl during the American Revolution.

Patricia A. Engebrecht, *Under the Haystack*

Nelson, 1973, $5.95; pap., Dell, 1975, 95¢

To this story of 3 young girls, abandoned and on their own on a dilapidated farm for a summer, Mrs. Engebrecht brings the first-hand experience of growing up on a farm. She has a sparse writing style and reveals a clear understanding of the emotions of the 13-year-old heroine. Ned Glattauer has done an attractive cover drawing of the 3 girls, their farm animals, and small shack. Girls from 8- to 13-years-old will empathize with this story of survival.

Sandy or Sondra, as she was named, lives with her mother and stepfather (Him) and two younger sisters on a rundown farm about 35 miles away from the manufacturing plant in which the parents work. More than 3 years ago when they first moved there, "Him" added 2 bedrooms to the 2-room shack which remain unfinished. There is an outhouse, but no plumbing. Eight-year-old Marie, who is big for her age, and 6-year-old June, who is small and scrawny, help Sandy with the farm chores. They love and care for their dog, Shep, and milk the three cows, Julie, Daisy, and Bess the leader. June weaned a young bull calf, Fred, by dipping her fingers in a pail of milk until he learned to drink from the pail. The children also feed the chickens, gather the eggs, and clean the barn. What they enjoy most of all, however, is hiding in their elaborate tunnels and secret place in the center of the bales that form the haystack. Often these serve as convenient places in which to hide from "Him."

One June morning, Sandy instinctively feels that they are uncomfortably alone. When she finds the suitcases gone from her mother's closet, she realizes that they have been abandoned and wonders what she will tell the girls. Sandy can't answer June's plaintive "Why doesn't mommy come home?" She gets angry at herself, which strengthens her resolve to rely on herself and protect her sisters by writing a note supposedly from their mother saying she has gone away to visit a sick aunt. Sandy counts the $22.87 in the coffee tin and their provisions: milk from the cows, eggs from the flock, hams in the barn rafters, and some beef and fruit in the rental food locker at Mr. Samuel's grocery store.

Sandy makes up her mind that no one is to find out they are alone because they may be split up and sent to an orphanage. She assigns the chores to the girls. She herself does the cooking and planning. Sandy believes that they can earn sufficient money picking fruit and vegetables to get them through the summer. They start by picking strawberries at Ferguson's farm hoping to average $30.00 a day, which together with the milk check should keep them solvent. Sandy's school friend, tall, gangly 14-year-old Joe Baxter who lives on a nearby farm, is once again one of the pickers. Only the appearance of a mangy-looking, rancid dachshund and her owner, Mrs. Holdermann, who has come to complain to their mother, mars things as the younger girls blurt out that their mother isn't there. Sandy bawls them out for squirting milk on the dachshund and telling people about momma.

Realizing that she is getting bossy just like momma, Sandy responds to June's plaintive plea for her mother's return by suggesting that they each write to their mother every night. They pull a wagon to Samuels Corners 2½ miles away to buy some supplies and take some provisions from their locker to vary their dreary ham and eggs diet. Mr. Samuels, who likes Sandy because some time ago she returned a $10.00 bill he gave her by mistake, sells them 3 cupcakes at a special 5¢ price because June wants one so desperately. On the pull home, they quench their thirst on a few frozen cherries.

These summer days revolve slowly around doing the chores, picking fruit and vegetables, swimming in the creek each evening, and keeping their mother's departure quiet. For Sandy there were the responsibilities of planning and making difficult decisions, such as which bills must be paid, whether to plant a garden in the hard clay and board a neighbor's goat for pay, and ultimately whether to use the fortress of baled hay that had been their refuge from an abusive stepfather. There are also emergencies: Mr. Ferguson locks up their meandering cows—Joe liberates them; Marie gets a nasty pitchfork thigh puncture—the doctor gives her a tetanus shot, and Mrs. Baxter, a ride home; and June is the object of a charge by a bull— her sisters and Shep save her.

After 4 weeks of being on her own, Sandy begins to be filled with self-importance because everything is going so well. Nevertheless, she has spells of crying, and not just because of her mother. Sandy still becomes angry at the thought of the desertion, but she keeps telling the girls, June especially, how much momma loves them. June, however, finds the unmailed letters to their mother, accuses Sandy of lying, and confesses her fear that they will be put in an orphanage. Resolutely, Sandy takes them to Mr. Samuels where she buys them a cupcake treat. For herself, she gets some tampons for the menses she expects. As a special treat for the despondent June, she gives them the Sears catalog from which to choose clothes. Although there is less than $7.00 in the coffee tin, Sandy does not hesitate to send the order. Some problems make her despair: the garden which sprouted is now dry and dead and the ham and egg meals are all that they have left. She refrains from killing the rooster because he is old and tough and a hen because she sees June shed a tear. Miraculously, a basket with crispy lemon chicken, bread, and fruit is found resting on their front porch.

Although the girls find picking beans easier than picking strawberries, they have a hard time because Tom Gregory, a bully, tries to steal Sandy's half-filled sack. Joe helps to get it back. A second box of good foodstuffs on the porch cheers them on their return from picking the beans. Later that evening, someone frightens the girls and someone else fights off an intruder while the girls run from the outhouse. In the morning, Sandy thinks she sees Joe sleeping near the house and protecting them.

As the days start getting shorter, Sandy rages against their mother and finally breaks down. Mrs. Baxter comes and shares her own story of leaving home. Before they part, she tells Sandy that her mother will need all Sandy's love when she gets back.

The Sears package arrives, including the bras Sandy ordered for herself. Everything the girls ordered fits and looks fine for school, which starts in 2 weeks. Sandy sees a sheriff's car at the house convincing her that he is coming to take them away. The next day the girls do their regular work, bathe, and change into their new clothes. They are ready. Unexpectedly, momma gets out of the car and starts up the walk alone. Marie screams, June sobs, and both run to her. Observing her mother's beseeching look, Sandy, remembering Mrs. Baxter's words, runs to her calling "mama."

Thematic Analysis

The value of compassion and forgiveness is well developed as a theme. Clearly expressed is the childishness of clinging to hatred and anger instead of showing a more mature understanding of unintentional hurts. Also well delineated is the value of being independent and industrious. Minor themes of female puberty and first love are tenderly, but strongly, interwoven.

Discussion Materials

Introduce the girls and the farm using study prints or overhead projections to show the farm animals and children; cows; bull; bull calf, Fred; chickens and rooster; bales of hay in the barn; outhouse; Sears catalog. Some readings or talks can be given on various subjects: abandonment (pp. 9-10); chores (pp. 10-13); the dachshund (pp. 26-27); Samuels Corners (pp. 28-34); making a garden (ch. 5); getting the cows (pp. 44–49); baths (pp. 61–63); fishing with Joe (pp. 66–69); the bull (pp. 72–79); choosing clothes (pp. 87–92); a night of terror (pp. 102–106); Mrs. Baxter's story (pp. 107–113).

Related Materials

A couple of books for the same readers are Norma Klein's *Mom, the Wolfman and Me* (Pantheon, 1972; pap., Avon, 1974) and Joan Robinson's *Charley* (Coward, 1969). Both treat some of the same problems. The film *Tara's Mulch Garden* (Wombat, 21 min., color) will be informative. Two books for younger readers are *Rita the Weekend Rat* (Atheneum, 1971) by Sonia Levitan and *Go and Hush the Baby* (Viking, 1971; pap., Penguin, 1976) by Betsy Byars. Also suggested for this group is the colorful *Rosie's Walk* (Weston Woods, 3 min., color).

Sharon Bell Mathis, *The Hundred Penny Box*
Illus. by Leo and Diane Dillon. Viking, 1975, lib. bdg., $6.95

In a lyrical style, Sharon Bell Mathis expresses the richness of understanding and eternal verities some children share with the old. This story of the strength a little boy draws from his great-great aunt will delight children from the age of 8 to 11 as well as younger children if they are good readers. The author has other fine titles, among them the ALA notable book, *A Teacup Full of Roses*.

The well-known artists use watercolor, water and bleach, cotton and brush, as well as a two-color separation process, to produce the sepia tones. Each full-page drawing is decorated at the top with circles of an appropriate size to contain the "Lincoln pennies" that appear scattered throughout the text. Notes "About the Author" and "About the Illustrators" follow the text.

Young Michael is fascinated by his 100-year-old great-great Aunt Dew, and especially by her hundred penny box. Since his father and mother, John and Ruth, brought Aunt Dew from her house in Atlanta to live with them and occupy his former room, Michael has never tired of hearing the story of her life which the box commemorates. In spite of her advanced age and occasional confusion over her presence with John, whom she raised after his parents drowned, and with Michael, who is the spitting image of John, she will often tell the story of the box as Michael drops each penny in and listens. Each penny represents one year of Dewbet Thomas's life from 1874 to the present. She says that she was born during the time of Reconstruction after slavery was abolished. She also relates how her husband, Henry Thomas, put the first 56 pennies in to celebrate each birthday, while she put in the rest. Michael's fondest wish is to put in the 101st penny himself.

However, he knows that Aunt Dew's presence and her need for care are making his mother miserable. Michael also knows that Aunt Dew understands this. Ruth, not realizing the human value of the scratched old wooden hundred penny box, wants to get rid of it. To Aunt Dew the box is her life (p. 19), and she tells Michael that ". . . your momma gonna throw me out soon" (pp. 16–17). Michael does not know what to do. He continues to visit Aunt Dew's room, often sitting waiting for her to wake up from her naps or finish softly singing her long song, "Precious Lord, take my hand . . ." and encourages her to live through her story. He finally talks to his mother, angrily accusing Ruth of making Aunt Dew cry, and all the while trying to think of a place to hide the box.

In an answer to Michael's questions at the end of the book, Aunt Dew, who is patiently waiting to die, explains that to live long and well someone special must give you a hundred penny box which you must then be careful to protect. Michael climbs on the bed and places himself lovingly beside her. The communication is complete.

Thematic Analysis

A young child's early exposure to the important value of reverence toward life and an understanding of its continuity underlie this story. Aligned with this is the conflict that can develop in a loving family situation when understanding is incomplete. The life history of one black person born just after the abolition of slavery in the United States is an added thread beneficial for all to hear and read about.

Discussion Materials

Tell the story by using the 9 illustrations (making transparencies and projecting them will add to the drama): Aunt Dew rocks as Michael watches (p. 8); Ruth watches Michael and Aunt Dew (p. 13); Dewbet Thomas's moving (p. 18); a large tree in the Atlanta yard (p. 22); images of Dewbet's life (p. 27); a tear flows (p. 30); Michael talks to mother (p. 35); Mother is angry (p. 39); more images (p. 43). Under wise leadership, a discussion about aged family members may be undertaken.

Related Materials

Two books about grandparents are suggested: for the young reader *Nana Upstairs and Nana Downstairs* by Thomas de Paola (Putnam, 1973), a story about an Italian family, and for older readers, *My Great*

Grandfather, the Heroes and I by James Krüss (Atheneum, 1973), about a German family. Two more books will also appeal: *My Street's a Morning Cool Street* by Ianthe Thomas (Harper, 1976) and *My Black Me: A Beginning Book of Black Poetry* (Dutton, 1974) edited by Arnold Adoff. The unique film *The Magic World of Whiselphasoon* (Films, Inc., 12 min., color) can be used to inspire art and creative writing. *The Trouble They Seen: Black People Tell the Story of the Reconstruction* (Doubleday, 1976), edited by Dorothy Sterling, is an entertaining and instructive book which tells the story of the Reconstruction through excerpts from letters, diaries, and accounts of the period.

William O. Steele, *The Man with the Silver Eyes*
Harcourt, 1976, $5.95

In an easy-to-read adventure story about a Cherokee boy who unwillingly lives for a year with a white man and discovers that he is not a pure Cherokee but is of "mixed blood," the author once again demonstrates his command of this genre. William O. Steele grew up in Tennessee, and is knowledgeable about the geography and history of the area. He has written many fine books, among them *The Year of the Bloody Sevens* (*Juniorplots* 1967) and *The Perilous Road*, an ALA Newbery Honor book. The title-page drawing for this book is by Paul Galdone from *Winter Danger*. It is symbolic of the early frontier days and the many skirmishes among the Tory, Loyalist Unegas (Whites), and the Principal People (Indians). Youngsters from the age of 9 to 14 will read this story eagerly.

Eleven-year-old Talatu (the Cricket) lives in Chota—the stronghold of the Cherokee nation before the Unegas leveled it 3 years ago—with his grandmother, Neeroree, and her brother, Old Coat, who tutors him. Talatu longs for his mother, Oconee, and his young uncles to come and take him to their new town, Running Water, and their leader, Dragging Canoe. To fight with the Canoe and return the land of the Principal People to its former greatness is Talatu's fervent wish. He knows that the Cherokees under the Canoe stand with the British in spite of Old Coat's admonition to live in peace with the Unegas. Although Talatu also knows it is the right of every Cherokee to do as he pleases, he accepts the Cherokee tradition that youngsters do not argue with their elders. In spite of his conflicting feelings, he loves the great old warrior, whose knees are now a home for the Intruder (arthritis), almost as much as the sympathetic Neeroree.

It is a shock when Old Coat embraces a tall, hatted Unega at Green Corn Festival time in October and sends Talatu and the Unega off together until the next Festival. Talatu, who understands and speaks English, nevertheless obeys and goes with his grandmother's farewell, "Na-hwun-yu-ga-i" in his ears (p. 15). Only the finding of Old Coat's amulet rolled up in his belongings stills his fears somewhat.

As the Unega Benjamin Shinn, a Quaker with the palest eyes the boy has ever seen, his horse Shucky, and Talatu travel on the Great Indian War Path along the frontier to Shinn's unfinished cabin, they have a couple of encounters that increase Talatu's unhappiness. When Old Coat's name and amulet are mentioned, the three Cherokees who tie Shinn to a tree release him to Talatu's disgust. Later, Talatu is doubly humiliated when a renegade Felty Tyce cuts his breechclout and the boy runs away. Old Coat's advice was always not to be goaded into cowardice. He feels better when Shinn catches up with him and gives him powder and a knife for hunting.

When they reach Shinn's unfinished cabin, Talatu also gets his own rifle "Miss Never," together with the promise of the annual hides. The late fall days pass as Talatu hunts and Shinn, singing Cherokee refrains, tries to get the cabin finished. The Tilson family and Adam Kirk come to give a hand with the building. Talatu bristles as Kirk refers to him as a "savage," one of the Tilson children throws a rock at him, and someone destroys a hide he is dressing. The final indignity, however, comes when Talatu becomes infected with virulent smallpox contracted from them.

Talatu is ill throughout a fierce winter in the lean-to rock shelter they had just managed to set up before the snows. In his delirium Talatu believes Shinn to be a conjurer who is riddling his body with fevers and pain. However, as he recovers he learns that Kirk's son had died of smallpox and that some of Talatu's nightmares of animals—even a bobcat—by the fire had been real during the worst of the snow and cold. Talatu says "wadan" (thank you) to Shinn for nursing him all winter. Although he is grateful, he longs now for the sight of Chota and his family.

They stay and slowly resume the building and hunting as Talatu recovers. The foraging is difficult after the hard winter. On one trip Talatu sees 3 Indians and one Unega scalp some settlers. As he goes to investigate, Tyce and his comrade, Crawford, capture Talatu and tar and feather him. Kirk arrives and saves him.

While Shinn cleans Talatu's tarred body, he starts to tell him about the white man's lore, and that his amulet may be from a meteor. When it is once again August, Talatu learns that they will soon leave. However, he is disappointed when instead of going south to Chota, they head east because

Shinn has promised to serve briefly as an observer for Colonel Sevier. Talatu waits for Shinn in Sycamore Shoals. The town is crowded with Unegas, increasing his yearning to be fighting with the Canoe.

Shinn rejoins Talatu 2 days later in the Quakers Meadows, where they prepare to travel light and fast together on Shuckey's back. They run into Tyce, now a Tory deserter, who has his rifle drawn. Talatu cleverly rams the butt of his rifle into him giving the two time to hide in a crowded Quaker meeting house. When they emerge, tragedy engulfs them. Although warned by Talatu, Shinn receives Tyce's bullet as Shinn implants his tomahawk in Tyce's skull. A man, Lusk, who promises to see Talatu home to Chota, helps Talatu take the dying Shinn to a cabin. In a delirium Shinn confides to Oconee that he misses her every day, and lucidly to Talatu that he is his father. Talatu is overwhelmed: a white man is his father! How can Old Coat stand the sight of him? He bursts into tears from the double shock.

Accepting the good man with the silver eyes and wearing his double heritage proudly, Talatu consigns his father's body to the river and performs the Cherokee ritual to the Long Person "With your head in the mountains and your feet in the lowlands . . . hold my father's body in your arms forever." Although a different boy, his heart is whole. His father was white, and in Native American matriarchal succession he, like his mother, is forever one of the Wolf Clan of the Principal People.

Thematic Analysis

The main theme is a youngster's developing ability to discriminate between cultural and individual differences and overcome prejudices. Other themes concern values of peace, respect for elders, and other things that are common to many cultures. Geographical and historical information about the countryside and the era are important topics that enhance this vital story.

Discussion Materials

An introductory talk can be fashioned to interest youngsters (pp. 3-10). The main characters can be introduced; Talatu, Shinn (pp. 9, 11, 25), and others through the episodes in which they play important parts. Some episodes are: goodbye to Chota (p. 15); meeting the war party (pp. 27-32); eating on the trail (pp. 33-36); Talatu's fear and Shinn's thoughts (pp. 44-45, 103-108); hunting (pp. 48-56); a savage (pp. 62-66); winter smallpox (pp. 74-80); tar and feathers (pp. 91-93); stealing food (pp. 131-133); the Quaker meeting house (pp. 127-129). Other topics for discussion include some Indian beliefs: the great vulture myth (pp. 5-6); freedom, death, peace, and treatment of elders (pp. 8-11); the Great Indian War Path (pp. 21-23); the first Cherokee hunter, Kanati (p. 45); dressing hides (pp. 59-60); burial song (p. 145).

Related Materials

Joyce Rockwood's *To Spoil the Sun* (Holt, 1975) tells the story of the Cherokee culture through the eyes and heart of an 11-year-old girl. It is lyrically written and is for more advanced readers. Suggested for the same audience as *The Man with the Silver Eyes* are *Navajo Slave* (Harvey House Pubs., 1975) by Lynne Gessmer, the story of a boy's slavery during the wars in Mexico, and *The Sound of Flutes and Other Indian Legends* (Pantheon, 1975), a book of poetry edited by Richard Erdoes, and illustrated by Paul Goble. Of interest to younger readers are *Somebody Else's Child* (Warne, 1976) by Roberta Silman and *Hawk, I'm Your Brother* (Scribner, 1975) by Byrd Baylor. *Arrow to the Sun* (Weston Woods, 9 min., color) is a film suitable for younger viewers.

William Steig, *Abel's Island*

Farrar, 1976, lib. bdg., $5.95; pap., Bantam, 1977, $1.75

Famous for his many award-winning masterpieces, among them *Sylvester and the Magic Pebble*, *The Real Thief*, *Amos and Boris*, and *Farmer Palmer's Wagon Ride*, William Steig has produced one more. In a beautifully told and illustrated morality tale, he relates the thoughts and events that thrust a contented and secure mouse on his own for a full year as he struggles to survive and fight his way back home. This timeless story about finding oneself is for all seasons and ages. It is straightforward and simple truth expressed and portrayed gloriously. More than 50 drawings— many full-page or half-page—are done in this illustrator's inimitable style in ink wash with pen outline.

To add to the book's luster, Jane Byers Bierhorst has found a perfect design in which to present it. Young readers of ages 7 to 11, as well as thoughtful adults, will savor it. Reading it to older elementary and junior high age children will not be amiss.

Abelard Hassam di Chirico Flint, an idle young mouse, passes his first year of marriage in 1907 fashion, playing croquette and picnicking with his lovely wife, Amanda. A dilettante who lives on an inheritance from his mother, Abel is caught in a sudden August storm on one of these pleasure excursions. In trying to grasp Amanda's fluttering scarf, he is blown by strong gusts into the surging river and tosses helplessly down a waterfall.

He finally comes to rest in a tree on an island in the middle of the river. Always gallant he has held onto the scarf.

Abel tries to get off the island. Walking across the flooded river is obviously impossible, and his two efforts to sail across are failures. Over the weeks during which he labors at building boats, Abel is surprised and slightly repelled to see that he is using his teeth in a natural way to make the second boat. With both boats lost, Abel sits dejectedly beside his cherry birch tree with long thoughts of Amanda and his former comforts.

Abel finally accepts the bitter truth. After all these weeks no rescue party is coming; he must provide for himself while he continues to try to find a way off the island. He cleans out a rotting hollow log and proceeds to stock it with seeds and mushrooms and other edibles for a long winter. He piles up small stones to use for a door to keep out snakes. Satisfied with these preparations, Abel turns unsuccessfully to building a rope bridge and a causeway of stepping stones. He also uncovers many somnolent skills: making a fire and sending smoke signals, firing clay pots to send notes and flowers downstream to Amanda at 89 Bank Street. The message always carries the promise of a substantial reward.

As Abel becomes lonelier, he begins to create sculptured likenesses of Amanda and his family. With practice he finally makes one that looks just like her as he dreams of walking again with her. Abel spends each starry night looking for his own favorite star of his childhood. However, some of his days are filled with the youthful zest of trying to fly with a catalpa leaf tied to his back or skimming pebbles across the water. His biggest coup is his discovery of a large watch and chain and a book which he reads faithfully each day.

The idyll ends when an owl snatches him, forcing Abel to slash at its toes with his penknife to make the owl release him. He stays in his log until he thinks it is safe to go out, even then affixing his penknife to a long stick and muttering incantations to a moulted owl feather. With winter upon him, Abel weaves a double coat of grass with a milkweed lining and makes a pair of snowshoes. Thus armed he continues to replenish his food stores and wind his watch and read his book. When the blizzard finally arrives, Abel retreats to the log emerging only during the intermittent thaws until spring comes.

A May flood tide washes Gower Glackens, an elderly frog, to the island. In spite of Gower's forgetfulness, Abel is delighted with his companionship and adds his likeness to the sculpture garden. Gower tells Abel that sculpturing is obviously his vocation (p. 93). In June Gower swims home promising to send help for Abel. However, as Abel suspects, Gower forgets.

Abel makes more sculptures as he waits for the driest part of the summer to swim across the river. Abel makes a supermouse effort in August. Before he drops under a rock on the far side, he looks back at the island that was his home for a year, remembering that he learned his own measure there.

He sleeps content only to be awakened by a cat who carries him away. Abel slips away from him, and climbs to the top of a tree from which the pursuing cat falls. Abel hurries to his elegant turn-of-the-century town house to leave Amanda's scarf, which has been his talisman, on the hall table. He bathes and dresses because he wants Amanda to see him as she best remembers him. When she returns home, they embrace joyously.

Thematic Analysis

One of the most important values of life—harmoniously balancing work and play—is subtly explained in this story. It shows that one must know her or his capabilities and be willing and able to work with them. It also shows that one must be able to let recreation be a part of existence. The combination of artistic imagination and practical rationality, is exalted. Industriousness, determination, and the ability to implement learning are stressed.

Throughout runs an excellent discourse on nature and the weather cycle of a river in the temperate zone.

Discussion Materials

A practical discussion about survival skills or nature study (recognizing edibles) can be encouraged.

The story can be introduced by showing several illustrations of the characters and their home: Mossville Park, 1907 (p. 114); 89 Bank Street (p. 116); Abel and Amanda (pp. 5, 6, 9, 12). The following episodes can introduce parts of the story and be combined, together with the pictures, to tell major portions: attempts to get off the island (pp. 15, 18, 21, 25, 39, 41); melancholy (pp. 27, 30, 31, 33); survival (p. 37); rescue hopes (p. 45); log home in fall (p. 47); dreams of longing (pp. 49, 50, 52); recreation (pp. 53, 55, 57); owl story (pp. 62, 63, 65, 66 incantation); winter (pp. 68, 70, 72, 75, 77, 80); spring (p. 83); Gower (pp. 84, 85, 87, 88, 91, 95, 96, 97); waiting to cross the river (pp. 99, 101, 102, 103, 105, 107); the cat (pp. 109, 111, 112); reunited at last (p. 117; epilogue).

Related Materials

The following titles and film may help inspire the development of lasting values: *Domenic* (Farrar, 1972; pap., Dell, 1974), winner of the 1975 William Allen White Award, and *The Real Thief* (Farrar, 1973; pap., Dell,

1974), both by William Steig; *The Cat Who Wished to Be a Man* (Dutton, 1973) by Lloyd Alexander; *The Fables of Aesop* (Rand McNally, 1975), edited by Ruth Spriggs; and *Martin the Cobbler* (Billy Budd Films, 27½ min., color). Complementary to this story is a book of poetry by Ada and Frank Graham, *The Milkweed and Its World of Animals* (Doubleday, 1975), about meadow ecology, with outstanding photographs. For humor, try a tall tale with comic sketches by Glen Rounds: *Squash Pie* (Greenwillow-Morrow, 1975) by Wilson Gage.

Colin Thiele, *Blue Fin*

> Pictures by Roger Haldone. Harper, 1974, lib. bdg., $5.79; pap., 1976, $1.50

One of Australia's most popular authors, Colin Thiele, tells an exciting story of a boy and his fisherman father in a sea adventure that is the 1970 Australian Book of the Year. The plotting is tension filled, the characterizations simple and honest, and the writing as alternately calm or storm tossed as the South Australian waters where it takes place.

The impressionistic sketches, done in soft pencil and outlined in pen, capture every quiver of the people and the ship at sea, as well as the harshness of the work at sea. Boys and girls from 9 to 14 will be so captivated by its easy style and fast pace that they will easily absorb the few Australian expressions.

The Pascoes live in Port Lincoln near Adelaide on the southern coast of Australia close to the other tuna fishermen who form the South Australian Fisherman's Cooperative (SAFCOL). It is a hard life to sail 2 hours out on the 50-mile continental shelf in a 20- by 50-foot, 25-ton boat for 10 minutes of fishing for the "chicken of the sea." Often the boats look like cockleshells in the Southern ocean. They know, however, that out of the $160 a ton the tuna brings, they have to pay for the boat, insurance, crew, and family. It is a short summer season, but a single good trip can bring in $5,000. They have to find a school, chum it with bait, pole in the fish, and wash them down. Each step is hard work; none more so than the open poling with a man slapping a huge southern bluefin (tuna) on the deck. To these tuna men, however, there is no more beautiful fish than the streamlined, bullet-nosed southern bluefin. It is their lifeline.

There are five in the Pascoe family: Bill, the captain of the *Blue Fin*; the mother; Ruth, a 17-year-old Government Produce Office typist; Wendy, an 11-year-old tomboy; and 14-year-old Steven (Snook) who is trying hard to earn his father's respect. Since the *Blue Fin* holds 40 refrigerated tons in its dual holds and it takes one man to land a 30-lb. tuna, the ship carries a crew of 7. Polers all are: Captain Pascoe, Herbi Anderson, Fritzie, Con (Kanopolis), Stan, Hodges, and sometimes Sam Snell who normally crews for the *Dog Star* and is Ruth's boyfriend. Two of the other ships, Bob Clutterbuck's *Dog Star*, and Rudi Obst's *Petrel*, often vie with the *Blue Fin* for top catches.

Snook, a thin, gangling fellow who feels that no one has any confidence in him, wants to gain his father's confidence during the school's winter vacation (equivalent to our summer vacation) and prove that he is not a financial burden. His chance comes when he is asked to chum for the crew. He performs well through the rocks and rips of the "Cabbage Patch" and Cape Catastrophe (the treacherous water between Thistle Island and the Mainland). All goes well until, in an effort to be first to unload, the *Mollyhawk* rams them, throwing Snook overboard. The *Blue Fin* comes in second because it stops to rescue him. Mortified, Snook is also despondent because his father will not accept his apology.

He spends the early spring back in school with his friends, Ockie, Bo, and Snitch Hankel, as well as their teacher, Mr. Smart, who is as "ruthless as a barracuda." At home, life goes on as usual with the tuna catch always foremost, especially in a year in which there seems to be a hex on both the *Blue Fin* and the *Dog Star*. Snook finally goes to work in the cannery and does some water skiing from the bay to Boston Island. Nonetheless, he is never far from his problem. Even Wendy taunts him about falling in the water.

In March, his friend Snitch and Ruth's friend, Sam Snell, sail on the *Dog Star* which is lost without a trace in spite of the SAFCOL air search and special VH5BA radio transmissions. It is a terrible tragedy and emotional burden for the folks at Port Lincoln. Meanwhile, Snook's father and mother argue about money, and especially about him. When Snook loses his job at the cannery because a mischievous fellow tosses a cooked tuna at him and Mr. Smart catches him with a note to another boy from the class flirt, Pamela Wenzel, the atmosphere of gloom deepens even more. Some poor luck for Captain Pascoe—the loss of two injured men—gives Snook an opportunity to get a place on the *Blue Fin*. Because of the *Dog Star* disaster and Snell, Snook's mother and sister Ruth are upset.

The *Blue Fin* spends Good Friday and the Saturday of Easter week looking for fish. On Easter Sunday the big fish appear right on the surface. The men catch more than 14 tons of the large 30-pounders. Simultaneously, the weather turns ominous and a once-in-a-lifetime waterspout almost demolishes them and sets them adrift on the Southern Ocean with only Snook and his father aboard. With an unflagging sense of purpose, Snook drags his delirious and severely injured father from the ammonia-filled brine tank in which he landed, turns off the valve in the leaking section, and uses a hand pump doggedly to pump out half of the water that has inundated the ship. On Easter Monday, having drifted for 18 hours while he was doing all this, Snook decides to balance the ship by placing half the catch in the empty brine compartment, put a signal flag on the mast, and set the signal light for searchers.

However, on the third day after Easter, the searchers begin to give up hope. Meanwhile, the sometimes conscious Captain Pascoe tells Snook how to repair the engine by copying one of the old connections. Snook is able to start the engine and set a star course N by NW. He sleeps briefly and wakes up to see Thistle Island. Snook is amazed because it means that they have sailed right past the Neptunes and Dangerous Reef—an area known almost certainly to cause calamity.

Rudi Obst in the *Petril* sights the *Blue Fin* at the Passage and escorts it toward the south entrance. Snook's gallant struggle is at an end, however, for the *Blue Fin* is out of gas. With the aid of life jackets, Snook and Rudi make the transfers while the *Blue Fin* sinks (p. 237).

After a good sleep, Snook goes to the hospital to see his father. He feels rewarded when he hears Captain Pascoe tell the nurse that Snook ". . . near saved the boat and the fish, me too, . . . he's a tiger!" Snook knows now that he will be a tuna man.

Thematic Analysis

Nothing is more important or often more poignant than earning one's own self-respect and learning an eternal verity, e.g., ". . . school was young and life was very old." These values are forcefully shown in this adventure in which the sea represents both literally and figuratively the essence of life. Another important value is earning your parents' respect and also gaining independence from them.

Discussion Materials

Some of the sketches together with the book descriptions make intriguing introductions: descriptions of tuna fishing and southern Australian waters (pp. 18-23); orange buoys (picture p. 87); the cannery (pp. 55-57); water skiing (pp. 58-61); the *Dog Star* (pp. 68-72); an ecosystem verse (p. 128); poling (picture p. 137); waterspout (pp. 145-149); the *Blue Fin* demise (p. 237). A project about or a discussion on tuna fishing as it is done on the continental shelf in South Australia will also be of interest.

Related Materials

Two of Colin Thiele's later books will appeal to the same readers: *February Dragon* (Harper, 1975) and *The Hammerhead Light* (Harper, 1976). A related story with an American flavor is Madeleine L'Engle's *Dragons in the Waters* (Farrar, 1975). Berniece Rabe's *Naomi* (Nelson, 1975; pap., Bantam, 1976) and Natalie Babbitt's *The Eyes of the Amaryllis* (Farrar, 1977) are both about the theme of identity and integrity; the former is set on a farm, the latter on the seacoast. Use the filmstrip *Sea Animals with Backbones* (BFA, 60 frames, color) from the series *Life in the Sea*.

4

Understanding Physical
and Emotional Problems

Children first become aware of physical differences among people during the middle years of growing up. Differences due to emotional variations also begin to come to their attention. They note that acceptance and approval by others may be determined by a youngster's physique or physical skills. This can prove extremely disheartening for handicapped children and members of their families. Similar unfortunate reactions may also be encountered by those who have emotional problems.

Children should begin to be able to assess their own physical assets and liabilities, and learn to accept them. They should also begin to understand, accept, and help those who have emotional problems.

The books discussed in this chapter deal with a wide range of both physical and emotional handicaps that young people may have, ranging from hearing loss to depression. Shown also are a variety of ways of adjusting to handicaps in a positive and courageous manner.

Rose Blue, *Grandma Didn't Wave Back*
> Illus. by Ted Lewin. Franklin Watts, 1972, lib. bdg., $4.90; pap., Dell, 1976, 95¢

Here is a thin, easy-to-read book about elderly family members that is both enjoyable and packed with a message with which many youngsters will identify. Boys and girls from 8 to 11 years of age will read it. The appropriate reading age can be extended to include slower older readers and superior younger ones.

The problems and peculiarities of "live-in" family members of advancing age (often labeled with the medical terminology, senile) are briefly shown through the eyes of a loving 10-year-old granddaughter during a winter and spring. Placing the grandmother in a nursing home—one way of handling the problem in a working 2-member family situation—is one solution that may continue to increase in a population whose greater number of citizens are already becoming "the elderly."

The setting among the high rises near the Atlantic Ocean enhances the emotional power of the story in its fidelity to the atmosphere. The author has been a teacher and is a native of Brooklyn, New York. The illustrations are unique and a definite asset from the cover rendition of grandma's favorite old-fashioned blue enamel clock to the frontispiece and the final decoration of a ceramic gull. In between, Ted Lewin has integrated 11 crisp pencil and brush sketches that highlight the story and 6 lower margin right hand-page pencil sketches of some of grandma's favorite figurines (tsotzkes).

Debbie, who is nearly 11, is the youngest in a professional family living in Brooklyn, New York. Her 2 older brothers, Mark and Alan, no longer live at home; Alan is married and Mark moved out a few years ago freeing a room for their maternal grandmother to move in. It is a good arrangement. Helen, Debbie's mother, is the only one of grandma's children who can find room for her. On the other hand, Helen is a practicing lawyer and finds her help with the child-sitting and cooking a lifesaver.

Debbie is delighted with Mrs. Green's presence because she loves her. Debbie can remember years earlier when she anticipated the special treat of the long drive to grandma's and grandpa's home. She can also remember indistinctly grandpa's death 5 years ago, even though she didn't go to the funeral. She does remember clearly when her friend Jennifer told of a burial and her own feeling of nausea when she heard the description.

When Mrs. Green moves in with many of her favorite possessions including some of her figurines, she and Debbie are close as only a grandparent and child can be. Debbie learns about her heritage and responds warmly to grandma's caring and loving. After Mrs. Green has been with them for 5 years, however, Debbie begins to notice changes in grandma's behavior. One of the first changes that Debbie notes is grandma's failure to wave back to her from the window in her usual goodbye as Debbie goes to school. Debbie is stunned. Then she notices that grandma occasionally wanders around in her nightgown and also talks about relatives who have been dead for 20 years as if they were alive. Debbie's mother calls Dr. Rappaport after grandma sets an extra place at the table for cousin George who died in the Korean war. The physician explains that medically Mrs. Green who is 75 is becoming senile. He also explains that it is a degenerative process that affects some people, and that it may occur at different ages. He suggests that one solution may be getting grandma into a suitable nursing home. Debbie in the center of this storm inwardly screams, "no"! However, the entire family begins to discuss the problem. Father's special birthday dinner with all the relatives is devoted to the issue.

Meanwhile, Debbie and grandmother remain close. Grandma shows and tells her about a beautiful shawl that Debbie's great-great grand-mother made in Europe. Grandmother is aware of all the talk and tragic excitement because of her. Debbie overhears her telling one of her friends that, "one mother can take care of ten children, but ten children can't take care of one mother." When Debbie is playing in the snow with her friend, Beth, they discuss the family situation with the other children. One of the group, Jennifer, comments that everyone knows that her grandma is crazy. Debbie hits her with a snowball. Debbie finally learns that they can't keep grandma. She angrily accuses her mother of trying to put grandma out of the way.

During the remainder of the winter, grandma has good and bad days. After a neighbor, Mr. Ricci, brings her home one night when he finds her wandering outside in her nightgown, Debbie begins to understand that she needs more care than they can give her. She begins to adjust to grandma's departure. In the late spring, grandma moves into the Shore Nursing Home to a room with the ocean view she enjoys. Debbie finds her departure a wrench and on the first Saturday fills a shopping bag with grandma's shawl, clock, and some of her precious tsotzkes to take to her. Grandma is happy to see Debbie and insists on giving her the clock and the gull. After a nice visit and the promise of many more, Debbie leaves with grandma's request to come again soon and a special message, "Remember life is to enjoy." Outside the tall building, Debbie waves to grandma and catches the bus home.

Thematic Analysis

The theme of understanding and accepting the physical limitations of life as seen in the advancing age of a beloved grandparent is one that many youngsters must face. Coping emotionally with the physical restrictions life forces on many human beings is difficult for young people, yet one that if dealt with will enable them to handle life crises more easily as adults. A secondary theme of appreciating parents' decisions is briefly but well shown. The nature of misunderstanding and taunts among young friends is made clear. The fulfillment that sharing family genealogical anecdotes between grandparents and their children can bring is also briefly shown.

Discussion Materials

If a suitable leader is available, this book can be a point of departure for a good discussion on aging, the family, and its many ramifications. A visit to a local nursing home (with the permission of the authorities) could also be arranged. Children's private opinions may also be explored.

An introduction to the story may be made especially effective by relating the pictures to the family members (e.g., p. 8). Debbie's remembrances of grandma can be characterized by: the montage (p. 13) together with a visit to the room (p. 17); setting the table (p. 28); at the stove (p. 32); rocking (p. 48); and her tsotzkes (pp. 45, 47, 51, 55, 57, 58). Evidence of grandma's aging behavior of wandering (pp. 21, 53) that confirms the doctor's diagnosis (p. 75) can be given. Emphasize Debbie's difficulty by reading about the snowball fight (pp. 42–44). Some of the tender moments when grandma tells Debbie about her shawl can be highlighted (pp. 36–39); the clock (jacket) and the ceramic gull (frontispiece).

Related Materials

Other titles on the same theme are *The House of Wings* (Viking, 1972; pap., Dell, 1973) by Betsy Byars; *A Paper Dragon* (John Day, 1968) by Marietta Moskin; *The Sugar Pear Tree* (T. Y. Crowell, 1961) by Clyde R. Balla; and *A Killing Frost* (pap., Avon, 1973) by Sylvia Wilkinson. The last two titles are for younger and older readers respectively. *Over the River and through the Woods* (Coward, 1974; pap., Scholastic Bk. Services, 1975) by Lydia Maria Child, illustrated by Brinton Turkle, is a celebration of going to visit grandparents—a lovely rendition of a beloved poem. Also suggested are Rose Blue's other books: *Nikki* (Watts, 1973), *A Quiet Place* (Watts, 1969), and *A Month of Sundays* (Watts, 1972).

Judy Blume, *Deenie*
  Bradbury, 1973, $6.95; pap., Dell, 95¢

The author, one of the most popular writers of juvenile books, is responsible for many titles. Her stories treat the problems of the young and their feelings. Many have been controversial because they deal with changing social conditions. This title, however, is concerned with a young girl's reaction to a physical handicap—adolescent idiopathic scoliosis. The words flow smoothly in this well-crafted, easy-to-read book that young girls from 9 to 14 will read eagerly. It is an excellent title to suggest for slower readers.

Thirteen-year-old Wilmadeene (Deenie) Fenner is the prettiest girl in her seventh grade, indeed in the entire school. Deenie lives with her mother and father, Thelma and Frank Fenner, in Elizabeth, New Jersey, where her father owns a gas station. Deenie has several good friends including Janet (Midge) Kayser and Buddy Broder. Midge Kayser's father runs a Kosher butcher shop, and Buddy is sometimes considered to be her boyfriend. However, Deenie secretly dreams of Harvey Grabowsky, the football captain, as a boy nearer to her romantic ideal.

For as long as she can remember, Deenie has spent every Saturday morning courting modeling agencies in "The Big Apple" with her mother. Thelma Fenner is a typical star-struck, though well-meaning mother. Deenie remembers that her mother has been telling everyone for a long time that, "Deenie's the beauty, Helen's the brain." The only redeeming feature of the Saturday travel is that Aunt Rae, Thelma's friend, usually accompanies them. Deenie also remembers that each agency comments on her poor posture. Until recently, Deenie tolerates the trips even though she isn't really interested in having a career as a model. She admires her sister, Helen, and would prefer to be her. Deenie has no desire to be on the cheerleading team the way Midge is. She accepts her natural beauty and would like to wear it quietly with dignity.

She gets the opportunity in a cruel way. An orthopedic surgeon who examines her because of her back discomfort informs the family that she is a victim of scoliosis that afflicts some adolescents. He further explains that she must swim regularly and wear an orthopedic aid—a Milwaukee Brace—for 4 years until she is 17. Deenie's immediate reaction is one of revulsion. She will never wear that thing. The thought that everyone will know about it sends her into a panic.

However, her friend Midge encourages her and double-dates with Buddy and Deenie. Everyone including her father supports her and urges her to face the necessity. She is measured with a plaster cast, goes on a buying trip to get larger clothes to fit over the brace, and starts to swim regularly at the "Y." Midge joins her whenever possible. Nevertheless, Deenie cries when she first wears the uncomfortable brace. Her modest aspirations about her future seem dashed because she thinks she will no longer be even slightly attractive to boyfriends. She finds out that some people, like Joe her father's gas station assistant, have a negative view of people with physical handicaps, while most, like Helen and her friends, have a positive and helpful outlook. Eventually, Deenie is confident about her continuing attractiveness when Buddy gives her a first kiss. Deenie realizes that she can wear the brace and live happily.

Thematic Analysis

Several themes are central in this story. First, the recognition and adjustment to a physical handicap that appears in later childhood are clearly shown through the handicap's effect on a beautiful young girl. Second, the idea of developing appropriate values about one's appearance runs parallel to this theme. The first stirrings of sexual feelings toward boyfriends are portrayed. Feelings about parents' values are stressed. Primarily, however, it is one girl's response to the awesome fact of having to correct a spinal condition with a heavy, awkward brace.

Discussion Materials

Introduce the main characters, and give some background information on Deenie's beauty and the Saturday morning modeling agency rounds. A definition of scoliosis is given (p. 56). Some episodes to use are: the medical news (p. 78); the plaster cast (pp. 84–86); the first wearing (p. 103); the presentation of the masturbation lecture in the gym (pp. 92–93). A before and after look at Deenie's dating life is given in her double date with Midge (p. 67) and her kiss from Buddy (p. 136).

Related Materials

Two books for the same audience that deal with physical appearance and its effect on youngsters are *Representing Super Doll* (Viking, 1974; pap., Avon, 1975) by Richard Peck and *The Cat Ate My Gymsuit* (Delacorte, 1974; pap., Dell, 1975) by Paula Danziger. More Judy Blume is always in order, especially *Blubber* (Bradbury, 1974; pap., Dell, 1976, 1978), which concerns the feelings of a fat fifth grader. Also suggested are Robert Lipsyte's *One Fat Summer* (Harper, 1977) and Jerome Brooks's *Uncle Mike's Boy* (Harper, 1973). For younger readers suggest *Goodbye, Funny Dumpy-Lumpy* (Houghton, 1977) by Bernard Waber, about a feline family.

Barbara Corcoran, *A Dance to Still Music*
Illus. by Charles Robinson. Atheneum, 1974, $6.95

The author combines some truths about the experiences of a 14-year-old girl who is deaf with the exotic setting of Key West, Florida, in an adventure story of self-discovery. The story covers the winter months during which a stranger helps the young girl set her life on course. It is an easy-to-read book and will be enjoyed by youngsters, especially girls, from the age of 9 to age 14.

The pencil-ink sketches are by Charles Robinson, a well-known artist. The sketches complement the story with their reflection of the setting and mood. They can be used effectively to enhance the book talk and discussions. The jacket painting of Josie in her high-crown hat playing the balalaika on the houseboat sets the scene.

Fourteen-year-old Margaret has lived her whole life in Maine with the grandfather who is "deaf as a cod," three great-aunts, and her mother. Her father disappeared before she was born. Her mother, a waitress, hears a traveler rave about Key West and decides late in December to take Margaret and go there.

The move poses many problems for Margaret because of her deafness. She has been totally deaf as long as she can remember. Unless people speak very slowly, she cannot read their lips. Her mother, for example, talks too fast. Margaret is also afraid to speak for fear she may talk too loud. She knows that she will miss the few friends she has, especially Becky who bought her a sign language book.

Margaret likes colorful Key West with its Cuban atmosphere and its "bollos" or donuts. She also likes Mrs. Parrish, their landlady, although she isn't happy about having time hang heavy for her as she travels from their room, to the beach, or to the restaurant where her mother works and Margaret takes her meals. She finally gets up her courage to go to the employment office to ask for a dishwashing or fruitpicking job. However, when the woman says, "no," Margaret is afraid she'll be asked about schools and quickly flees. Although she likes to read—*The Changeling* is one of her favorite books—she is afraid to go to the library. She spends some time watching the New Year's Eve parade, dancing, and stumbling along with the revelers.

Meanwhile, her mother is increasingly irritated with her for not talking. When her mother becomes engaged to Big Ed, a retired Navy man who owns some shrimp boats, she explains that Big Ed is willing to pay for Margaret to go to the School for the Deaf in St. Augustine. Margaret makes up her mind to return to Maine. On New Year's Day she writes Becky that she is coming home, makes a hitchhiking sign, "Temporarily Deaf," leaves her mom a note not to worry and, unseen, gets in the back of a pick-up truck headed north.

When the truck runs over something, Margaret jumps out to discover a small white-tailed Key deer. As Margaret tries to comfort the fawn, a woman in a straw hat riding a three-wheeled bike with a basket filled with cleaning mops, dust cloths, and cleansers, pulls up and sets the fawn's broken leg, bracing it with a broom handle. The woman offers to take the fawn and Margaret to her houseboat nearby on the Gulf. Margaret celebrates the New Year on the houseboat by giving "Sonny" the deer some palm leaves to eat.

Slowly Margaret adjusts to life on the houseboat and its easygoing owner. Sixty-three-year-old Josie is a part-time cleaning woman at a local motel on this resort Key and a full-time enjoyer of her life-style. Josie, and old Conch (Konk, a native of the Keys), whose father used to make cigars in Key West, ran away at 16 with a sailor who died of influenza right after their boy Danny was born. She speaks slowly and makes Margaret feel happy and free. Danny, who is in the Merchant Marine, sent his mother a balalaika which she plays. She encourages Margaret to dance to the rhythm; Margaret remembers that Beethoven was deaf.

Margaret spends her time cleaning the houseboat and helping to cook native Floridian dishes, swimming in the Gulf beside the houseboat, and picking palm leaves for Sonny along the mainland. While she is swimming alone one day she sees a wild-looking woman and a fierce dog. Josie tells her that this woman, Maisie Carter, who lives in a nearby shack is harmless, but the dog is not. She adds that Maisie Carter thinks Margaret is a witch and is afraid of her.

As April approaches, Margaret decides to give Josie a birthday celebration. She forces herself to go into the local variety store to purchase her a gift. It is difficult. However, she talks with the owner and smiles a lot to cover the nervousness. She finally chooses a pair of $42.00 binoculars for the nature-loving Josie. On her way back she muses that she could always be happy with Josie, Sonny, and perhaps a dolphin. She prepares Josie's favorite turtle steaks and a chocolate cake. After a swim together, Josie and Margaret eat and Josie opens the present. In return Josie plays and Margaret tries to dance to the "still music."

As summer approaches, Margaret has some adventures. In her explorations, she meets an old man feeding an alligator on a desolate strip of beach and also meets Josie's friend, Eva Winthrop, a teacher. She is bitten on the wrist by Maisie Carter's dog when she fights off his attack on Sonny. Luckily, she doesn't need a rabies shot. She joins Josie in her cleaning chores at the motel and is unfortunately caught in some hijinks between a girl and boy at the poolside. At the houseboat, Josie pays her and refuses to pay any attention to her feeling of inferiority. Josie very clearly pronounces, "Don't be dramatic about your deafness." When Margaret protests about meeting any more people at the motel, Josie sagely retorts, "Skipper, I think you need more people, not fewer" (p. 149).

Meanwhile, things begin to happen faster once a policeman comes, as

Margaret suspected he might, about her schooling. In a tempestuous incident on the shore, Margaret not realizing that Maisie is hunting for her meal throws the raccoon that the woman shot in the water and steps on a rattler. Maisie performs the necessary cutting and drawing of blood and carries the bitten girl to her shack where she treats her through the days of raging fever.

When Margaret is finally back with Josie, Eva Winthrop comes with the news that the University Workshop will enroll Margaret. Her mother and Big Ed come to the houseboat in reply to Josie's letter telling them the news. Ed leaves $500 to pay for school and keep. Before she leaves for school, Margaret goes to thank Maisie Carter and writes to her friend Becky in Maine that, "I may get up to Maine someday, but not for a while."

Thematic Analysis

This is a splendid example of how crippling deafness can be to an ordinary girl: the necessity of aids such as sign language and lip reading; the fear of talking abnormally loud; the sense of frustration and inferiority. If, to this situation, any of life's far-too-common problems that arise when a parent makes sudden changes in location are added, only the happy intervention of another understanding person can alleviate the potential disasters.

The story shows well the differences between young people with and without hearing in the section on the youngsters at the pool (ch. 18).

The book also demonstrates a difference between love and need in relation to Margaret's mother and "Sonny," who appears in different stages of growing up in the drawings.

Discussion Materials

The pictures can be related to the episodes: Margaret in a Key West house (p. 19); eating and daydreaming (p. 29); Big Ed, mother, and Margaret (p. 47); fawn (p. 63); deer watching (p. 81); cleaning motel room (p. 144); saved (p. 165). Other episodes: Key West food (p. 114); Maisie to the rescue (pp. 157–161). A fruitful discussion with the help of a hard-of-hearing person or expert might be started by talking about Margaret: her problem and her reaction.

Related Materials

Other books about deafness are *Anna's Silent World* (Lippincott, 1977) by Bernard Wolf; *Axe-Time, Sword-Time* (Atheneum, 1976) by Barbara Corcoran; and Eleanor Spence's *The Nothing Place* (Harper, 1973). *Handtalk: An ABC of Finger Spelling and Sign Language* (Parents'

Magazine Press, 1974) by Remy Charlip et al. uses color photographs to display the language of the deaf and provides useful discussion or training material. The following films are suggested: *Understanding the Deaf* (Perennial Education) and *The Only Thing I Can't Do Is Hear* (Gallaudet College, Washington, D.C., 27 min., color, free rental).

Julia Cunningham, *Come to the Edge*
Pantheon, 1977, $4.95; lib. bdg., $5.99

Here again is the talented author who writes a child's story with a deft mixture of reality and imagination that comes directly from her enjoyment of both. In many ways this mixture is a road map in the actual life of some children. The author often writes of the lives of quiet desperation led by some youngsters, as in this novella of a young orphan who must travel to the edge of sanity in order to build his self-worth. It is a story of a child's depression, a phenomenon far too common in our society. The author writes in a crisp, easy-to-read style with deep perception.

The jacket art by John Cayea portrays a confused, lonely youngster in a gloomy, gabled attic looking through a window toward a cheerful, serene town. Youngsters from 10 to 14 will find the story compelling.

In 16 brief chapters, 14-year-old Gravel Winter undertakes a perilous journey to build trust of others in himself. A red-haired boy who was deposited at a foster farm when he was 10 by an alcoholic father who pleaded that he wanted to make a new start, Gravel has been visited only three times by the man who finally tells the principal that he frankly doesn't want his son. As Gravel overhears this final confession of total abandonment, he feels the grayness of despair settling firmly around him.

Gravel had spent his first 10 years desperately trying to help his sodden parent across the landscape, although he knew in his inner recesses that it was impossible. Any shred of trust that the 14-year-old Gravel has left is irrevocably destroyed both by overhearing his father and by losing his one friend at the farm, Skin. Fat Skin used to listen to Gravel's stories, and once told Gravel that he stayed fat to annoy the hated principal. When Gravel awakens one morning in early summer shortly after realizing he is abandoned to find that Skin has been adopted and is gone, he feels the grayness totally encase him. He flees for his life.

Gravel lands five towns away at the home of friendly Mr. Paynter, who happens to be a sign painter and was also once a runaway. Mr. Paynter accepts Gravel easily, absorbing him smoothly into his way of life. He gives him food, shelter, and work answering the business phone and learning to paint signs. After 3 weeks, Gravel's sadness and inability even to say Skin's name make him decide to leave the kind man. Mr. Paynter's parting words are, "I trust you to come back" (p. 22).

Gravel walks the highway to a new town and stops to stare at a 3-story gabled Victorian mansion when he is stopped by a thin old man with a white cane whom he mistakenly thinks might be his father. Mr. Gant is the town rich man and miser and lives in the mansion with his butler, Williston. Mr. Gant gives Gravel a room in exchange for having Gravel do morning chores and serve as his eyes during the evening. As Gravel explores the town, he meets feeble, plump Mrs. Prior who offers him food in return for doing her marketing. He forces himself to accept these arrangements, and eventually agrees to the request of the deaf spinster, Ethel Ransome, to talk to her in the afternoon. His existence falls into a pattern and toward the end of summer begins to develop into an image of helpfulness that is difficult for Gravel to accept, especially when all the people involved begin to talk about his future.

Gravel becomes involved unwittingly in the sinister bondage under which the murderer, Williston, is held captive by Mr. Gant who was a witness to his crime. Williston, who tries to divide Gant's money, which he has finally found in the cellar coal bin, with Gravel, is killed finally by Mr. Gant. Gant immediately tries to enslave Gravel. Gravel, however, leaves the Gant mansion. He says goodbye to the ladies and goes back with Miss Ransome's rose in his hand to Mr. Paynter's house. He realizes he is returning because Mr. Paynter trusted that he would. Through his summer experiences in the far town, he has learned something of trust. He has also started to learn how to discriminate better those he can trust. But, most of all he has learned how to accept friendship. He is now ready to practice extending it.

Thematic Anaylsis

The classical search-for-self theme here follows Christopher Logue's poem as quoted in the book, "Come to the edge/We might fall/Come to the edge/It's too high, and they came, and he pushed, and they flew." The story deals with the symptoms of depression (characterized as grayness in the story) at a level of understanding appropriate to the readers. From the point of view of the child, it treats the pain and anguish involved in restoring a child's psyche. On an external level, the story is a timeless adventure detailing the escapades of a young orphan as he meets different individuals. On either level it speaks directly to the spirit of a child.

Discussion Materials

A brief book talk covering Chapter One, to introduce the story, together with a discussion about the jacket picture should be more than enough to encourage readers. The jacket will also help youngsters to draw their interpretations of the main characters (not illustrated): Mr. Paynter, Mr. Gant, Williston, Mrs. Prior, and Miss Ransome.

A query about what Gravel's eventual decision will be, based on Mr. Paynter's comment, "I trust you to come back," will also stimulate curiosity. Any discussion should be undertaken with professional assistance. Individual responses should be handled reassuringly to help build strong feelings of self-worth.

Related Materials

Any of the author's previous books are suggested, such as *The Treasure Is the Rose* (Pantheon, 1973), about love and understanding greed. Three books on similar themes are *George* (Atheneum, 1970; pap., 1974) by Elaine L. Konigsburg; *Three of a Kind* (Franklin Watts, 1970) by Louise D. Rich; and *Teetoncey* (Doubleday, 1974; pap., Avon, 1975) by Theodore Taylor. *The Silver Pony* (Houghton, 1973) by Lynd Ward, a dreamlike picture story about a boy who delivers dream gifts to other lonely children, is also suggested. The nonfiction title *Madness, Magic, and Medicine: The Treatment and Mistreatment of the Mentally Ill* (Lippincott, 1977) by Elinor L. Horwitz presents an historical survey. *Stoneflight* (Viking, 1975; pap., Avon, 1976) by George McHargue describes a young girl's flight into a fantasy world; it is suitable for older readers.

Constance C. Greene, *The Ears of Louis*

Illus. by Nola Langner. Viking, 1974, lib. bdg., $5.95; pap., Dell, 1977, 95¢

In an easy-to-read story about a fifth-grader who, like many other youngsters, faces the problem of adjusting to having protruding ears, this recognized author writes with sympathy and simplicity about the boy's pluckiness and personal resolution. It is a tale about facing reality that many can emulate. Conversely, it shows to those who do not have this particular physical problem some of the torment that their thoughtlessness may cause. Youngsters from 8 through 11 will find it satisfying reading.

The soft pencil wash drawings on the title and other pages (pp. 23, 29, 36, 58, 78) complement the text. The colorful primary-color jacket design that portrays Louis in a football helmet provides an expressive introduction.

Ten-year-old Louis is normal and bright. The eldest in his family, he has a 6-year-old brother, Tom, and a baby sister. He has a best friend, Matthew, who is also in the fifth grade. Louis, however, feels he is different because of his protruding ears, which he hates. He is sick of being called "elephant boy" or "Dumbo" and having recurring dreams of crossing the finish line or winning in a flying race or flying to Alaska. He is tired of hearing the question, "Why do you wear your football helmet all the time?" One reason why he likes Matthew so much is that Matthew tells him his ears are nice and not to pay any attention to those who taunt him. Matthew, who has a round face that makes him look like the man in the moon, is an authority on wildlife. He even interests Louis in catching animals in Havaheart traps. The boys are inseparable and are known in school as the "silent wonders." Louis stays carefully away from Calvin Leffert, the biggest kid in school, and Mr. Anderson, the principal. Fortunately, he is rarely in trouble. He is consumed, however, by the desire to play football which is the reason why he has a helmet in the first place.

Louis has two other friends, Mrs. Carmichael, his teacher, and Bertha Beeble, a neighbor. Bertha is responsible for teaching Louis to play poker using candy mints instead of chips. They have delightful times with this activity. Bertha also gives him a good luck charm that he treasures.

Meanwhile, the early fall passes slowly while the two boys have many adventures. One weekend Louis goes to a garage sale and buys himself some barbells. He thinks about getting a present for Bertha but postpones it until Sunday when he returns with his wagon for a more thorough expedition. He searches and finally buys a sapphire-like ring for her. By the time Louis convinces Mrs. Beeble to go to the sale, however, the garage sale man has moved. Matthew gets into difficulty when he catches a skunk in one of his traps and cannot get rid of the tenacious odor. He spends a lot of time sitting outside the classroom in the hall. Louis also catches a skunk, fortunately without encountering the problem of the odor. However, his good fortune slips away when someone steals his good luck amulet.

In the midst of these weekend activities, Louis continues to try to get a place on any after-school football squad. He stands around watching each day, on the ready with his helmet. Even receiving a thrown football in the stomach and throwing up in the toilet from the blow doesn't discourage Louis. He plays in a couple of games and hangs around hoping to be called. Louis does not even mind when an older player calls him to substitute by saying, "You with the big ears." While some youngsters still taunt him, Louis realizes his heart's desire when he is recognized as the kid who subbed the last time and is chosen for a game.

Thematic Analysis

The external and internal life of an elementary school youngster who is ostracized by some physical difference, no matter how slight, is well portrayed in this tiny slice of life during the fall term of a fifth-grader. The sheer fortitude that this young hero shows in facing his "otherness" and surmounting it should be helpful to readers who suffer from similar physical differences that seemingly detract from one's appearance. Protruding ears or large noses are common in both boys and girls. Their own attitudes toward themselves, as well as the helpfulness of having special friends and a desire to join with social or group activities, are essential keys to acceptance.

Discussion Materials

Introduce Louis and his problem. Follow this with noting some of the typical taunts he receives (pp. 1-11; 31). Mention Mrs. Beeble and the poker games (pp. 19-22); the amulet (pp. 34-37); Matthew and his traps (p. 27); the smell (pp. 40-44); the garage sale (pp. 47-53). Give some emphasis to Louis's wish to play football: Louis plays and feels good (pp. 77-79) and Louis is actually chosen (pp. 87-90). Contrast the reality with the jacket design showing Louis wearing a helmet to hide his protruding ears. This subject lends itself to a discussion. Ask how the youngsters feel about appearances, and how they feel about taunting others. The discussion content is volatile and directing it will take capable, calm leadership. Attempt it only in instances when you know the group well.

Related Materials

Other books that deal with physical appearance problems are: (acne) *I Was a Ninety-Eight Pound Duckling* (Dell, pap., 1976) by Jean Van Leeuwen; (freckles) *Freckle Juice* (Scholastic Bk. Services, 1971) by Judy Blume; (eyeglasses) *Guards for Matt* (Walck, 1961; pap., 1961) by Beman Lord; (tallness) *Johnny Long Legs* (Little, 1970) by Matt Christopher; and (shortness) *The Runt of Rodgers School* (Lippincott, 1971) by Harold V. Keith. An interesting film concerning small stature is *The Amazing Cosmic Awareness of Duffy Moon* (Time-Life, 32 min., color).

Arnold A. Griese, *At the Mouth of the Luckiest River*

Illus. by Glo Coalson. T. Y. Crowell, 1973, $5.50; lib. bdg., $6.50

The author of this story, which is based on an actual incident in an Athabascan Indian boy's life, has been a teacher in Alaska. Like many

Alaska residents he has piloted his airplane over much of the state and in this book he has reported geographical and historical details that are accurate. The story concerns a courageous clubfooted Indian boy caught in the struggles among the Eskimos and Indians and whites in the fur-trading business of not so long ago. It is crisply written, and will be thoroughly enjoyed by youngsters from 8 to 11.

The illustrator, himself the author of the book *Three Stone Women*, has lived in Kotzebue, an Eskimo settlement near the Arctic Circle. His vital charcoal and ink sketches parallel closely the high points of action, as well as portraying the energy of the characters. The book is lavishly illustrated with 26 double, single, and top- or bottom-margin drawings, many of which are bled over to suggest the landscape or the action.

The tale covers the late winter and early spring of one Athabascan Indian group who live between the 60th and 65th parallels at the convergence of three rivers below the town of Nulato in an encampment called "At the Mouth of the Luckiest River." The story opens in the height of the coldest season when the Athabascans honor the year's dead at the Nutsil feast. Although Tatlek, a stout-hearted boy who was born with a turned-out foot, lost his own father 2 years ago, he is still anxious to take part in the festivities—particularly the wrestling. In spite of his mother's fears, he believes as does his grandfather, that some strong yegas (spirits) work on his behalf. To the derision of the medicine man, he wrestles an older heavy boy, Tano, who in spite of his victory finds Tatlek a strong adversary who uses his deformity to every physical advantage.

Tatlek, a good hunter who has killed caribou, was taught by his father to use bows and arrows. He has also learned to train sled dogs. As a result of a chance meeting the previous year with an Eskimo boy from the "land of the little trees" he has adopted their method of training the dogs by voice signals. This has infuriated the medicine man who provokes jealousy against Tatlek's family for not sharing food in the time of hunger. The people fear Tatlek. Tatlek, who is sensitive about his deformity, asks his grandfather why the medicine man doesn't like him. The old man explains patiently that he uses his yegas (spirits) to disrupt. His grandfather expresses the hope that someday they will have a medicine man who is kind and uses his yegas to help the people. The old man believes in the lore of the Athabascans that many who become medicine men have weak bodies; he thinks Tatlek may become one.

Meanwhile, as the time for the return of the ducks and geese approaches, Tatlek and his friend, Sayo, train the dogs in Eskimo style and endure the misery and hunger of the winter months. The first caribou is finally brought in by a warrior. Then the medicine man calls all the men to his hut where he outlines the information given him by the owl spirit that the Eskimos are coming to this side of the mountains. He says that they must be killed in a surprise attack. As they leave, Tatlek is told not to go with the war party.

Not to be deterred, Tatlek and Sayo set out in advance to see what the medicine man is up to. In spite of the medicine man's powerful yegas, they plunge ahead checking Tatlek's snares far from his encampment. They stop the first night in a spruce woods, traveling all the next day until they hear some Eskimos singing. Tatlek sees the medicine man join 6 Eskimos and tell them they are in danger from the men in his village who are coming to kill them. He advises that they hide and kill the Indians. Tatlek reasons that the medicine man doesn't want the two groups to trade because the white man at Nulato will buy all the furs the Athabascans can bring to Nulato.

Tatlek confronts the medicine man (picture p. 51). The sled dog twice saves Tatlek as he deflects the medicine man's spear and knife, but not before the knife wounds Tatlek's arm. Sayo brings the sled and together they bind and hide him while Tatlek tells the Eskimos and Indians about the plot against them both. He asks his Eskimo friend (Ilyak) to translate. Finally, the two small groups are reunited. The Eskimos give presents (pictures pp. 62, 63) and the destitute Athabascans demonstrate their "Dance of Welcome." Tatlek has rid his group of an undesirable medicine man. In the years to come, he would become one.

Thematic Analysis

This story focuses mainly on a congenital defect, a clubfoot, and the stern conditions it imposes on a boy who lives in a harsh climate. The brand of courage, stoutness of heart, and confidence required to gain ascendancy over its limitations reinforce the type of attitude that is required to deal with a physical handicap. Also interwoven is a secondary theme of social justice that is simple and idealistic, but not inappropriate to the age of the readers.

Discussion Materials

Successful book talks can be given by using the superb illustrations and keying them to some central ideas. Use the following pictures and amplify them with the written descriptions in each chapter: Tatlek (pp. 1, 3, 6, 9-12, 19, 24, 29-30, 47); grandfather (pp. 14, 15, 27); medicine man (pp. 21, 23, 51-54); the journey toward Nulato (pp. 29, 30, 35); the landscape (pp. 32-33, 37, 59, 64-65); Eskimos (pp. 40, 41, 44); the solution (pp. 57, 62-63).

A discussion about the clubfeet and medical advances in today's treatment will be valuable. Also Alaskan topics, both geographical and social, are useful.

Related Materials

Other stories set in the same geographical area are *Eskimo Songs and Stories* (Delacorte, 1973), edited by Edward Field; James Houston's *Ghost Paddle: A Northwest Coast Indian Tale* (Harcourt, 1972); and Jean George's *Julie of the Wolves* (Harper, 1972). *Don't Feel Sorry for Paul* (Lippincott, 1974) by Bernard Wolf is a photographic essay about a boy's cheerful attempts to lead a near-normal life despite having been born with deformed extremities. Three other titles dealing with deformity are suggested: *The Jazz Man* (Atheneum, 1966) by Mary Hay Weik; *Johnny Tremain* (Houghton, 1943; pap., Dell, 1969) by Esther Forbes; and *The Witch's Brat* (Walck, 1970) by Rosemary Sutcliff, about a hunchback in twelfth-century England.

Sharon Bell Mathis, *Listen for the Fig Tree*
Viking, 1974, $6.50; pap., Avon, 1975, 95¢

To be blind in a sighted world is bad enough, but to also be a female adolescent Black living in Bedford-Stuyvesant, Brooklyn, fatherless and trying to cope with a bereaved and childlike mother makes the blindness just one of the handicaps. A noted writer for young people, the author of this story celebrates life and especially the lives of Black youngsters. She salutes them by dedicating this book to 3 beautiful women. Her insight into youngsters' feelings and thoughts and the social conditions that surround them is exceeded only by her ability to express this in tough, explicit yet easy-to-read prose that has a cadence and life of its own. Some will call it Black English. The good and bad coexist as they do in reality but unflinchingly the joyousness of survival and conquering pervades.

The jacket art design shows the attractive heroine beside a large, leafy fig tree that encompasses a typical "Bed-Stuy" multistoried apartment house side by side with the strong profiles of 3 female progenitors. Youngsters of all races, especially girls between the ages of 10 and 16, will be attracted by this powerful slice-of-life novel.

Sixteen-year-old Marvina Johnson has been blind from glaucoma since she was 10. Her father, Marvin a cab driver, bought her a braille watch when she started to lose her sight at the age of 6. However, since last Christmas when he was beaten by a couple of Blacks and bled to death before the ambulance arrived, Marvina (Muffin) has had to stand by and try to help her always dependent mother who has become increasingly childlike. Everyone except her mother, Leola, who wants both Marvin and Marvina, calls her Muffin. To make matters worse, Leola is an alcoholic who does not need much to make her ill. Unfortunately, the Midnight Club, which is open until 4 A.M., is just across the street. Between keeping the pills from the Mental Health Clinic away from Leola when she is drunk, taking over the finances, and managing by careful organization to be independent, Muffin is preoccupied.

Luckily, Muffin has many kind friends in the apartment house and neighborhood: Mr. Dale, the owner of the Club who is an upstairs neighbor; Mr. Thomas who lives next to him and soundlessly often peers out his door; the Reverend Willie Williams, her father's best friend; Miss Geneva, a downstairs spinster neighbor; and Tank, a young neighbor who is always "high" on drugs and greets her with the refrain, "Hi, Miss Cupcakes, Miss Pie." Muffin's two special after-school friends (Mr. Osahar, a blind math teacher is her "in-school" friend), however, are Mr. Dale and Ernie. These friends, together with her strong wish to celebrate at long last the 5 days of Kwanza this year at the Black Museum, are the ever-present visions in her active mind.

Mr. Dale, a prosperous club owner, is an exotic person and a demonstrative admirer of Muffin. He sews and keeps marvelous fabric pieces like his special pale pink suede for his own pleasure and that of his "sweet Black Plum." Ernie, a steady, industrious young man with graying hair, works in a Black grocery store and is Muff's boyfriend. It is a case of first love for Muffin (he smells like wet wood, wet grass, and wet flowers). Leola, Mr. Dale, Ernie, and the imminent approach of Kwanza—an African festival of communal celebration—are at the center of the pressure points that finally erupt around Muffin. Her own conflict of wanting something for herself and feeling responsible for her mother serves as the fuse.

Leola vacillates between deciding to have their best Christmas ever and having none. Only 5 days before Kwanza, Mr. Dale agrees to give Muff a yellow velvet dress and to plait her hair when she goes with Ernie to the Black Museum on December 26. However, Ernie, the oldest in a family of 6 sisters, bawls out Muffin for not realizing that Leola is getting worse. Muf n retorts that she is still going to Kwanza.

Meanwhile, Leola is vomiting. Ernie arrives and silently cleans her and the apartment, but refuses to take Muffin downtown on Christmas Eve to buy a long slip because he has a food delivery to make. Desperate, Muffin gives Leola her medication and goes downtown after sharing a hasty Christmas dinner with her mother.

Ignoring Ernie's ring because she knows he will be back, Muffin gets dressed in the yellow long wraparound, kisses her mother, and goes up to show Mr. Dale. As she starts up the steps, she hears someone whisper "Little yellow riding hood" in her ear. Then everything explodes around her as her assailant unsuccessfully attempts to rape her. Mr. Thomas, who is a mute, hears the noise and tries to help by swinging an old belt buckle at the attacker; in return he is savagely ripped by a knife. Miss Geneva calls the police. Finally, Mr. Dale carries Muffin back to her apartment and helps to place her bruised body in a soothing tub while preparing her for the police and hospital ordeal to come. While she is gone, Mr. Dale sews his precious pale pink suede into a duplicate of her ruined dress which together with the silver cane he gives her and the advice "to strut," help her pass through this terrible time. Unflappable Ernie, who only comments realistically that "people are people; they do what they do," and she goes to the museum to fulfill her fervent desire. The following day, Muffin goes to Mr. Thomas's door and embraces him. She also tells Leola for the first time, "I love you, Momma." Out of her world of darkness, Muffin looks forward to beholding the fig tree and providing others with some of the strengths they may need.

> Behold the fig tree,
> And all the trees; when they shoot forth,
> Ye see and know of your own selves
> that summer is nigh at hand
> —Jesus of Nazareth

Thematic Analysis

The theme is fundamentally about the richness of courage and inner resources that a severely handicapped person can have. Although the heroine is blind, she demonstrates enough courage to share with others. Black culture in large urban areas is well developed and integrated into the story. It serves as a parallel theme. The Kwanza festival is an integral part of it along with the religious and social fabric of Black neighborhoods.

The theme of responsibility—common among many young adolescent concerns—completes the triad.

Discussion Materials

The tantalizing cover with its portrait of Muffin and the fig tree can provide a good graphic point of departure, together with the fig tree verse, for a history of Muffin's blindness (pp. 10–11) as well as her description (pp. 13-15). Other episodes are: Ernie and first love (pp. 40-42); a sympathetic Black salesman (pp. 49-55); Mr. Dale, the tailor (pp. 62-74); the Christmas "battle" (pp. 75-81); Ernie's viewpoint (pp. 82-90); Muffin's response (p. 104). Also explain the Seven Principals of Kwanza (pp. 167-168). Discussions about blindness and alcoholism as handicaps can be generated using this title.

Related Materials

Connie's New Eyes (Lippincott, 1976) by Bernard Wolf can be used. For younger viewers, try the film *Apt. 3* (Weston Woods, 8 min., color) about a blind man, a harmonica, and a small boy. For older readers interested in exploring Black culture, try *Bongo Brody* (Hawthorn, 1973) by Barbara Glasser and Ellen Blustein. For a title on rape, try Richard Peck's *Are You in the House Alone?* (Viking, 1976; pap., Dell, 1977). Other titles of interest are *Chief* (Dutton, 1971; pap., Dell, 1973) by Frank Bonham; *Sound of Sunshine, Sound of Rain* (Parents' Magazine Press, 1970) by Florence P. Heide; and *None of the Above* (Dial, 1974; pap., Avon, 1975) by Rosemary Wells.

Colby F. Rodowsky, *What About Me?*
Franklin Watts, 1976, lib. bdg., $5.90

The author of this first novel, herself a mother of 6 children, effectively expresses the hopes and fears of a young girl in turmoil because of the conflicts that come from having a severely retarded brother living at home. Drawing on her own observations, she writes knowingly about the ambiguity of a love-hate relationship in the life of a youngster. Fifteen short chapters cover the events that occur and the feelings that the heroine experiences during the final spring of her brother's life. Told from the vantage point of remembrance, this poignant story is written with style.

The jacket design by Chuck Friedman immediately signals the observer that the story is black and white and gray in its complexities. The gray cover carries a double silhouette of the protagonist set on an overexposed photograph of a Mongoloid child. Youngsters from 9 to 14 will enjoy it.

No matter what the state at any given moment of 15-year-old Dorrie Shafer's feelings of love or hate and the accompanying guilt feelings, she has to accept the fact that things will always be the same for her 11-year-old brother, Fred. Fred is a Mongoloid who has a mental age of 3 years. Dorrie remembers calling him Piglet when he first came home from the hospital because she was interested in the doll, "Winnie the Pooh," and was reacting to his strange little eyes. Feeling her mother's discomfort, she dubs the baby Fredlet. Dorrie, who has inherited her mother's artistic talent, lives and breathes art, and is encouraged by the school art teacher, Guntzie. Guntzie is a downstairs neighbor in their apartment building.

Dorrie feels sorry for her mother who has given up her interest in art and almost everything else to stay home with Fred. Although her folks seldom go out, Dorrie definitely resents being asked to baby-sit when Mrs. Moran is ill. She does, however, so that her parents can go to the school dinner-dance. At a disastrous predance cocktail hour Fredlet manages to demonstrate all of his habits that irritate Dorrie. Fredlet bows to everyone and says, "How do *you* do," repeatedly, reads continuously from his favorite 1964 Sears catalog, and drools constantly. He finally ruins the cocktail hour by scattering cracker crumbs and throwing the fancy cheese ball his mother had prepared. He has a habit of hugging and lugging around the green ceramic cat Dorrie sculpted for her mother's Christmas present to the words, "Poor cat." In spite of knowing that Fredlet has a congenital heart defect, Dorrie sometimes hates him and compares him to an animal with her in the cage (pp. 25–26).

Each time when things become overwhelming, Dorrie retreats to slapping around her sculpting clay (wedging) or talking with Guntzie, a loner who understands the problem. One day, for example, Dorrie helps her mother take Fredlet to the dentist to have his teeth cleaned. While he continues to scream, Dorrie flees to the Guggenheim Museum. She finds Guntzie studying a Kandinsky painting. After explaining different ways of looking at art (p. 38), Guntzie tries to convince Dorrie to start working hard at her art work. In preparation for the Spring Art Festival, Guntzie convinces Dorrie that she should enter her green ceramic cat (pp. 46–47).

Calmly, Dorrie tries to tell her father about her feelings of hate. He, however, is more concerned about her mother. He declares that mom has carried the brunt far too long and that he is thinking of going back to a family law practice in Tunbridge, Maryland, so his wife will have the help of her mother and family. Dorrie is horrified to think that she cannot finish her last 2 years at school. As the school year ends, things get very busy. Dorrie's friends, Ann and Pat, nominate her for class president. Her election only adds to her worries. Dorrie asks to have her work-study week changed so she can work at Fredlet's school for exceptional children (Bellringers) to assuage her conscience. Mrs. Sherwood, the head teacher at Bellringers, shares her philosophy with Dorrie, but the repetitive, physical nature of the work disgusts Dorrie. She spends much time trying to train Marie to negotiate stairs normally without success. She is so revolted that she decides not to report on her final day. Being responsible, however, she just shows up late.

By the night of the Spring Festival, Dorrie is exhausted from helping Guntzie set up the displays and warring against her own feelings of conflict about her brother and family. When her mother says they cannot go to the Festival, Dorrie is crushed. From the stage, however, Dorrie sees her mother, father, and Fredlet in the audience. When Fredlet starts to mimic the musical conductor from the aisle, not even the good-natured approval of the crowd can make her feel better. Even receiving the first prize for her ceramic cat does not diminish the torment she feels, especially when later at home she hears her mother cry.

Her mother puts Dorrie's two blue ribbons on the kitchen bulletin board as she makes more calls in preparation for moving to Maryland. Meanwhile, Pat gets Dorrie an invitation from a Naval Academy freshman to attend June week. Her mother says she may not go. Instead, she asks Dorrie to stay with Fred while they go to her father's twentieth anniversary reunion at his law school. Dorrie's mind intones, "Dorrie do this, Dorrie do that."

In the meantime, there are many family conversations about moving to Tunbridge. Dorrie decides she will not go and goes down to talk to Guntzie. Guntzie explains how one can look at a family in almost the same way as pictures, seeing the whole and the pieces (p. 102). She also responds to Dorrie's inquiry that being independent requires high payment in being alone and without a family (pp. 99–102). When Dorrie gets back to her own apartment, she yells at Fredlet to put down his favorite green ceramic cat (which had won the first prize). He drops it. As it shatters Dorrie screams, "You idiot," at him (pp. 103–104). She runs brokenhearted to her friends. Ann and Pat sympathize with her and call Mr. Shafer who tells Dorrie to come right home. She is grounded for a week. However, her father also tells her that she can spend her last 2 years at Miss Benson's and take advantage of Guntzie's offer to live with her.

Somewhat relieved by this new development, Dorrie puts a new yellow ceramic cat, made especially for Fredlet, in Guntzie's kiln and stays with Fred while her folks are at the reunion. Unfortunately his heart fails, scaring him and terrifying Dorrie who calls Dr. Weinberg. An ambulance takes the two to the hospital intensive care unit. Fred dies moments before mom and dad arrive.

They all go to Fred's burial in Tunbridge. Mom finallys breaks down and has to stay in bed. When she is better, Dorrie shows her Fred's new yellow ceramic cat. Mrs. Shafer tells Dorrie that "Poor cat" means love, and that Dorrie loved Fred in spite of herself. On the train back to New York City, Dorrie listens as the wheels sing the refrain "Hate, your brother; got your trunk; love your brother," all the way home.

Thematic Analysis

The main theme revolves around the difficulties of living with a retarded child, especially for a sibling close in age. The normal pressures on a teenager compounded by those brought on by the presence of a retarded sibling add to the inner turbulence of adolescence. The inner conflict between love and hate is well delineated. Also well portrayed is the Mongoloid child in all his complexity. This book will help youngsters to appreciate the daily life in such a situation.

Discussion Materials

The jacket alone, with a brief introduction to Dorrie and her family, will easily set the mood for a book talk. For a description of retarded children at school tell about Dorrie's week at Bellringers (pp. 62–67). Also describe any of the following: Fredlet (pp. 1–14, 21–25); in action (pp. 5–14); "Poor Cat" (pp. 18, 103–104); at the dentist (pp. 35–36); as an orchestra leader (pp. 78–81); effects on family (pp. 50–54; 83); Dorrie's conflicting feelings (pp. 25–26). Emphasize Guntzie's prescriptions for "looking" at pictures (p. 38) and at the family (p. 102).

Related Materials

Some interesting books about the problem of retardation are *But I'm Ready to Go* (Bradbury, 1976) by Louise Albert and *Me, Too* (Lippincott, 1973; pap., New Am. Lib., 1975) by Vera and Bill Cleaver, both about girls. *The Hayburners* (Delacorte, 1974; pap., Dell, 1975) by Gene Smith is about a boy. For younger readers, suggest Harriet Sobol's *My Brother Steven is Retarded* (Macmillan, 1977). For more sophisticated readers, use E. L. Konigsburg's *Father's Arcane Daughter* (Atheneum, 1976) and Roy Brown's *Find Debbie!* (Seabury, 1976).

5

Forming a View of the World

IN THE MIDDLE YEARS of childhood, youngsters have started to relate to and become interested in the community, the country, and the world. At the same time when they enjoy finding out about other people around them, they are also curious about people in other countries and ultimately about the countries' histories. Moreover, their developing sense of historical time gives an immediacy to events of the past and a shape they may never again assume.

Endless is a youngster's curiosity about how others around the same age live in different parts of the world. The lives of young people of the past as well as those of the present also excite them. The quest for information and an understanding of the values of the past and of the current situation in other countries may be partially satisfied by the indirect experiences provided in children's books.

Some examples of books that fulfill these requirements appear in this chapter. There is an equal mixture of history and current affairs in these stories about different countries. The titles reflect the wide-ranging taste of this age group and there has been some attempt to include stories about lesser-known places.

Betty Cavanna, *Ruffles and Drums*
> Decorations by Richard Cuffari. Morrow, 1975, $6.50; lib. bdg., $6.01

This prolific author is responsible for many books that are enjoyed by young girls. Here she writes of the American Revolution's impact on a 16-year-old girl who lives in Concord, Massachusetts, where the opening salvos where exchanged in April 1775 at the bridge over the Assabet River. The author lives in Concord and knows the area and its history, and the romantic nature of many young girls well. Although it is a fictional tale, the research into the events of that fateful year are accurately reconstructed around the imaginative, yet possible, family events. Girls from 10 to 15 will find this 5-part story covering the time from the spring of 1775 to the spring of 1776 stimulating fare.

The colorful portrait of the heroine in her ruffled bonnet serves as a centerpiece for the smaller background figures of a young Tory shouldering a musket and a young British officer in his redcoat uniform. The trio symbolizes both the romantic and the larger conflict of that year for Sarah Devotion Kent.

Sarah, a stubborn and curious girl who had been something of a tomboy until this fateful year, sees her world change in 1775. Although there has been talk and ferment about freedom and about England in the rural village of Concord, it isn't until Sarah sees her dog, Obadiah, shot at Concord bridge on April 19 that she fully realizes the personal impact of the coming struggle. In her horror at the scene, she believes that she sees a young British officer actually kill the dog. As she carries her dog's dead body home for burial, her neighbor and boyfriend, Tom Fletcher, helps her. At a later meeting, he tells her that he is leaving to join the Revolutionary Army and kisses her. Before they part, she realizes numbly that she has agreed to marry him on his return. Although she has occasionally thought that she might marry Tom in the future, she is shocked by the suddenness of her action.

At home, Mrs. Kent explains that she has agreed to billet, in the kitchen bed, a delirious British soldier who has been shot in the leg. Several other Concord families also are caring for the wounded. Sarah learns that her younger brother, Amos, and her father, Nathaniel, have joined the forces as fifer and soldier. Sarah envies Amos because he can serve. In spite of her strong feelings against the British, she and her mother take turns nursing Lieutenant James Courtney Butler of the King's Own Regiment whom Sarah recognizes as the soldier who shot her dog. Although the stench from his leg wound permeates the entire house and sickens Sarah, she tends him and when the fever breaks she is somewhat grateful to know that he will live.

Meanwhile, she rolls bandages with her girl friends, one of whom, Mary Quill, is deeply in love with Amos. Young Amos, however, does not reciprocate. When he returns home on one occasion, he reports on the fighting at Bunker and Breed's hills, as well as the annihilation of the King's Own Regiment. James Butler overhears, and he and Sarah argue over the relative merits of the American and British points of view. As summer arrives, there is a letter from Tom and talk of General Washington and of Mr. Emerson who comes to preach in Concord.

After a discussion on women's fashions following a town meeting, Sarah and her mother return to an empty house. Lieutenant Butler, now on crutches, has been rounded up with the other military prisoners and put in jail. Deploring the miserable conditions in the jail, Mrs. Kent goes about getting him released. She sends Sarah to Cambridge where the soldiers are camped to see her father and Amos. While she is there, she also sees Tom toward whom she feels loyalty, but not love. Mrs. Kent is successful in getting Lieutenant Butler released to her custody and a teaching position in the Concord one-room school. Sarah and she, however, must tend to the farm work because James is lame.

To Sarah's relief, Nathaniel Kent returns to help finish the harvesting. James spends all his free time doing woodwork and talking good-naturedly to Sarah. She is interested in his former life in England and finds him stimulating company. He in turn likes her. Sarah receives an occasional letter from Tom full of misspellings and far less satisfying than her conversations with James. The letters are filled with Tom's great liking for army life and his desire to move to New York. This upsets her.

James proves to be an excellent teacher as Sarah observes one day. When there is some talk in early winter of dismissing him because he may be exerting undue influence on the school children, Sarah goes to President Langdon of Harvard whose school has moved to Concord for safety. As a consequence, a committee visits the class and goes to the Kent home to talk with James. At the conclusion, Sarah blurts out, to her acute distress, that James shot her dog at the Concord bridge skirmish. James explains calmly to her that Obadiah was caught in the cross fire, which is far different from being singled out. Sarah is beginning to understand that she has feelings of love toward James and feelings of guilt about being affianced to Tom.

The committee decides to let James continue to teach. When Amos comes home during the first snowfall, he ignores Mary who comes to call. James gallantly offers to walk her home. The jealousy this act provokes brings some understanding, at least to Sarah. James receives a packet of long-delayed mail from England informing him that his mother has been dead a year and granting him the smaller portion of the family inheritance that traditionally goes to a second son. After this sad news, Mrs. Kent and Sarah both recognize a definite desire on his part to stay in America. On Christmas day he surprises Mrs. Kent with a small gift of a wooden box he has carved. He also perplexes Sarah by giving her a cherrywood replica of her mother's courting mirror. Sarah knows intuitively that it is a proposal of marriage.

James reads aloud to them in the evening and answers Sarah's numerous requests for help in her spelling and reading. He has become one of the family. When he kisses her and tells her he wants to stay and buy a house, Sarah is not surprised. She is surprised, however, by the depth of her feelings toward him. After much deliberation, she tells James that she will marry him.

Thematic Analysis

Although this is a romantic love story for younger girls, it has a strong thread of American history during the first year of the Revolution as witnessed by a young girl entrapped by her ambivalent feelings of patriotism and her love for an enemy soldier. The historical reconstruction of the year 1775 in Concord, Massachusetts, is worth noting. A flavor of feminism is also implicit, showing realistically a range of feelings among girls and women.

Discussion Materials

Introduce the main characters (pp. 1-33). Follow this by using the chapter headings and drawings to tell the story that parallels the seasons from spring 1775 through spring 1776. Dramatize by paraphrasing an incident from each: spring, Amos reports on the battles (pp. 87-92); summer, life in England (pp. 127-130); autumn, farm work (pp. 130-132); winter, snow and complications (pp. 163-178); spring again, a thaw (pp. 206-208). Other good book-talk material: nursing Lieutenant Butler (pp. 47-51, 82-84); Tom proposes (pp. 57-62); girl talk (pp. 68-75); romance begins (pp. 93, 142-145); romance flounders and flourishes (pp. 154-162, 180-182, 185-199).

Related Materials

For the same readers, try *Rebecca's War* (Warne, 1972; pap., Dell, 1976) by Ann Finlayson, a book which makes a strong statement about women's rights and feelings. The acclaimed *My Brother Sam Is Dead* (Scholastic Bk. Services, 1974; pap., 1977) by James Lincoln Collier and Christopher Collier gives an unbiased view of a boy caught between revolutionist and loyalist sympathies. Younger readers will enjoy the humor and humanism of several Jean Fritz titles: *And Then What Happened, Paul Revere?* (Coward, 1973); *Will You Sign Here, John Hancock?* (Coward, 1976); and

Why Don't You Get a Horse, Sam Adams? (Coward, 1974). For readers who want more facts, suggest *The Tavern at the Ferry* (T. Y. Crowell, 1973) by Edwin Tunis and *The Colonial Cookbook* (Hastings House, 1976) by Lucille R. Penner.

Kornei Chukovsky, *The Silver Crest: My Russian Boyhood*
>   Tr. from the original Russian by Beatrice Stillman. Holt,
>   1976, $6.95

The author of this autobiographical reminiscence is a translator and writer of scholarly works, as well as a famous Russian poet (1882–1969). "Grandfather Kornei" as he is affectionately known wrote the verse tale, *Dr. Ouch,* which delights Russian children. He was a popular children's storyteller and a distinguished man of letters. In the tradition of writers of children's stories, he kept a deep sense of his own childhood which is recounted here in 26 brief chapters that recapture the bittersweet joy of a boyhood in the seaport of Odessa in south Russia. It will be enjoyed by children from 10 to 14.

The jacket painting by Gloria Singer reflects the Russian setting in its use of the typical domes of Russian Orthodox churches and earth colors. A mischievous-looking boy in a black sailor cap with a silver school crest is the author as a schoolboy and two classmates are standing in the background. This portrait emphasizes the importance to Kornei and his mother of the crested cap which cost 30 kopecks.

In 1893 in pre-Communist Russia, the school system or gymnasium for 9- to 17-year-olds was segregated by sex and cost money for tuition, books, and special uniforms. It was, however, a precious thing for the bastard son of Katerina Osipovna (Katya). The Ukrainian-born mother of 11-year-old Kornei who is a fifth-year student is proud of her intelligent son and knows that to get anywhere he needs a certificate from a gymnasium. She takes in laundry in their rooms in the once fashionable home of the Makerys on Rybnaya Street. Marusya, his older sister, who is also intelligent, spends much of her time reading, studying, and tutoring others.

Kornei's Odessa remembrances include some friends and some enemies. He counts among the former: his mother; sister Marusya; uncle Foma Osipovich; a best friend, Timosha Makarov; Top Hat, a thief befriended and redeemed by his mother; and Finti-Monti, a friendly teacher who is an opponent of clericalism and therefore dismissed from the gymnasium even before Kornei is expelled. Kornei's enemies are Proshka and "Six Eyes"

(Mr. Burgmeister, the principal); Zuzya Kozelsky, the worst student in class; Tuntin, the son of a well-to-do customs official; and Zhorka Drakondidi, a racketeer.

Two years earlier when he was in the third-year class, Kornei set up a string-foot telephone with his row mates to help them pass a dictation test on punctuation. Unfortunately, the boys didn't respond properly to the leg jerks, and they all failed. They rewarded him with a sound beating. Kornei also recalls the priest, Father Melety, catching him eating a meat pie on Friday and Zusya changing a low mark of one to a high mark of 4 and blaming Kornei for suggesting it. When he is threatened with expulsion and having his mother called in, Kornei doesn't know what to do. Because he knows his mother's great fear is that he will be unable to finish the gymnasium, he is paralyzed by this tragedy. He easily avoids telling her because uncle Foma is there visiting when he gets home. As Foma and Katya sit drinking tea Russian style in their glasses, Kornei decides to try to brave it out at school hoping he will not be noticed.

On the way to the gymnasium, Kornei passes the girls' Kroll Gymnasium where his secret love, Rita Vadzenskaya, goes to school. He thinks about how the boys in his school have often communicated with these girls by putting notes in the galoshes of the teachers who taught in both gymnasiums. Kornei is shocked when he finds that his favorite teacher, Finti-Monti, has been replaced. In a low moment he tells Timosha that he not only loves Rita, but he also writes poetry. His epic poem about school is aptly entitled, "Gymnasiada." However, his hope that he will be overlooked at school is in vain. Proshka and "Six Eyes" expel him; for good measure, the porter at the door strips his cap of its school identification of silver oak leaves. As he walks home dejectedly, he thinks many thoughts: how a gymnasium certificate guarantees a profession; how Marusya is always more serious than he; how the "Makrukies" (the boys in the large Makery home) regularly fight the "Pechonkies" (the boys from the Wagner house together with the young blacksmith, Pechonkin); how dying would wreak vengeance on everyone. He goes to Tuntin's house to ask for help. He is refused. At Zuzya's home, his former classmate will not retract his false statement blaming Kornei because he is afraid of his father's beatings. Timosha is not home, nor is Finti-Monti. Finally, at the home of Monsieur Racquet—the 96-year-old French former dancing master—and his two aged spinster daughters, who make salable trinkets, he is given a carved woodpecker to give to his mother when he tells her. His last stop before he goes home is at Drakondidi's on Uspenskaya Street. There, in the back-room bar, he finds Finti-Monti who tells Kornei that he has been expelled because ". . . You're not good enough for them—you're low class." Telling his mother is easier now, and he falls asleep on her lap.

He quickly gets a job as a sign-painter's apprentice as a roof (spatula) painter. Katya congratulates him for getting a job so fast. Meanwhile, he keeps up with his studies and teaches himself the English language. Edgar Allan Poe's poem, "Annabel Lee," reminds him of his yearning for Rita until one day when she calls him a "creep." He retaliates by "falling in love" with a school friend, Lida. He continues tutoring and reading novels to the elderly. He soon masters the required sixth-year school curriculum. However, he falters in his seventh-year studies, and goes on a loafing binge which torments him. Life begins again, however, when Kornei starts to tutor Timosha after the boy's illness with the flu.

Pleasant occasions such as a trip with Lida on Tuntin's father's customs launch and free opera tickets come his way. He witnesses many changes in old friends the summer before he goes to the university. Top Hat, who has been framed by Drakondidi and put on trial, is restored to his family; Katya turns to doing fine needlework that brings a better living; Marusya and Kornei work as tutors and Kornei passes his third examination for university entrance at the Richelieu gymnasium where Finti-Monti teaches.

His mother's dream of her son attending the university comes true. Further, Kornei becomes a famous writer, and she often tells people, "My son, you know is a writer."

Thematic Analysis

The pre-Russian Revolution atmosphere and life of people transplanted to the cities from the provinces (Ukraine) give a remarkable glimpse of the histosociological conditions in south Russia at the turn of the century. It is nonetheless a school and family story, although not a typical one for many. It can be enjoyed either as a narrative of slices of school life or as a retrospective look at a culture that may no longer exist except in cases of in-migration.

Discussion Materials

Set the scene by reading Kornei's poem, "Gymnasaida" (pp. 126–129) which explains how he revered his schooling. Introduce him by displaying his portrait on the cover. Explain the historical setting in Russia in 1893, with special emphasis on Tsar Alexander III and the school system. Also emphasize that Katya comes from a province, the Ukraine. A large map will be useful. Good incidents to describe are: the string-foot episode (pp. 1-6); Kroll gymnasium (pp. 40-48); Kornei's confusion (pp. 79-83); Kornei tells his mother (pp. 117-124); the poem, "Gymnasiada" (pp. 126-129); "Doing Nothing" (p. 149).

Related Materials

Aleksandr M. Linevski's *An Old Tale Carved Out of Stone* (Crown, 1973), the winner of the 1975 Hans Christian Andersen Award, and William Kurelek's *Lumberjack* (Houghton, 1974), about a passing way of life in Canada, will be appreciated by the same readers. The latter has the artist-author's wonderful paintings. Younger readers will like reading or listening to a collection of tales by Isaac Bashevis Singer about his childhood in Warsaw, *Naftali the Storyteller and His Horse Sus, and Other Stories* (Farrar, 1976). Two other exciting tales are Barbara Schiller's *Hrafkel's Saga: An Icelandic Story* (Seabury, 1972) and Oliver Butterworth's *The Narrow Passage* (Little-Atlantic, 1973). For older readers who are interested in early Greek and Byzantine history, suggest both Peter Dickinson's *The Dancing Bear* (Little, 1973) and Jill Paton Walsh's *The Emperor's Winding Sheet* (Farrar, 1974).

Erik Christian Haugaard, *A Messenger for Parliament*
Houghton, 1976, $6.95

This book has the sense of excitement and the style that have made its prolific author internationally acclaimed. Danish born, Mr. Haugaard has lived in Canada and presently resides in Ireland. He is noted for the historical research of his settings and of the eras involved that help to make his stories so vital. This one recalls vividly the events of a young life lived in England by the older Oliver who in 1865 is living in Boston. The story begins in 1642 in Cambridgeshire and covers the English Civil War of Cromwellians against Royalists. It will interest both girls and boys from age 9 to 13. The jacket displays a line drawing reminiscent of a woodcut of a young messenger eluding a soldier.

Oliver Cutter was born in 1630 in Cambridgeshire, England. His father a penniless carpenter who could read and write but who preferred to discuss politics rather than work was impressed with Oliver Cromwell, Alderman of Huntingdon and Member of Parliament. He named his son after this important townsman. Oliver's mother, Mary, died of consumption when he was 11 years old. Although his mother, on her deathbed, made him promise to "mind" his father, Oliver knew that with her gone his childhood was at an end. Oliver had a low opinion of his philosopher father and was not surprised when he decided that they should pack up and go along with the fringes of the Army of the Parliament under Cromwell against the Royalists under Charles II, the Stuart King.

After the sacking of Worcester, Oliver, who is barely 12, is forced to join the growing gang of children (the Children's Army) because he loses his father. He joins a small group among the boys: Ezra, the leader; William, who believes he is the bastard son of the Earl of Essex; and Easy Jack who is 14. Jack's parents are shopkeepers in Oxford where the Royalists have their headquarters. He is easy to get along with and Oliver and he become fast friends. Although Oliver unexpectedly bumps into his father who is working as a scrivener for a lieutenant, he does not hesitate to stay with Jack and the boys. Soon they talk about the widespread rumors about the coming battle.

The Battle of Edgehill takes place beside them. Ezra flees and William dies, forcing the others to take the road to London. The boys look with eager eyes on the metropolis and arrive finally at Master Walden's house. His daughter, Antonia, is deranged and Master Walden is a hunchback. He prints the newsheet "Mercurius" and is happy to have two ready-made messengers to carry the paper to Oxford.

Oxford, which a Puritan cooper calls "ungodly Oxford," is bustling with Royalists and spies. Master Powers, the owner of the tavern, *The Unicorn*, is a spy for Cromwell. Oliver meets his Master Powers's daughter, the barmaid Faith, when he delivers the papers and is smitten with her. He eagerly observes Christ Church College and Cathedral where King Charles II is in residence. Most of all, however, he enjoys the pageantry of the royal table and kitchen. While in the kitchen he meets Master Michael Perry, the actor, who captivates him with his good-natured and witty style of begging food. Oliver occasionally tends bar at The Unicorn until Master Powers needs someone to carry a message for Oliver Cromwell to Cambridge. The boys go.

On the way, they are almost trapped in a hayloft by a farmer and his sons. They escape only to be beset by highwaymen. Jack is wounded and turns over the letter packet to Oliver to deliver alone. On the 3 nights' journey from Oxford to Cambridge, Oliver spends one night at the home of the Vicar of Brill whose wife is suspicious of him. He is searched by men alerted by her as he takes the Ampthill Road to Cambridge. Eluding them at the crossroads, he meets Michael Perry who is on his way to London. When he tells Master Perry dramatically, "I am a messenger for Parliament," the actor exlaims that, "It is how you deliver your message that counts." Through all of this, Oliver reviews the many experiences he has had since he parted from his father.

By the time Oliver reaches Cambridge, Cromwell is in Ely. Oliver goes there and insists on delivering the message personally.

Forty-three years later, from across the seas in Boston to which Oliver emigrated and where he now lives, he thinks back to this early period in his life and the one time following when he became Cromwell's boy (a sequel). The older Oliver appends a fable, ". . . tyrants will always be with us, until we look into our souls and find there the reason why they flourish and the true seat of their power."

Thematic Analysis

As in all of the author's books, the nature and variety of humankind are explored through the eyes of a youngster. The complexities of the human condition are well illustrated. The insight shown by the author in revealing a young person's thoughts is startling. Also brilliantly expressed is the flavor of the historical period. The times are recreated in a crisp prose, the countryside so neatly described that one might even feel confident enough to walk the road from Oxford to Cambridge or tend bar in The Unicorn or do many of the other things the young hero does. The book provides an intriguing look at and an understanding of one brief historical moment on a foreign soil.

Discussion Materials

A brief retelling of the events during the period of the Civil War in England is appropriate. An encyclopedia can be referred to for a digest. Make it clear that the story about 11-year-old Oliver in England is told as a flashback by the 43-year-old Oliver who lives in Boston. Give some of Oliver's history (pp. 1-28). Describe the sacking of Worcester (pp. 30-32), the Children's Army (pp. 33-35), and London (pp. 110-113). Introduce the boys: William (pp. 33-35); Ezra (pp. 40-43); Jack (pp. 46-51, 101-105). The following episodes are good for book talks: the Battle of Edgehill (pp. 65-67); Master Walden, the printer (pp. 89-101); Oxford and The Unicorn (pp. 114-120); King Charles II in residence at Christ Church (pp. 121-129); and the royal kitchen (pp. 130-134). The excitement of carrying a message to Cromwell is seen in these two close calls: almost trapped (pp. 143-155); and highwaymen (pp. 157-170). The fable and promise to tell the next part of his story, "Cromwell's boy," is a fitting conclusion (pp. 216-218).

Related Materials

Eloise Jarvis McGraw's *Master Cornhill* (Atheneum, 1973), set in Restoration London in 1665, makes good additional reading. For readers interested in historical fiction, any of the following books, arranged chronologically by historical period, may be suggested: Rosemary Sutcliff, *The Capricorn Bracelet* (Walck, 1973); E. L. Konigsburg, *A Proud Taste for Scarlet and Miniver* (Atheneum, 1973); Cynthia Harnett, *Writing on the Hearth* (Viking, 1973); Hester Burton, *Riders of the Storm* (T. Y. Crowell, 1973); Barbara Willard, *A Cold Wind Blowing* (Dutton, 1973); and Sonia Levitin, *Roanoke: A Novel of the Lost Colony* (Atheneum, 1973).

Moses L. Howard, *The Ostrich Chase*
Illus. by Barbara Seuling. Holt, 1974, lib. bdg., $5.95

Musa Nagenda, the African name of this author, published his first book in English under the title, *Dogs of Fear*. Although he now lives in the United States, he has taught in Kampala, Uganda, and knows the setting of this story well. Of special interest to American readers is the author's recognition and treatment of the universal desires and interests of little girls even in an African country that has been one with a traditional role by gender culture.

The author writes economically in 12 short chapters about the yearning and determination demonstrated by a young Bushman girl who, contrary to the custom of her tribe, wants to hunt with a bow and arrow. A glossary is included to give the reader some guidance with unfamiliar words and concepts, for example, morro (hello) and Gao Na (god of the Bushmen). Young readers from 9 to 12 will enjoy this story.

The illustrations and frontispiece map of Africa employ a crosshatching style in their pen-and-ink directness. Each of the full-page illustrations shows the heroine in a pose that graphically explicates the text. The map detail of the Guatscha Pan or flat salt area in Botswana is helpful in explaining the desert climate in which the story takes place, namely the Kalihara Desert in South-West Africa.

Khuana who measures her age by the 9 dry seasons she has witnessed, lives with the other members of her immediate family among a tribe of Bushmen on the fringes of the Kalihara Desert. She has a younger brother, Gishay, and a still younger 6-year-old sister, Ungka. Her mother is busy with the traditional woman's work of the tribe including taking care of the youngest baby. Khuana's best girl friend, Nsue, who has seen 10 dry seasons is content with her rigid role as a female. Nsue only yearns for the powder scent from the Sjaae bush that she can keep in a tortoise shell box. It is one of the small vanities of many Bushman women. Khuana, however, longs desperately to hunt ostrich with a bow and arrow as the men do—a task forbidden to women. Although Mrs. Samgan interrupts and reprimands Khuana who watches the men prepare their poison-tipped arrows, her grandmother, Gaushe, sympathizes and supports her.

The Bushmen live in a harsh climate. The reality of hunger and thirst together with an oppressive heat pursues them relentlessly during the annual dry season. These tribes follow the dry river beds of the desert once a year to the Guatscha Pan where they congregate on the salt flat. It was on such a march a few seasons past that the tribe was forced to abandon Gaushe's ill husband. In such a primitive environment one can rarely afford the niceties of civilized behavior.

As the tribe's water hole drys up and becomes foul, the crippled storyteller, Guike, collapses from the heat of the desert whispering that he has sighted game, a large chamois. The men hurriedly withdraw to prepare for the hunt. Khuana steals away to watch them and learn. Afterward, she persuades Gaushe to help her search for the black beetles whose crushed cocoons exude the fatal poison. They dig up four cocoons and Gaushe promises to help apply the poison and give her granddaughter her deceased husband's bow. Meanwhile, Khuana loses one of the cocoons while hunting for her brother who is scatterbrained and uninterested in hunting.

As Khuana and Gaushe finally slip off to prepare the arrows, Gaushe tells her granddaughter about the pain of leaving her ill husband to die in the desert. Khuana carefully rubs each stone arrow tip across the crushed cocoon. The final tip, however, slips from her hand and enters Gaushe's leg. Khuana is terrified, especially when Gaushe can't move her leg the next morning. The tribe decides that she must be left behind.

With the water hole completely dried up, the tribe sets out on the long trek. Khuana decides to stay and help her grandmother. Together with her injured grandmother whom she half-carries, Khuana follows them. The distance between the tribe and the two increases. For them it becomes a ruthless battle of two against the desert. They spend one entire evening's journey going around in a circle. Khuana leaves her grandmother in order to look for game and finally shoots a rabbit which they eat. As days pass, the maggots that invade Gaushe's wound cleanse it so well that when they do come across some curative salt water, the leg is almost healed.

As they approach the salt flat, Khuana sights nesting ostriches. She secures one of the large eggs that the Bushmen use to carry water (decoration on last page). As her grandmother explains later, Khuana was sure to be chased by one of the parents who faithfully tend the eggs. Khuana is trapped in a cave with only 3 arrows. Two arrows miss, but her third attempt kills the ostrich. Khuana and Gaushe dry and pack most of the ostrich meat to carry to the tribe. When they arrive, the other members greet them warmly. Everyone is astonished that Gaushe is alive and surprised that Khuana has brought them ostrich meat. They will stay and visit with the other tribes until the rains come.

Thematic Analysis

Interwoven in this story are the realities of a traditional African culture and the beginnings of change. It is a story of survival of the most elemental kind, and will be enjoyed as such. A girl's overwhelming love for her grandmother and desire to hunt game show dramatically the strong surge of civilization across the face of the globe.

Discussion Materials

The story can be introduced to youngsters by using the map, glossary, and illustrations: Khuana (p. 12); watching the men prepare arrows (p. 13); Khuana draws a bow (p. 19); Khuana and Nsue search for Ungka (pp. 34–35); the leg wound (p. 44); the tribe marches (pp. 62–63); Khuana hunts a rabbit (p. 74); the ostrich (p. 97); trapped (p. 107); decorated ostrich egg (p. 116). Give some background material (pp. 12–13). Several exciting episodes can also be described: Gaushe is poisoned and left behind (pp. 40–50); Khuana leaves Gaushe and returns (pp. 59–67); they are lost (pp. 82–91); ostriches (pp. 96–98). The story can be used to discuss another and more primitive culture. Use an atlas to trace the journey.

Related Materials

For older readers use another engrossing story of the Bushmen, *The Harmless People* (Knopf, 1959; pap., Random, 1965) by Elizabeth M. Thomas. Also try *Mukasa* (Macmillin, 1973) by John Nagenda, a story set in Uganda. For younger readers and as an aesthetic treat for all ages, display Margaret W. Musgrove's *Ashanti to Zulu: African Traditions* (Dial, 1976), a portrayal of 26 African tribal cultures heavily illustrated by Leo and Diane Dillon. Also use the Weston Woods filmstrip and the 13″ x 18″ SVE prints, 28 of them, of the same title. Two other filmstrips are useful: *Africa's Niagara* (Multi-Media Productions) about northwestern Rhodesia and *Desert People* (Urban Media Materials, *Places People Live* series). The latter is non-narrated. *Alex Haley: The Search for Roots* (Films for the Humanities, 18 min.), a 16mm adaptation of an interview with Alex Haley, is appropriate. Two survival stories set in Australia are also suggested: Joan Phipson's *The Way Home* (Atheneum, 1973) and Bill M. J. Bunter et al., *Djugurba: Tales from the Spirit Time* (Indiana University Press, 1976). For a magnificent ostrich poster write Pomfret House, Pomfret, Connecticut, who also produce the filmstrip *From Reptile to Bird* which will fascinate the same audience.

Lee Kingman, *The Meeting Post: A Story of Lapland*
Illus. by Des Asmussen. T. Y. Crowell, 1972, $3.95; lib. bdg., $4.95

In an easy-to-read story for youngsters from 8 to 11 and older slow readers, Lee Kingman writess movingly about a little boy who spends the beginning of his school life in a state-run boarding school. The author is well known for her books both for children and about children's books. This title, about the little-known and rarely studied country of Lapland that is administered by Finland and located close to the Soviet Union and within the Arctic Circle, is one of the books in Crowell's series "Stories from Many Lands."

The illustrator, a Dane, has contributed numerous bold pen-and-ink renditions that enliven the text. They are strategically placed, covering areas ranging from a portion to a double spread. A striking cover portrays the joyful reunion at the end of the story when Hilma meets Matti on his return to the 120-kilometer post marker as the blue and red northern lights shine in the background sky. A note about the author and illustrator is given.

Eight-year-old Matti Kitti lives with his beloved grandmother, Hilma, on a riverbank in northern Lapland 30 kilometers from the main road in one of the loneliest spots in the world. His parents were drowned when he was a baby while they were stringing a fishing net across a nearby river. He has kept his father's unique Lapland belt. Matti carries on in the family work by fishing in the river with Hilma and tending their reindeer, including the favorite Old Parrak. It is Old Parrak who brings their sled to the post marker on the main tarmac across the tundra where the state bus picks him up when he sets out for school.

Matti waves goodbye to Hilma who like him is dressed in national Lapp costume. Matti wears the traditional "cap of the four winds" for men and reindeer skin slippers. He has packed his father's belt to carry with him. As they pass Mr. Saari's "baari grilli" (roadside variety store and grill) at 10 kilometers, Matti becomes very dejected. He remembers that the tarmac on which he travels is 6 feet above the tundra in some places and was originally put down as a supply route by the Germans in World War II. He has never been south of the "baari-grilli"; the large evergreens are his first introduction to the new landscape. Although he realizes that the Finnish government requires more than 100 boys and girls from northern Lapland to attend the state school at Ivalo, the size of the 3-story building is still a shock. Matti has only seen 3 stairs before.

At school, his roommate is Petri Peltonen, a Finn who speaks Swedish, but not Lapp. His teacher and room supervisor is Miss Rütta Salmi who teaches the geography and languages of Europe by using maps and a short-wave radio. Matti jumps out of bed on his first morning in response to the disembodied voice saying "Good morning and time to get up" over the intercom. Soon afterward he becomes familiar with his classes, participates in the air raid drills and uses the sauna, and discovers the enjoyment of listening to the radio in Miss Salmi's room. Matti is very lonesome, and takes great pleasure in the radio and solace from crying undisturbed in the sauna showers.

Remembering that Hilma told him to look up his cousin Jussi in Ivalo, Matti goes to the inn where Jussi Kitti, a maitre d'hôtel who speaks 6 languages, is packing to go to work in Spain for the winter. Jussi welcomes him and shows Matti his exotic Lapp dress which the tourists all admire. As the inn manager gives Jussi souvenir pins to take to Spain to encourage summer visitors to visit Ivalo, Matti, who has been trying to think of how to get Hilma a powerful radio for their home, asks if he can sell his father's belt. When Jussi says "yes," Matti runs to get it and meets Jussi as his bus departs. Knowing how much it will bring, Jussi gives Matti the money while commenting, "You're a Kitti all right, tough and stubborn."

Miss Salmi drives Matti 295 kilometers to her home in Rovainiemi for the school fall break. They travel through the historic World War II village of Sodänkylä, and Rütta takes Matti's picture at the Arctic Circle marker. From the Salmi home in a seventh-floor apartment in the "land of the midnight sun," 12-year-old Seppo Salmi shows Matti the ski lift and brilliant flowing northern lights. However, the biggest adventure comes as Matti packs his purchase of a radio in his duffle bag as a surprise for Hilma.

After they return to school, it isn't long before the headmaster distributes the bus tickets to the students to return home for Christmas. Matti and the other youngsters are excited as they dress and depart exclaiming "Hauskaa Joulua" (Merry Christmas and Best Wishes for a Happy New Year). All the way home, Matti wonders if Hilma will be waiting. The bus deposits him at the "baari-grilli" where he has hot soup and cookies. Mr. Saari takes

Matti on a thrilling ride to the meeting post on his new motorized sled. They wait 10 suspenseful minutes for Hilma to appear with 2 sleds: one with Old Parrak for him alone. Matti's adventurous step into the world south of the Arctic Circle has been a mixture of pain and pleasure, but worth it all, especially when Matti opens Miss Salmi and Jussi's present— his father's belt.

Thematic Analysis

This story is an excellent vehicle for talking about an alien culture in an extreme climate that is populated by human beings who share universal characteristics. On one level it is a school story, on another a family story. Finally, however, it is primarily a vehicle for expressing the unique environmental qualities of an area of the world.

Discussion Materials

A little background will make the story more appealing (pp. 1-3, 20). Use the illustrations and a large map to describe the action and surroundings. Introduce the main characters and show the exotic Lapp national dress (cover); "caps of the four winds" (pp. 30-31); cousin Jussi's dress (pp. 32-33); father's belt (pp. 22, 63). Also describe any of these: school, roommates (pp. 11, 13, 15, 17, 18, 24, 26, 27): trip to Rovainiemi (pp. 39, 40, 42, 46, 47, 48, 49 northern lights); goodbye to school (p. 54); leavetaking and arrival (pp. 1, 3, 4, 5, 7, 56, 59, 60, 61).

Related Materials

Lee Kingman's novel about medieval Iceland, *Escape from the Evil Prophecy* (Houghton, 1973), is suggested for older readers. Also try Nathaniel Benchley's World War II novel, *Bright Candles: A Novel of the Danish Resistance* (Harper, 1974). For younger readers, Elsa Beskow's *Peter's Adventures in Blueberry Land* (Delacorte, 1975) has been reissued in a new edition. Middle readers will enjoy *All This Wild Land* (Viking, 1976) by Ann Nolan Clark, about Finnish settlers in Minnesota in 1876. Several of the titles by Canadian author-artist William Kurelek are also suggested: *A Prairie Boy's Summer* (Houghton, 1975); *A Prairie Boy's Winter* (Houghton, 1973); and *A Northern Nativity: Christmas Dreams of a Prairie Boy* (Tundra, 1976).

Scott O'Dell, *Zia*

Houghton, 1976, $7.95

The writer of this story about an Indian girl who is caught between her mother's world—island of the Blue Dolphins—and the mission world of

Spanish California is himself a Californian and winner of the Newbery medal for the book *The Island of the Blue Dolphins*. This title is a sequel. Through his careful research and fine writing for young people, Mr. O'Dell has also garnered the first Hans Christian Andersen Medal given to an American and has written 3 ALA Honor books. He writes exciting and moving tales that are easy reading, such as this book which will be savored by girls and boys from 9 to 13.

The jacket portrays the heroine surrounded by the symbols—Indian, religious, and artifacts of nature—that circumscribe her world at the height of the mission history in California.

Fourteen-year-old Zia Sandoval and her 8-year-old brother, Mando, have come on their mother's death from their Cupeño village, Pala, to the mission at Santa Barbara. The journey takes 3 days of traveling northwest. The missions from San Diego to San Francisco were situated one day's distance apart. At Santa Barbara, the mission is located on a low bluff overlooking the Pacific Ocean and the islands of Santa Cruz and Santa Rosa. The missions are supervised by the Roman Catholic See in Mexico and Father Merced is in charge at Santa Barbara. Beyond them Zia can visualize the island where her mother's younger sister, Karana, still lives. It is her deepest wish to rescue Karana.

Zia and Mando soon fall into the routine of the place, working, eating, and sleeping under the strict rule of Father Merced who works everyone extremely hard. Although the girls, particularly Rosa and Anita, immediately become her friends and Gito Cruz, the young major domo, has a crush on her and favors her, Zia continues to long to go to the island of the Blue Dolphins. Finally in the summer she secures a drifting "long boat" and persuades Mando to set out in it with her. Mando who lives to fish—his hero is pez Señor Espada (Sir Marlin)—is easily convinced. They have several exciting escapades: Mando catches and Zia releases a giant marlin and they spend the night on an island in the lagoon. However, the whalers of the *Boston Boy*, to which the "long boat" belongs, capture them and set them to work on shipboard. Mando likes the work on a whaler, but Zia can think only of her thwarted desire to rescue Karana. After careful planning and good fortune, they escape and land in Ventura near a Chumash Indian village.

They make their way to the mission only to discover that Gito or Stone Hands, who is the son of an Indian chief, plans to take all the younger people north to Box Canyon in revolt against life at the mission and Father Merced. Zia will not abandon her island dream. However, she agrees to open the dormitories with the key Stone Hands gives her. When Father

Merced reports the revolt to the nearby garrison, after putting her in jail El Capitan Cordova questions and tortures Zia by exposing her to the cold and threatens her with blows delivered in iron gloves. Mando who has also stayed manages to bring her a little meat to vary her near starvation diet. Suddenly, one day Zia sights a sail from her cell window and hopes that it is Captain Nidever, a retired seaman, and Father Vincente, a friendly curate at the mission, returning from the island of the Blue Dolphins. They had left for the island in the early fall in a catamaran-type vessel with a sail Zia wove. To Zia's delight the two together with Karana and her dog, Rontu-Aru, climb the low bluff to the lonely garrison cell and release her.

Karana recognizes Zia's resemblance to her older sister. She cannot speak the language, nor is she understood by everyone, and she finds it difficult to adapt to life in the mission and sleeps on the floor. When Rontu-Aru is put in the courtyard, she sleeps there with him. When Father Merced suddenly dies, Father Vincente takes over and things are better for a while.

When the mission gets reports in the spring that there is trouble among those who went to Box Canyon, Father Vincente, Zia, Karana, and her dog go to the canyon where they find the people starving. While they are talking, a cooking fire is fed by a Santana (hot wind) which spreads it. All must flee. Some take the land route back to the mission; Karana, however, insists on following the rock-strewn coast because it is her natural terrain.

Soon after many people return, Father Vincente is sent to the Monterey mission. Mando also goes to Monterey to look for work on the *Boston Boy*. No one else is pleased, however, for Father Malatesta who replaces Father Vincente is stern. In protest Stone Hands leads another band north. Karana goes to live in a cave on the shore. Zia knows from Karana's touch when they try to communicate that she will never go back to the mission while Father Malatesta is there. Meanwhile, Karana takes ill in her cave. Zia and an old former medicine man from the mission try to help. It is no use: Karana dies. She missed her island home and found her new one inhospitable.

Zia tells Father Malatesta that she is going home with Rontu-Aru to Pala where she belongs. She runs toward home in the delight of feeling free with her blessing of "Vaya con Dios" still reverberating from her lips.

Thematic Material

The personal feeling of freedom that being in sympathy with your own heritage gives is highlighted. A young girl's realization that she must live at peace with herself is well delineated.

The story shows the mission system in Spanish California as it existed for some. The conflict between cultures—Indian, Gringo, and Anglo—is well drawn. This look at an earlier period on the west coast will intrigue youngsters and give them a deeper appreciation of their own heritage.

Discussion Materials

Introduce Zia Sandoval and her brother, Mando, and tell about her relationship to Karana, the heroine of *The Island of the Blue Dolphins*. Emphasize her desire to rescue Karana. Describe the mission system (pp. 1-25). The "long boat" escape to the islands makes a good book talk (pp. 26-27); pez Señor Espada (pp. 28-44); working on the whaler (pp. 47-50); spermaceti (pp. 54-56). Other episodes are: torture in the garrison (pp. 119-125); Karana and the medicine man (pp. 163-169). Almost any part of this story makes an exciting anecdote.

Related Materials

Any of the author's books are suggested, such as *The Black Pearl* (Houghton, 1967; pap., Dell, 1977) and *Sing Down the Moon* (Houghton, 1970; pap., Dell, 1976). Be sure to recommend that the youngsters read Scott O'Dell's *The Island of the Blue Dolphins* (Houghton, 1960). Two filmstrips are appropriate: *The Coast Ranges*, from the series *California: The Natural Regions* (BCS Educational Aids), and *The Life of the American Indian* (National Geographic). *The Girl Who Married a Ghost and Other Tales from the North American Indian* (Scholastic Bk. Services, 1978), edited by John Bierhorst, and *Groundhog's Horse* (Holt, 1978) by Joyce Rockwood are both appropriate for the same readers.

Katherine Paterson, *The Master Puppeteer*
Illus. by Haru Wells. T. Y. Crowell, 1976, $6.95

In an engrossing story for which she received the 1977 National Book Award for Children's Literature, the author has blended a literate mix of adventure and Japanese history with a subtle knowledge of young people. Out of her own background and interest in the Orient, she has fashioned 3 stories about feudal Japan, the latest a gripping tale for youngsters from 10 to 14. The pencil and ink brush drawings by Haru Wells complement the prose by depicting the character's expressions and actions. They lend an appropriate air of authority to the meticulous text and can be used effectively to explain many of the techniques of the Bunraku puppet theater which is the focus of the story.

Times were particularly hard in eighteenth-century Japan. Present with regularity were plagues, famines, and the oppression of the Shogun and their political deputies, the Daimyo, to say nothing of the merchant class who controlled the distribution of the poor rice harvests. The legend of a Japanese "Robin Hood" was popular. In the city of Okada, he who commandeered rice and monies from the wealthy by night to share with the starving masses was called Saburo. In the safety of the Bunraku puppet theater, even the beleagured merchants would cheer his name as they watched a play that lionized him. Outside the night rovers or rabble swirled about the streets in the hysteria of their hunger.

Thirteen-year-old Jiro who is always hungry even though his father Hanji, a skilled puppet maker, occasionally sells a 4½-foot doll to Yoshida, the master puppeteer, finally apprentices himself to the master's Hanaza theater because he has seen plenty of food there. Seemingly disliked by his mother, Isako, because he alone among his brother and sisters survives, he still hears her curse upon him as he asks the blind chanter, Okada, for a place at the theater. Okada is the overseer of the East Wing of Hanaza musicians and he listens because Yoshida had once commented on Jiro's spirited nature. Because Yoshida had once been the old blind man's apprentice at the famous Takemoto Theater, Okada has influence with him. At Okada's suggestion, Yoshida who presides over the West Wing of puppeteers adds Jiro to the group of apprentices. Wada is the eldest; Minoru, a handsome peasant, Teiji, a small-sized stutterer, and Yoshida Kinshi, the idealistic son of the master, complete the group. Jiro feels an immediate kinship to the friendly Kinshi who had originally let him in the Hanaza and directed him to Okada. His liking for Kinshi was strengthened when he witnessed him unflinchingly withstand a beating from Yoshida.

Jiro begins his apprenticeship by pulling stage curtains, learning the scripts, and studying the careful synchronization of the movements of the 3 black-hooded men who operate the puppets. He painstakingly develops his natural talent for puppetry, especially as the foot operator for the female doll Akoya (frontispiece drawing), and gains the respect of Yoshida. As he learns the rules of the Hanaza, he begins to notice the straw-hat baskets in Yoshida's quarters that bring recollections of one recent story about Saburo's band who appeared in similar headgear during one of their forays.

When Haniji fails to arrive with a doll he is repairing, Jiro gets permission to go home. There he finds that his sick father has been taken to a cousin's farm near Kyoto. Meanwhile, the pressures of the Hanaza nightly schedule of plays for the wealthy merchants keep Jiro occupied. Nagging worries persist; none are more irksome than the regular nightly absences of Yoshida Kinshi to whom Jiro confides his recognition of his mother's voice from the midst of an angry mob that is attacking the compound. An announcement that Saburo will be present at a performance of Okada's newest play about a thinly disguised Saburo hero figure to be played by Yoshida brings the assistant magistrate from the Daimyo and his underlings to the after-dark performance. Added to his worries about his family and Kinshi, his best friend, is Jiro's discovery in the Hanaza storage attic of the crested samurai sword that was stolen from the assistant magistrate the night Saburo's disembodied voice spoke out in the darkened theater before the lights went on to show the defrocked and bound officials and police.

Finally, Jiro is catapulted into action the night the city is set afire. In memorable prose that maintains a delicate balance between humor and tragedy, the author describes how Jiro ventures into the burning streets looking for his crazed starving mother only to find his father who is not ill, but one of Saburo's band. Haniji helps Jiro to elude the authorities by disguising him as a fireman of the brave Nambo Cho Brigade.

Back at the Hanaza, Jiro eludes the blind Okada in the attic storeroom after he has confided to him his belief that Yoshida is Saburo. Jiro's proof is the samurai sword he discovered in the attic. Jiro finally confronts Yoshida only to learn that like the Japanese saying, "The puppeteers act like the shadow of the doll and become its victim in manipulating it," Yoshida, as his old teacher's eyes, is only the reflection of the true Saburo—Okada.

Thematic Analysis

Jiro's struggle to master his own physical and emotional hunger, together with his strong feeling of attachment to his friend Kinshi, is a dramatic recreation of the childhood pattern of many children. His personal growth in having to discipline himself within the rules of the Hanaza community while dealing with his family problems and the surrounding world serves as a fine example for today's young. Also important are the secondary themes concerned with the values of learning a skill and occupation and of understanding that young people living in historical times and belonging to other cultures often faced problems and had feelings similar to those of today's youth.

Discussion Materials

A good introduction is Haniji and Jiro's delivery of a doll to the Hanaza (pp. 8-15). Follow this with a technical description of how the Bunraki puppeteer work (pp. 27, 80-83). The drawing of Akoya (frontispiece) can be shown to indicate the lifelike quality of the puppets in the famous

Japanese Bunraki theater. This book is rich in ancedotes and yields many episodes for book talks: Yoshida Kinshi bemoans his fate (pp. 38–39); life and practice in the Hanaza quarters (pp. 40–44); *The Battles of Coxinga* (pp. 50–53), a paper nailed to the door (pp. 86–87); night rovers (pp. 103–111); the fireman (pp. 159–169).

Related Materials

Suggest the author's earlier books about young people in feudal Japan: *The Sign of the Chrysanthemum* (T. Y. Crowell, 1973), about a 13-year-old boy caught in the wars between powerful classes, and *Of Nightingales That Weep* (T. Y. Crowell, 1974), about a 13-year-old daughter of a samurai who finds a place at court. *The Wicked One: A Story of Suspense* (Harper, 1977) by Mollie Hunter may also be used. A lovely collection of Haiku, *Flower Moon Snow: A Book of Haiku* (T. Y. Crowell, 1977) by Kazue Mizumura can be useful. The 16mm film *Full Moon Lunch* (Japan Society Films, 57 min.) presents an intimate portrait of a Japanese family and shows conditions in contemporary Tokyo.

Siny Rose Van Iterson, *Pulga*

Morrow, 1971, lib. bdg., $6.94

The author who has lived in Central and South America lives now with her family in Bogotá, Colombia, and knows her subject well. She has had many other books published in Holland as this one was originally. *Pulga* and some of the others have been translated into German and Danish. This edition was translated from the Dutch language by Alexander and Alison Gode. Siny R. van Iterson was the 1973 Hans Christian Andersen medal recipient for the corpus of her work.

This exciting story told in 23 chapters parallels the journey a poverty-stricken boy takes across Colombia as an independent truck driver's helper. It encompasses both the external and internal realities of this South American country. The young protagonist's many adventures will attract readers from 10 to 14 years of age.

The jacket painting by Lydia Rosier illustrates the malnourished 14-year-old boy placed prominently against a night scene that includes the Andes mountains and a truck. A detailed route map of the trip from Bogotá north to Medellin and back to Bogotá through Tolima is included in the frontispiece.

Francisco José or Pulga, which means flea, lives with his grandmother and 3 younger siblings in one room in a slum quarter that once housed the first families of Bogotá. He wears threadbare clothes, lacks shoes, and is always hungry. After their mother died his father abandoned them to dire poverty. His brother, Pedro of the twisted foot, for whom he feels deeply is coerced into begging with a band of children by an older man, Tio Pepé. Pulga is unable to help Pedro because he is only a street urchin who vies with grown men for a living by "watching" cars.

On one of his forays for work near the theaters he notices a trio of wealthy youngsters getting into a Mercedes. While he is wondering about them, two older street boys force Pulga to join them in a burglary. When they refuse to pay him as promised for slipping into a wealthy house and unlocking the front door, Pulga sits dejectedly under a parked truck. When the driver, Gilimon Naranjo, and his friend, another truck driver, Polidoria, come back to the truck, Gilimon hires Pulga as a helper for tomorrow's run to the Caribbean. Pulga's only regret is leaving his lame younger brother.

On the first leg of the trip to Cúcuta, Gilimon stops at his godmother's place just off the highway. Mamá Maruja feeds them and comments that she needs a boy like Pulga around now that she is older and Gilimon is gone. Pulga compares his life to what it might be with Mamá Maruja as he goes on with Gilimon.

As they head down to Páramo del Almozadero, Gilimon explains that they have had many holdups in this area. He warns Pulga to protect the suitcase which contains Gilimon's clothes and money. It is one of the more important chores for a trucker's helper. Fortunately, when they do stop and are held up, Pulga sits on an axle under the truck hugging the suitcase. The robbers are unable to find anything and Pulga and the terrified Gilimon escape.

In Cúcuta Gilimon delivers his cargo and tries to get another truckload. In the process he meets a friend, Fermin, who looks prosperous. Fermin takes them to Don Ramon where they are caught up in a treacherous escapade in which Don Ramon discovers that Fermin has been cheating him while delivering his cargos.

They finally leave to face a series of adventures before they get back to Bogotá. They transport a small boy, Eduardo, a short distance with a bag of rotting meat for his grandmother. Pulga warns Gilimon about a clever thief and once again saves the truck. They take the ferry across the Magdalena River. Gilimon buys Pulga his first pair of shoes (tennis) which Pulga finds have been stolen while he naps. They carry a family and their household possessions a short distance only to have them refuse to pay. After delivering the payload of cement they have carried from Cúcuta to Monteria, they take a detour to Las Palmas to pick up a load of cattle bound for Copacabana. They are so loaded that Pulga must sit on the tailgate where he survives a flash flood. After this close call with death, Pulga thinks seriously about trying to improve his life.

As they start to double back on the road from Copacabana to Bogotá, "the trunk of the Devil," they hear more talk about the Sombra Negra (black shadow) of Tolima. A sudden landslide slows them down in this territory. While they are stopped Pulga goes to investigate and sees Sombra Negra and Jorge Gabriel, who is about his age and was one of the boys in the trio Pulga saw at the theater in Bogotá. Pulga tells the village police who refuse to believe him until Jorge's father reports his son's kidnapping. They then find the boy and return him to the fabled and wealthy hacienda at his ranch, La Virginia. The father, Don Gabriel, wants to reward Pulga, but he and Gilimon have long since left for Bogotá. They meet Polidoria in his truck on the treacherous mountain roadway and learn soon afterward that his truck crashed down a ravine.

They arrive in Bogotá in time for Christmas and decide to go to Mamá's for trees to sell before they part. To Pulga's delight, he is paid and asked to continue as Gilimon's truck helper. Pulga goes to his old home only to find that his grandmother has died and his sisters have been placed in homes. He looks all over for Pedro. He finally finds him and takes him along to Gilimon remembering Mamá's wish. The new life Pulga has been daydreaming about has started.

Thematic Analysis

Pulga is a story of survival that is also a series of exciting adventures in a country in South America. At its most elemental it speaks directly of the harsh conditions the hero and others like him face and surmount. It deals with the bravery and love of the young, as well as the brusque affection toward children of some who are older. The landscape of Colombia is drawn on a large canvas from a child's-eye view, making it dramatic in spite of its grinding poverty. The scenes of the Colombian countryside are superb. A boy's will to succeed is deftly characterized.

Discussion Materials

The map detail on the frontispiece can be used to introduce this story of a Colombian journey. A large map of the country (a transparency of Colombia will do) can be used to retrace the trip of the truck bearing Gilimon and Pulga from Bogotá to Medellin and back. Follow the truck route on the detail map in front. Introduce Pulga and his background, emphasize his encounter with the rich children from the ranch, La Virginia (pp. 1-18). Relate the way Pulga meets Gilimon (pp. 34-38), and Polidoria (p. 41). The trip episodes make good talks: Mamá Maruja's place (pp. 43-50); the highwaymen (pp. 57-60); Fermin (p. 63); the house on Rio Seco (pp. 74-76). Don Ramon traps Fermin (pp. 102-106); Codazzi, the cotton center (pp. 107-109); Pulga and Gilimon (pp. 110-114); the Ferry (pp. 118-126); the tennis shoes (pp. 130-133); Old Menadro's funeral (pp. 149-154); loading cattle (pp. 155-160); a flash flood (pp. 160-167); Sombra Negra (pp. 170-173). The kidnapping and Pulga's story form the central climax (pp. 190-196, 197-203). Pulga's first thoughts about the future (pp. 94-95) and his first awareness of his own worth (pp. 136-137) can also be used.

Related Materials

An amusing story to suggest to the same audience is Patricia Beatty's *The Bad Bell of San Salvador* (Morrow, 1973). Other survival stories about children trying to live in a hostile environment are *Slake's Limbo* (Scribner, 1974; pap., Dell, 1977) by Felice Holman; *Midnight Is a Place* (Viking, 1974; pap., Simon & Schuster Pocket Bks., 1975) by Joan Aiken; and *Jonathan* (Dutton, 1972) by Margaret Lovett. The first has a contemporary New York setting, the latter two portray nineteenth-century England during the era of child exploitation. Other titles by Nicholasa Mohr—*Nilda* (Harper, 1973; pap., Bantam, 1974); *El Bronx Remembered* (Harper, 1975); and *In Nueva York* (Dial, 1977)—are compilations of short stories that deal with the harsh realities of Puerto Rican migrants' lives. Edgar White's *Sati, the Rastifarian* (Lothrop, 1973) does the same for a West Indian boy. Two filmstrips are also suggested: *South America: Land of Many Faces* (SVE) presents a current view, and *Stories of Latin America, Set II* tells colorful stories of several countries and is especially good for slower or younger learners. A 7-minute color film, *Imprint* (New Yorker Films), has echoes from the bleak world of the little boy in *Pulga*. It is a sophisticated film for thoughtful older viewers.

6

Respecting Living Creatures

MANY YOUNGSTERS find pleasure in caring for a pet. The ability to understand and give comfort and care to an animal is an indication of the child's developing capacity to love. This attitude and behavior ideally should be extended to all living creatures. Although many young people are unable to have the experience of caring for a pet, the opportunity to read about living creatures can be provided for all.

In this chapter, the books explore the nature and habitats of many different kinds of animals. One deals with a youngster's dependence on several small animals, one with a different way of thinking about small animals, one with an experimental animal's observations about us, Homo sapiens, and several with animals that are not commonly thought of as pets.

Byrd Baylor, *Hawk, I'm Your Brother*
Illus. by Peter Parnall. Scribner, 1976, $5.95

In their usual fortuitous styles, the author has created poetic prose and the illustrator has produced simple line drawings portraying a young Indian boy who longs to fly and does so through the magic of love for his pet hawk. It is a direct and profound story that will appeal to youngsters from the age of 5 up and readers from 8 to 10. This team composed an ALA notable book, *Everybody Needs a Rock*, and a Caldecott honor title, *The Desert Is Theirs*. The author has other books, notably another Caldecott honor book, *When Clay Sings* illustrated by Tom Bahti. All will be enjoyed by the same readers.

The illustrator, who is also well known for his contributions to *Audubon Magazine* and *Scientific American*, has echoed the lyricism of the prose with simple pen-and-ink dots and lines. The jacket, front to back, highlights, in shades of bright yellow, the boy's home in the Southwest near the Santos mountains. Both of the heroes, boy and hawk, are shown. The frontispiece, dedication, and double title page all show the boy, the hawk, and the mountains from different perspectives. The text is set in narrow double columns on the left-hand pages opposite the numerous drawings.

Rudy Soto is an Indian boy of about 11 years whose one consuming passion has been to fly like the hawks, smoothly. It is the only wish of the dark skinny boy who spends his time climbing up and down the high rock outcrops of the Santos mountains. His first word was flying, and he often asked his father, "When do I fly?" Although his father patiently said that people don't fly, Rudy is sure that some do. However, he soon decided that it must be a secret and stopped asking. Nevertheless, he is determined to fly and often on the mountain feels that he almost is. In his mind's eye, he is a hawk.

He knows the nests of the hawks and when they learn to fly, and he hopes to share their magic. From the old stories, he knows that if the hawk is his brother he will fly. He shamelessly steals a young hawk from its high nest. The hawk screams and resents the string Rudy ties to its leg. Although Rudy exclaims that the hawk will be happy with him, the hawk continues to scream and tear at the wires of his cage. He sees other distant hawks learning to fly, but cannot go high enough himself. Rudy takes the hawk walking through the desert hills, sandy washes, canyon trails, and to the water, always saying, "See, you're happy." Finally Rudy realizes that it is not true, and that the hawk must fly.

Rudy takes the hawk high up in the Santos mountains and stays with him while he jumps, flaps, rises, and sinks many times in his attempts to fly. It is not uncommon for 100 jumps to be made by hawks in learning to fly. Finally, the hawk soars with a long cry to Rudy. Rudy waves and calls to his brother. At this moment of release the magic begins. Rudy in his mind is also flying.

Although Rudy doesn't tell anyone, people notice that a hawk calls to him from the Santos mountains. Rudy also has a different look; his eyes flash like the eyes of a young hawk and one can see the sky in them.

Thematic Analysis

The tale carries messages on two levels. On the external level, showing regard for nature's way—the hawk is born to fly—it is explicit. There is also a more profound statement that humans must be as kin with other species, and it is only through mutual respect that people can become part of the spirit of the universe and share in the accomplishments of all.

Discussion Materials

This title is best read aloud with the youngster or a group. Interest can be generated by showing the jacket and title page and explaining that it is about a boy who wants to fly. An interesting discussion on geography may ensue from talking about Santos mountains and the Southwest and its Indians. Both the tale of Icarus (Greek) and Indian folktales of Navajo and Hopi can be used. A natural science lesson on desert flora and fauna is also indicated. The book will serve as a good departure point for the artistic and literary activities it can foster in youngsters.

Related Materials

Several titles about Indians relate: James Kirkup's *The Magic Drum* (Knopf, 1973); Elizabeth Coatsworth's *Pure Magic* (Macmillan, 1973); Katy Peake's *The Indian Heart of Carrie Hodges* (Viking, 1972); and Christie Harris's *Mouse Woman and the Mischief-Makers* (Atheneum, 1977). For older readers, Hal Borland's *When the Legends Die* (Lippincott, 1963; pap., Bantam, 1972) is suitable for younger readers in filmstrip (Current Affairs). The slide set *Understanding Natural Environments: Swamps and Deserts* (Science and Mankind, 2 units, 80 each, color) can also be used. Peter Dickinson's *The Blue Hawk* (Little-Atlantic, 1976; pap., Ballantine, 1977) is historical fiction set in Egypt and Babylon and is for older readers; *A Great Big Ugly Man Came Up and Tied His Horse to Me* (Little, 1973; pap., 1974) by Wallace Tripp presents humorous nonsense verses good for the young read-aloud audience. A nonfiction title on another type of hawk will also be useful: Burke Davis's *Biography of a Fish Hawk* (Putnam, 1977).

John Donovan, *Family*

Harper, 1976, $5.95; lib. bdg., $5.79

The author who is well known for creating provocative juvenile stories writes here of apes who are brought together for experimental purposes. In his usual taut readable style, he presents a morality tale about 4 apes who escape and form a family. The titles of the 4 parts describe the content: The Experiment; Freedom; Home; and Joined. The plot is rich and exciting, and is, in fact, unbounded by age restrictions. However, it will especially tempt young readers from 9 to 14.

Sasha, a fully grown male ape who was born in captivity at the San Diego Zoo, is only too happy to leave his fifth and boring language experiment at one university to become one of the group of 23 apes who have been sent to another. He quickly learns that 18 of them are 2- to 3-year-old

captives or "naturals." They differ from him and Myrtle, a good friend
from a former experiment, especially in having a forest odor, better bone
joints in their backs, and a more highly developed language. Those born
in captivity sometimes call the others "jungle bumpkins" because of their
magnificent physical strength and their awkwardness in confinement, as
well as their innocence of the world. Sometimes the naturals take a long
time to regress in their language to the point of being able to talk with
those like Myrtle and Sasha. The apes talk and laugh about the things
humans think the apes know about, such as the Scopes trial, and about the
names they give the apes. What they understand and the humans do not
is the type of communication that Myrtle and a graduate student engaged
in while they were playing. The graduate student was dismissed from the
project.

When Sasha overhears the scientists in the large old gym that houses
this project talk about manipulating bodies to put parts together, he remembers hearing other futurists talk about the same idea. He begins to
worry. However, Myrtle tells him he is crazy.

Meanwhile, Sasha helps protect Lollipop, a young motherless ape, and
tries to become friendly with Moses, a natural who was obviously a leader
in the wild. Moses, however, stays apart from the group, preferring the
solitude of the cave the scientists have simulated in the gym. Soon the
examinations begin. Each ape is taken downstairs to the metal table and
the machines. Moses has to be tranquilized. Eight new scientists join the
project and one who is 70 years old (apes can tell human age by degree of
drowsiness) rubs Moses's head and receives the same greeting in return.
However, when Sasha tries to talk to him, Moses falls asleep.

The scientists tickle (a favorite ape pastime) Otto, a young captive who
is always bragging about his achievements, and they throw him a basketball before deciding to take him downstairs again. The apes begin to worry
about him and Hortense roars at the humans, "Where's Otto." However,
the scientists think only that the apes are acting strangely. Sasha convinces
some that they must leave because the humans have a terrible plan. Sasha
leads a small group to the outside door where he watches Lollipop, Moses,
and the young female, Dylys, go out. He is saddened, however, to see Myrtle
turn to go back at the last moment.

The 4 apes have many adventures on their flight to the hills away from
the university. They eventually settle in a tree, while Sasha goes off to find
a better place. He gets lost and is attacked by a wild animal. When Sasha
awakens, he finds that the others have found him and licked his wounds.
After a couple of days of searching, Moses finds a high place beside a
waterfall.

In their new home, Sasha reflects about the ways of man and ape and also recalls some of the ancient legends of the apes. As they settle in their new life, Moses teaches the group the natural habits of the ape. They spend their time by rising early, talking, digging for sweet ants, grooming and playing, taking naps, and eating again. Moses teaches them ape "sounds," such as the "dry savannah" or danger call, and ancient stories about why apes can't swim. Lollipop continues her infant antics and falls in the water. They save her by forming a chain with Moses's strength sustaining them. They are a family. When Dylys becomes ripe or able to give birth, Moses goes off with her after biting Sasha's hands gently in the ape friendship fashion.

Soon after their return, the family is joined by a 25-percent drowsy male who has a beard, no shoes, and no smell. They recognize Man from living among humans, Sasha bites his hands and Lollipop exclaims, "I love Man." Their brother plays and communicates with them and brings them food from his trips below. He also leads them to a cave to hide in when there are hunters and guns around. While waiting for his return from one of his trips, Lollipop thinks she sees him near the waterfall. When she runs to him, she is hit by a hunter's bullet and Moses who goes after her also falls from the stunned hunter's volley. Sasha reassures Dylys, who now carries Moses's unborn baby, by saying they will find another place. The two adults and the one unborn baby are still a family. Many weeks later, they make their way to a hill overlooking the university. As they lumber toward the gym after their sojourn in the wild, Sasha hopes that Man is not lost.

Thematic Analysis

There are several themes interwoven in this story, among them man's ceaseless and futile struggle to improve the world and the ethics of subjecting living creatures to experiments. Overriding, however, is respect for a species of animals and the insight their respect can give to our own species. The story is full of information about the nature and behavior of apes and fanciful legends constructed to explain certain ape traits, for example, why they don't swim. Although it is an animal story only on a superficial level, it satisfies a young person's need to build respect for all life.

Discussion Materials

Introduce the setting (p. 11) and the famly; Sasha (pp. 1-11); Lollipop (p. 15); Moses (pp. 18-19, 24); and Dylys (pp. 29-30). Describe the naturals (pp. 10-11); the Myrtle-graduate student episode (pp. 9, 34), and the story of Dr. April Showers (p. 35). Talk about the final leave-taking (pp.

37-42); the creatures' struggle (pp. 65-69); Moses's teachings (pp. 81-83); and Man (pp. 102-109). Retell the legends: to the center of the earth (p. 80); dry savannah (pp. 84-85); why apes have many fathers (p. 100). For reflective use: home (pp. 75-79) and home to the gym (pp. 115-116).

Related Materials

There are some science fiction and fantasy novels that also deal with moral and ethical concerns. They are suggested for the same readers: *Z for Zachariah* (Atheneum, 1975; Hall, Large Print Bks., 1976; pap., Dell, 1977) by Robert C. O'Brien; *Noah's Castle* (Lippincott, 1976) by John Rowe Townsend; and *Beyond the Tomorrow Mountains* (Atheneum, 1973) by Sylvia Engdahl. Chester Aaron's *An American Ghost* (Harcourt, 1973) treats survival and wild animals in a compelling tale that helps to build greater knowledge of and respect for wild creatures. Ted Hughes's collection of poems, *Moon-Whales and Other Moon Poems* (Viking, 1976), illustrated by Leonard Baskin, adds a nice touch for sharing and reading aloud.

Carol Fenner, *Gorilla Gorilla*

Illus. by Symeon Shimin. Random, 1973, $4.95; lib. bdg., $5.99

The author started studying gorillas when she first spotted a magnificent male in Tokyo's Ueno Park Zoo. She continued her observations when the Air Force family was shipped to Battle Creek, Michigan. In this title she describes the youth of a male gorilla in East Africa and his experience living in a zoo after his capture. George B. Schaller's *Year of the Gorilla* (University of Chicago Press, 1964) is credited as the basic reference source.

Symeon Shimin, a famous painter and illustrator of children's books, is responsible for a compelling artistic treatment of the text. Using charcoal, pencil, and brush, he depicts the moods of the gorillas; the text is placed beside the drawing on each page. There are about 26 illustrations, several double page. The jacket also carries a gorilla illustration. The medium captures the natural look of this animal and adds an exciting dimension. Children as young as 4 years will enjoy looking at the pictures as well as having the story read to them. Eight- to 10-year-olds can read it themselves.

Gorilla Gorilla was named by the zoo keeper who posts a large sign in front of the cage area that says, Gorilla—Gorilla berengei. As he lies on the floor of his indoor cage, Gorilla Gorilla remembers the nightmare of being trapped in a net, pushed into a box with bars, and eventually landing in this large zoo in America next to a red orangutan and 3 baboons who also came from East Africa. He has not felt like eating and spends most of his time lying on his back thinking about his earlier life in the wilds of East Africa.

He was close to his mother as a baby and used to ride on her back while she gathered food—wild cherry, thistles, and bamboo—on their daily foraging expeditions through the large area they called home. Naturally, he tried to eat everything before he made his nest for the night next to his mother or in a tree. When he was a year old he could wrestle and roll about playing with the other youngsters. As he grew, he kept watching and trying to imitate the silver-backed leader. He also tried to hoot on a leaf, thump his chest, and run sideways in a thrashing ritual. He began to feel a power surging inside. However, when the silver-backed is disturbed, the leader becomes violent, swatting at any youngster in his path.

When the "young lord" is 8 years old and almost fully grown at 300 pounds, he is trapped by a party that is shipping animals to a zoo. The capture, journey, and arrival are upsetting. His outdoor area, with a tree and a moat, and his food do not tempt him. After a short while, however, Gorilla Gorilla stares out at the crowd. He also sees the orangutan steal his apples. Gorilla Gorilla comes outside and starts to eat, showing contempt by presenting his backside to the orangutan.

Soon the orangutan is removed and a young female gorilla is placed in the next cage. Gorilla Gorilla lies by her side next to the bars. Although she is listless the way he was, he likes her smell that reminds him of his forest home. This feeling gives him both pleasure and an aching feeling in his chest. By Sunday when the zoo is crowded with people, the ache has increased until Gorilla Gorilla suddenly goes out into his open area. He gives his hoot-hoot call, hurls himself up his outdoor tree and, standing at the top, thumps his chest. As cries of "a magnificent animal" spread throughout the onlookers in the zoo, Gorilla Gorilla appears to doze. The young female, reassured by his behavior, eats as the zoo closes, while Gorilla Gorilla dreams he is home in the forest foraging and eating wild cherry and bamboo.

Thematic Analysis

Respecting a wild animal's nature is the only theme in this short but satisfying story. Sufficient factual information is presented to show that a gorilla can be jarred out of his regular ways by being removed from his forest home to an artificial environment or zoo. Just as clearly, the story suggests that with proper attention and understanding, a gorilla will reestablish its pattern and nature regardless of its habitat. The story allows the reader to gain insight into animal behavior, and at the same time, into man's.

Discussion Materials

The illustrations can be used to tell the story. They are grouped here for use in 4 separate talks. *Childhood and Youth in East Africa:* the baby hides behind some shrubs (frontispiece); mother love (pp. 1–2); foraging (pp. 3–4); playing (pp. 5–6); watching the leader (pp. 7–10); "no nonsense" (pp. 11–12); aping the leader (p. 13); and the "young lord" (p. 15). *Caught:* hand in net (pp. 17–18); trapped (pp. 19–20); caged (pp. 21–22); and transported (pp. 23–24). *At the Zoo:* behind bars (title page); listless (pp. 25–26); the crowd (pp. 27–28); female arrives (pp. 29–30); side by side (pp. 31–32); home (pp. 33–34); ache increases (pp. 35–36); and confused thoughts (pp. 37–38); *Gorilla Gorilla on Display:* outside (pp. 39–40); climbs tree (pp. 41–42); and dozes and dreams (pp. 43–44, 47–48).

Related Materials

Suggest the author's other books for the same readers: *Tigers in the Cellar* (Harcourt, 1963); *Christmas Tree on the Mountain* (Harcourt, 1966); and *Lagalag, the Wanderer* (Harcourt, 1968), set in the Philippines. Betty Dinneen's *A Lurk of Leopards* (Walck, 1972), set in Kenya, and Anne De Roo's *Cinnamon and Nutmeg* (Nelson, 1974), set in New Zealand, both lend an international flavor. *The Peppermint Pig* (Lippincott, 1975; pap., Penguin, 1977) by Nina Bawden has a 9-year-old boy hero and is set in turn-of-the-century London; it is suggested for the same readers. Two books that have animal protagonists and encourage readers to stretch their thinking are: Emilie Buchwald's *Gildaen: The Heroic Adventures of an Unusual Rabbit* (Harcourt, 1973), for the same readers, and Richard Adams's *Watership Down* (Macmillan, 1975; pap., Avon, 1976), for older or better readers.

Michael Fox, *The Wolf*
Illus. by Charles Fracé. Coward, 1973, $5.95

Written by a veterinarian, who is also a professor and psychologist, this fictionalized account of the life of one pack of wolves is a frank and moving plea for the conservation of wildlife. The author has written other books that readers will enjoy, including *Understanding Your Dog*. Without a trace of anthropomorphism, he details the life cycle of the wolf by following the birth of 6 cubs to Silver and Shadow who together with old Uncle Two Toes spend a year raising the cubs, joining the main wolf pack, and finally seeing one of the cubs become the alpha leader. Youngsters from 8 to 12 will find the story and authentic facts above wolves exciting fare.

The illustrator, who is himself a naturalist, has many drawings for the National Wildlife Federation to his credit. Here he has done 13 magnificent pencil and pen illustrations in black and white, four of them on double pages, of the wolves mentioned in the book. The front jacket illustration shows Silver lying down surrounded by her 5 cubs while her mate and leader, Shadow, stands imperiously on the back of the white jacket.

Five-year-old Shadow, a wolf from the Alaskan Brooks range, lives with his mate, 3-year-old Silver, and his Old Uncle Two Toes, who when young and incautious was caught in a trap and had to bite off part of a foot to get out of it, near the Salmon River in the far North. As the story opens in early May, Silver has led Shadow and Uncle Two Toes to an old den that has been used for generations for the birth of cubs. She enters, but keeps Shadow out with a low growl. Old Two Toes has seen this procedure before when he was the alpha leader of the pack. He and Shadow go instead to eat the remains of the last caribou that they had stored for the winter. They are joined by another predator and friend, the raven, Hop-a-long, who also eats. When they return, Silver, who intermittently groans and licks something, by dawn produces 4 male and 2 female cubs.

She suckles and cleans the cubs by eating everything, as many animals do to keep their homes clean. For 3 days she does this until, forced by hunger, she goes to their empty larder and smells only Rastus the wily red fox. All the cubs huddle together for warmth, except for the sickly one that crawls into a corner and dies. Finally Shadow returns from hunting and enters the den where he seizes her muzzle in an affectionate greeting and stepping back regurgitates food for her. Old Two Toes also does this.

Shadow finally gets far enough into the den to meet his cubs when they are 2 weeks old. He nuzzles them in delight until they try to nurse. By 3 weeks of age, the cubs have their milk teeth and are exploring. One is nearly snatched from the den entrance by Talon, the golden eagle. Fortunately, the cub is pulled from danger by Silver who had lost a brother that way and had stored the experience in her memory. Wolves learn readily from experience. Each cub is unique: Blackie is the biggest and boldest; Tundra, the most active and forceful; Dusky, the smallest male and the most cautious; Blondie, alert and fierce; and Dawn, playful and clever.

Until late August when they are 5 months old and ready to meet the main pack, the 3 wolves educate the cubs. Old Two Toes pins them to the ground to teach them survival manners. They learn the sounds of friendship (low whine) and danger (growl) from their parents. Tundra assumes first place over his siblings by winning a fight over Blondie and Blackie. Silver saves Dusky from being taken in a clearing by the diving Talon. All learn to cooperate in tearing off chunks of meat from a kill.

When they move to a new home under some tree roots on the bank of a river nearer the game, the cubs learn to identify and respect others such as, Mr. Grumbly, the wolverine; Lady Amblethorn, the porcupine; and Caesar, the moose. They also participate with Silver and Shadow in their first kill. Shadow rolls in the musky-odored remains of the caribou carcass in an age-old ritual, followed by the cubs. They bay to the moon on full stomachs.

In September they meet 15 miles downriver with another pack: Grayface, who is Shadow's mother; and Storm, Shadow and Silver's father, and their 4 offspring; and Gale and Swift, Shadow's grown sister and brother. Two others had perished during the winter from starvation. After the greeting ritual they stay together for a week, killing a moose and being strafed by an airplane hunter. As winter approaches, they break into two search parties, one commanded by Old Two Toes, the other by Storm.

The New Year dawns for the 9-month-old cubs in the land of midnight sun, bringing adventures and hardships. Old Two Toes breaks out of line over an ice lake when the hunter in an airplane returns. He is killed and left for the carrion eaters: foxes, ravens, wolverines, and starving wolves. Shadow, unchallenged by his father who has been the leader for 5 years, becomes the alpha, and Storm is the second in command. Tundra bests Swift to become a future great leader.

The females, who have become tense as the breeding season arrives in February, take their natural place in the new formations. Gale and Blondie go with Tundra and Swift under Silver and Shadow. Storm and Grayface take the other three. That spring Silver and Shadow do not mate probably because the hunting range will not support a large pack. During the short spring and summer the two groups meet. Two planes come hunting, and Storm's entire pack is killed. A wildlife biologist in the other plane takes pictures of the slaughter to put in a national magazine. Shadow and his pack are safer now because hunting from the air has been outlawed because of the outcry. The wolves multiply. Four years later, Tundra becomes the leader of 12 and a father.

In the afterword, the author states that Tundra was the leader of a pack of 20 for 6 years. The wilderness had healed.

Thematic Analysis

The story deemphasizes many of the anti-wolf myths with a factual interpretation of their caution and wariness. It also shows the natural rhythms of their lives so in harmony with nature, and makes a plea to prevent their extinction. Respect for the wolves' way and conservation are the two main themes of this instructive and delightful story.

Discussion Materials

A display of the jacket, front and back, will attract readers. Further, a display of the illustrations keyed to parts of the book will be exciting, for example: Shadow nuzzles Old Two Toes (picture p. 9; p. 19, customs); cubs eat (picture pp. 42–43); first kill (picture pp. 60–61; pp. 60–61, learning). Describe birth of cubs (p. 12; picture p. 18); the cubs (p. 24; picture p. 15); and wolf facts (pp. 13–16). Also useful are: Talon (picture pp. 24–25); Mr. Grumbly, the wolverine (picture p. 51); and Caesar, the old moose (picture p. 56). For factual information talk about the wolf's nature and environment (pp. 13–16, 17–20, 21–27, 31, 36, 42–43, 46–48, 51–56, 63–65, 72–75, 80–83, 84–86; Afterword and Author's note).

Related Materials

There are 4 films that can be used: *Wolf Pack* (NFBC, 19½ min., color); *Where Timber Wolves Call* (Wombat, 25 min., color); *Biological Rhythms: Studies in Chronobiology* (EBEC, 22 min., color); and *Stop* (IFB, 10½ min., color). The latter is on conservation. A filmstrip and slides will also serve, especially for the younger viewers: *Visiting Nature* (Learning Tree, 4 strips) and *The Lure of Fall; Winter; Spring; and Summer* (Outdoor Pictures, 1 cassette and 26 slides each set, color). *Julie of the Wolves* (Harper, 1972; pap., 1973) by Jean C. George is recommended for the same readers. Jane Rockwell's *Wolves* (Watts, 1977) is a complementary information title.

Isabelle Holland, *Alan and the Animal Kingdom*
Lippincott, 1977, $6.95

The author brings the advantages of a varied background, as well as talent, to her writing. The daughter of a career diplomat she was born in Europe and traveled widely. Since returning to the States for college, she has been in publishing and lately has had 5 of her juvenile books published. This sixth book, in 7 chapters that are easy reading, explores a period of several weeks during which a vulnerable boy, whose only relative dies, tries to keep his pets from being taken from him. Boys and girls from 8 to 11 will identify with him.

The jacket illustration by Ted Lewin carries an attractive drawing of the hero in a blue jacket sitting cross-legged on the floor surrounded by his animals—a dog, a cat, two gerbils, a hamster, and a pet white rat sitting on his head. Set on a white background, this pensive pose appears on both front and back.

Twelve-year-old Alan MacGowan, a nervous stutterer, lives on the top floor of a renovated tenement in the west nineties with his great-aunt Jessie MacAndrews. He has had a nomadic life since his Scottish and English parents died when he was 3 years old. Alan has been raised mainly by his uncle Ian in Scotland, Canada, and Detroit except for the brief times that he spent with others while Ian was working in Japan. He learned some karate from his uncle who figured that a small skinny boy might need it. Alan also started to keep pets, a hamster in Scotland and a dog and cat in Detroit. When uncle Ian was killed, Alan, who has since vowed in blood ". . . never tell any adults anything," lost his animals to the pound before aunt Jessie came to get him. Alan, who wants to be a vet, quickly acquired his "animal kingdom," as aunt Jessie called them when he came to New York. The kingdom includes a dog, Winchester; a cat, Muff; Mr. and Mrs. Gerbil; a hamster, Wallace; and a white rat, Alexis, who likes to sit on Alan's arm or head.

When he is suddenly called to the hospital to find that aunt Jessie has died of a heart attack, Alan runs home to protect his animals from being taken away. In spite of his guilt feelings, Alan is mainly concerned about keeping things as they are.

He goes to school at St. Albans as usual and evades the questions of the headmaster, Mr. Laurence (The Sludge) and those of his pretty wife who teaches English. At home he tries letting the phone ring and gives garbled answers when he must respond, while the downstairs neighbor complains about Win's barking. Outside he is saved from the local gang by David Haines, a big Black kid from St. Albans. He jogs with David for a while and meets Mr. Lin a retired professor and his old dog, Ming. When they are about to be attacked by the gang again, The Sludge, a former athlete, and 8 students who are jogging save them. The Sludge tells Alan how he also moved around a lot as a kid with missionary parents. Nevertheless, Alan lies to him again about aunt Jessie.

When the rent bill arrives, Alan tries to find his aunt's strongbox. He remembers fondly many of her traits—neatness and an insistence on rights for both young and old—and also her strong bias against banks. While he searches unsuccessfully in the closet for the strongbox, Betsy Howard, a schoolmate, calls and soon arrives. Although she is surprised by Alexis, she tells Alan she likes the rat better than him (p. 69) and demands to know what is going on (p. 70). Alan introduces all the animals and then tells her everything. They find the strongbox filled with some jewelry and $223.00. The rent is $175.00.

Although Alan has $48.00 left for food, things soon revert to the same old pattern of lies and evasion. Mr. and Mrs. Laurence are genuinely worried about aunt Jessie, one of St. Alban's faithful parishioners. Alan cleans up the messy apartment, as Betsy suggests, and promises David to keep an eye on the old people in the park. He shops carefully and burns his hand while cooking (p. 98). The Laurences notice the burn and treat it the next day. Soon everyone is busy rehearsing for the parish fair concert which is only a couple of weeks away.

When the money runs out, Alan is despondent about buying animal food until he notices and opens aunt Jessie's Social Security check. However, no one will cash it. The phone, which he no longer answers, continues to ring. Muff becomes listless and ill. In desperation, Alan phones several vets finally getting Dr. Harris. He carries the cat 10 blocks to 105th Street only to find that Dr. Harris is drunk. Nevertheless, the doctor treats Muff with shots and pills, tells Alan he owes $20.00 and to bring the cat back. The next day, Dr. Harris talks about his alcoholism. Alan reciprocates by telling him about aunt Jessie's death and his fear for his animals. Dr. Harris calms his fears and promises to cash the Social Security check. He also starts cooking meals or taking Alan out to dinner. When Alan confides that he prefers animals to people (p. 135), the doctor explains that investing all your love in animals can be an escape. Alan helps out in the office and they become good friends.

Alan explains to The Sludge that Muff's sickness caused his absences. He feels guiltier about failing Mr. Lin. He worries the most, however, about Dr. Harris's alcoholism. When Alan and the doctor argue about it, the doctor tells him that he is only trying to excuse himself for failing to check on Mr. Lin.

When David tells him that Ming is nearly dead and Mr. Lin has been robbed of $6.00, Alan feels so terrible that he forgets to take Winchester out for a walk. By the time he dashes home, Winchester tries to relieve himself in the doorway. The landlord hits the dog sending him into the street.

Winchester is run over and has to be operated on by another vet because Dr. Harris does not answer. Fortunately, the man who is responsible for injuring Winchester gives Alan a check for $200.00.

The day of the fair, Alan sings a Scottish solo and helps David put the collection basket containing $134.00 in the rectory desk before he goes home to feed the animals and to Dr. Harris to cash his $200.00 check. When he finds the doctor drunk, he returns to the fair and takes the collection money to pay for Winchester. Alan returns home to sit disconsolately among his kingdom. Suddenly the door opens and everyone, David, The Sludge, and the Super burst in. Alexis dashes out, and Alan breaks into tears. However, everyone finally understands. David takes the gerbils who have just had babies; Betsy takes Muff and Wallace and issues Alan a standing invitation to visit; Mr. Lin takes Winchester; and the assistant pastor takes the rescued Alexis. Alan moves in with the Laurences who buy him a poodle for his birthday (the only kind of dog the allergic Mrs. Laurence can have around). Finally reconciled, Alan takes Ichabod, the poodle, to Dr. Harris for his shots. Dr. Harris says that he now goes to Alcoholics Anonymous and is coping one day at a time. He tells Alan, "You and Ichabod come back."

Thematic Analysis

A lonely youngster's emotional dependence on animals is skillfully drawn as a main theme. That such a youngster can be realistically helped to achieve a better balance is a positive and encouraging view. A secondary theme of adult alcoholism and its consequences coexists. The idea of a healthy respect for living creatures, in this case, pets, and the emotional support they can lend a deprived child, however, is all important. The hero's love and respect for animals transcend time and place and reach into an adult desire to be a veterinarian.

Discussion Materials

Introduce Alan and his background (pp. 9-34), and use the jacket portrait to name the animals and highlight his thoughts of trying to survive with the animal kingdom by finding aunt Jessie's strongbox (p. 105). Describe the important people in Alan's life: the Laurences (pp. 40-45, 52-57, 99-103, 177, 183-184); Betsy (pp. 63-79, 120, 177); the gang and David (pp. 35-37, 46, 49-50, 85-86); Mr. Lin (pp. 47, 90-93); Dr. Harris (pp. 115, 116-119, 122-126, 127-135, 136-139, 143, 146-148, 152, 154-156, 182-183). Follow with: aunt Jessie's strongbox (pp. 61-62, 105); Winchester's accident (pp. 160-164); and the school fair (pp. 103-104). Save the ending to the poodle story (pp. 183-189) for the readers.

Related Materials

Isaac and Snow (Coward, 1974) by Sally Edwards, about an industrious Black youngster who decides early on a career, is suitable for the same readers, as are 5 other books: *San Domingo: The Medicine Hat Stallion* (Rand McNally, 1972) by Marguerite Henry; *The Winged Colt of Casa Mia* (Viking, 1973; pap., Avon, 1975) by Betsy Byars; *Captains of the City Streets: A Story of the Cat Club* (Harper, 1972; pap., 1973) by Esther Averill; *Something Queer Is Going On* (Delacorte, 1973) by Elizabeth Levy; and *The Case of the Elevator Duck* (Random, 1973; pap., Dell, 1975) by Polly Berends (also in 16mm, LCA). Michael Bond's *The Tales of Olga da Polga* (Macmillan, 1973; pap., Penguin, 1974) and Lynn Hall's *Riff, Remember* (Follett, 1973; pap., Avon, 1975) are for younger and older readers respectively.

Judith Kohl and Herbert Kohl, *The View from the Oak: The Private World of Other Creatures*
Illus. by Roger Bayless. Sierra Club, 1977, $8.95; pap., 1977, $4.95

The Kohls are teachers; Judith Kohl is also a student of ethology, and Herbert Kohl is the well-known author of *Open Classroom* and *Thirty-Six Children*. Inspired by Jacob von Uexkull's *A Stroll through the World of Animals and Men: A Picture Book of Invisible Worlds*, this California team, who are also parents of young children, have produced a jewellike book that will encourage youngsters to look at the smallest animals in a new way. This winner of the National Book Award for children is one of the Sierra Club books that attempts to bring the earth, its creatures, and man's role to young people. Youngsters from 8 to 12 will enjoy it if encouraged. Younger folk should explore it with an adult reader or guide; older readers can perform some of the experiments it suggests.

The beige jacket on this ódd-size book carries a detailed pencil drawing of a large tree and the ground as the scene might appear to a small creature looking down from the tree. The book is full of drawings that also suggest visually unusual angles of observation; in addition, there are the more conventional close-up views of tiny insects or other creatures. The beige paper is a mechanical reproduction of handmade laid paper which lends a charming and elegant quality.

The authors credit many books. It would be worthwhile to check the following to read along with this title: Sally Carrighar, *Wild Heritage*; Konrad Lorenz's *Materials of Human and Animal Behavior* and *King Solomon's Ring*; and Franz Kafka's *The Penal Colony*. The Kohls have enabled us to view the world (*umwelt*) of tiny and small creatures, such as flies and birds, through their senses. The authors have stimulated us to revive some of the visual and imaginative ability that we once may have possessed in childhood. They have also encouraged us to experiment with our surroundings by asking questions such as, What it is like to live in . . . ? This sense of inquiry hopefully should be part and parcel of human beings from childhood to adulthood.

This informational book on nature is divided into 5 distinct yet interrelated parts: Worlds, Having a Place in the World; Time and Change; Tone, Mood, and Response; Values of the Oak. Each part is preceded by a page bearing a brown leaf design; the whole is followed by an index.

Part one introduces von Uexkull's concept from *Theoretical Biology* that there is not just one space and time as egocentric humans tend to believe, but a separate environment for each creature in which it has its own space and time. Also defined and used throughout is his concept of *umwelt* as the world around a living thing as the creature experiences it; for example, the ant and bee live in the same environment, but live in different *umwelts* (p. 14). This idea is illustrated by Sandy, the family golden retriever, who defines his *umwelt* chiefly through his senses of smell and sound.

Further, Niko Tinbergen's studies of the bee-killing wasp point up the nature of observing (pp. 16–18) as a means of exploring *umwelts*. Readers are told to look for special, temporal, and responsive signs in their observations in order to get an idea of how a creature functions.

Part two develops the reader's thinking about the place of each creature in the world by comparing human semicircular ear canals or balance mechanism with the ant's leg hairs. This part tells how the scientist Lorenz, an ethologist who studies animals in their own places or habitats, had to quack and waddle with his ducks in order to try to understand their place. It also explores the nondimensional (for example, the paramecium) and two-dimensional (for example, the water spider) qualities that form our spaces, suggesting that eliminating our senses will help us to inquire. The water game "Marco Polo," played with one's eyes closed in order to hear space, is recommended.

The touching of rats, cats, and moles, as well as the senses beyond our imagining, such as the heat sensitivity of rattlesnakes, is treated. Using one's eyes and understanding the territory of the animal under observation contribute to the importance of understanding space. Poincaré's measurement exercise (pp. 54–56) concludes this part.

Part three explains that the passage of time comes from the changes we perceive. Our sense of the passage of time is illustrated by the Afikpo people's 4-day-week rhythm (p. 60). Focusing on animal time is suggested: for ticks (pp. 66–69), snails (p. 72), spiders (p. 73), and people, dolphins, and bees (pp. 76–77). That there is no absolute time, only lived time becomes clear.

Part four explains and illustrates a variety of situations and signs of recognition that help to increase our understanding of living creatures. The creatures referred to are: hermit crabs (p. 84); cats (p. 88); dog, fish (p. 89); moths, dolphins, and fish (pp. 91–92); rattlesnakes (p. 94); and monkeys (p. 95). Tone, mood, and response are shown in each creature's development toward the goal of freedom and choice especially through the famous story of Buridan's Ass (p. 97).

Part five gives a summation by relating the *umwelts* of all creatures to the oak tree: from the fox, owl, and bark-boring beetle who live there, to the tree itself and those who use it, including loggers, a lost child seeking shelter and an aerial photographer mapping for conservation. The authors propose the question, What is the *real* oak? In whose *umwelt* is the oak big, small, hard, common, terrifying? They suggest that the answers are to be found by youngsters and others through observation and discovery.

Thematic Analysis

Respect for other forms of life through understanding each creature will help us preserve the world we share (p. 109). Conservation as a natural consequence of this type of study is the primary theme of this book. The scientific information and new ways of thinking about small living creatures are tremendously beneficial.

Discussion Materials

This book has many uses. It should encourage the child who is already interested in nature to observe and read the titles mentioned. It will, with the help of an enthusiastic leader who acts out the experiments, lead children not only to read this book but also to pursue other books on the topic. It can also be used for reading aloud, experimental inquiry about animal *umwelts* (p. 14), and book talks. For the younger readers, display the illustrations and tell a little about each. Also suggest the following: what to look for (pp. 19–20); balance (pp. 25–27); using your eyes (picture p. 44); difference between behaviorists and ethologists (pp. 53–54); rhythm of life (p. 60); the movies (pp. 70–71); time (pp. 78–79); Josh's fangs (p. 89);

city and country monkeys (pp. 95-96); evolution (p. 97); a remarkable jewel fish (pp. 99-100); and the oak tree in legend (p. 107). Some famous experiments: wasp-watching (pp. 16-18); duck-waddling (p. 28); can you hear space? (pp. 34-36); measurement exercise (pp. 55-56); Buridan's Ass (p. 97).

Related Materials

The authors' previous titles and the titles mentioned above are recommended. Read also from Franz Kafka's *The Metamorphosis*. The same readers will enjoy *Animals Come to My House: A Story Guide to the Care of Small Wild Animals* (Putnam, 1976) by Esther Kellner and two films, *The Morning Spider* (Pyramid, 22 min., color) and *Beekeeper* (ACI). Hilda Simon's *Snails of Land and Sea* (Vanguard, 1976) is recommended for the interested student. Three stories for younger readers are: Beverly Keller's *Fiona's Bee* (Coward, 1975; pap., Dell, 1977); Berneice Freshet's *Bear Mouse* (Scribner, 1973); and Lillian Hoban's *Arthur's Honey Bear* (Harper, 1974).

Jill Krementz, *A Very Young Rider*
Photographs by the author. Knopf, 1977, $8.95

This author is a recognized photographer of literary figures for newspapers and national magazines. She has served as the photographer-illustrator for several documentary style books by well-known authors. In this title, she exercises both talents in the sequel to *A Very Young Dancer* in what will obviously become a series with the forthcoming publication of *Young Gymnast*. Here she presents in text and photo a factual diary that reveals the reality and hopes of a youngster and her preoccupation with and love of horsemanship. Her family and her pony are also well portrayed. Youngsters, especially girls from 9 to 13, will savor the easy reading and pleasant viewing.

There are 169 photographs, all of them crisp and expressive. The title page alone, which shows the heroine in full riding regalia beside her pony, is deliberately grainy. The jacket photo is a warm color close-up of the two; the jacket design is by Elissa Ichiyasu.

Ten-year-old pigtailed and green-beribboned Vivi Malloy, who started riding her first pony, a Shetland named Fifi, at age 3, hopes someday to be on the U.S. Equestrian Team (USET). Presently, she rides her pony, Ready Penny, whom she has had for 2 years and loves. Penny is 13.1 hands high from the ground to withers (base of neck) and enters the medium pony hunter divisions at shows. Soon Vivi will need a larger pony and finally a horse over 14.2 hands high.

All but the father and two older Malloy brothers are active in horsemanship at the family Edition Farm in Purchase, New York. Mom still fox hunts and accompanies Vivi on the show circuit. Mark, who is 13, is a member of the Pony Club along with his sister and often accompanies her as Penny's groom. Seventeen-year-old Debby who has gone Vivi's route has 2 horses and has been in the prestigious Madison Square Garden Maclay Finals for 3 years.

Vivi goes to school where math is her favorite subject. Every day she has to see that the chores are done. Cleaning the stall involves mucking or seeing that the manure is shoveled out and that warm and dry bedding replaces the old. Edition Farm uses the less expensive sawdust instead of hay for bedding. Penny also has to be groomed. This means currying, vacuuming, brushing, rubbing legs, and picking dirt from the hoofs and treating them with oil. It takes almost 40 minutes to groom Penny before Vivi can get into her riding breeches, jacket, and boots to ride her. Even then Vivi has to tack-up or get Penny ready by putting her bridle on and tightening the saddle girth around the pony's stomach. At the final moment, mom sometimes gives Vivi a leg up when she is ready for her daily riding to practice equitation or horsemanship, although Penny is usually judged on her own movements in the hunter division.

Vivi has lessons once a week at the Farm or at the nearby riding stable from Jonathan, who is a pupil of the famous George Morris who also trains Debby. George won the 1960 Olympics Medal for Jumping. Jonathan teaches Vivi both jumping and flat riding (dressage). After each ride, she has to cool out Penny, feed her, and on hot days bathe her. Once a week, the family participates in the barn chores of scrubbing the buckets and raking the practice ring. On weekends, there are the Pony Club events in which Vivi, Mark, and mom are involved. Once a month, or when necessary in between, Bill Bradley, the vet, and Michael Lynch, the farrier and blacksmith, arrive to give shots or float (file) teeth and trim hoofs and shoe them. Occasionally Vivi has a special treat when she gets something for her outfit to replace something she has outgrown.

However, competing in the spring to fall horse shows is a special delight. In the spring mom drives the van with Vivi and Mark to nearby shows such as the one at Boulderbrook. Penny's hunter course has 8 jumps. Jonathan sees Vivi win a ribbon. Penny is also the champion at Syracuse. During the summer there are trips to shows farther away, such as the Lake Placid show and the C. W. Post show on Long Island. Vivi puts pressure on herself while riding, so meeting old friends her age and seeing famous professional riders like Rodney Jenkins are treats. She enjoys hearing George and Debbie talk about Debbie's winnings and seeing and remembering the lead line class for the little kid's first show. Vivi also has fun at the fairs attached to most shows; in fact, she eats so much she has to diet.

By August, Debby has again qualified for the Maclay Finals in the Garden and both she and Vivi can go to the big shows in Harrisburg and in Washington, D.C. However, Penny's leg goes lame and Vivi must borrow a horse for the nearby Pony Club Rally. By the time Penny's leg is better, they all go to the Garden to see Debby who gets a ribbon and a silver dish. She does not win the Finals, but George who won it when 14 tells her she rode well. She has another year to try.

Jonathan says that Vivi should get a bigger pony. Although it saddens her, she agrees to sell Penny to a nearby family before Christmas. On Christmas morning, Vivi receives a green-and-white horse blanket from her grandparents and finds in her stall a large pony, Fresh Paint, a gift from her family. She hugs Paint thinking about the good times they will have.

Thematic Analysis

Respect and responsibility toward one's domesticated pet is the theme with a strong definition of the reward of self-satisfaction that comes from proving you have treated another creature well. The practical aspects of caring for a horse are clearly outlined in words and pictures, as is the bond of love that develops between youngster and animal. It also serves as a good manual on show care for ponies.

Discussion Materials

The very large full-color cover picture of Vivi and Penny together with the title page photo can be shown to introduce this story of a young horsewoman who cares for her own animal. Also introduce Edition Farm and the family members (pp. 2–3). Photographic highlights of the everyday chores, daily riding, lessons, cooling out Penny, and barn chores should be shown. A list of local and area shows can be obtained for your location by your largest local stable or club. The 5 pictures of the tiny tots (one crying, one clapping) will provide a visual experience for telling that Vivi started this way. Conclude with pictures of the USET of four and the Royal Canadian Mounted Police (RCMP) of thirty-two at the Garden. Hint that Jonathan suggests just before Christmas a larger pony for Vivi. For the boys in your audience, use the photographs of the many men in the story. Boys also like to ride.

Related Materials

Two films are suitable: *Horses* (EBEC, 16mm) and *Look at Animals Series* (IFB, 3 films, 15½ min., color). Mary Stolz's *Cat in the Mirror* (Harper, 1975; pap., Dell, 1978), a fantasy about a modern girl in ancient Egypt, will be enjoyed by the same readers. *A Certain Magic* (Dial, 1976) by Doris Orgel concerns a girl's discovery of her aunt's childhood journal and a mystery, and will also appeal. The rich fantasy *Fly by Night* (Farrar, 1976), composed by Randall Jarrell and illustrated by Maurice Sendak, adds a special dimension for youngsters. Arline Strong's *Veterinarian, Doctor for Your Pet* (Atheneum, 1977) is a fine nonfiction title.

Laurence Pringle, *Listen to the Crows*
Illus. by Ted Lewin. T. Y. Crowell, 1976, $6.95

This prolific author of more than 20 books on nature and ecology has a degree in wildlife conservation from Cornell University and is also a photographer. In this latest title, he discusses the theories and experiments that concern the clever crow. Youngsters from the age of 9 to 12 will find it fascinating.

The illustrator, who is well known for his work in magazine articles and children's books, uses soft pencil to produce lush shaded black pictures of this large bird. His worldwide experience in observing nature is a bonus that shows particularly in the rectangularly framed jacket picture of the black crow. Here on a white background the bird's profile shows the true sheen of its feather in sudden bursts of blue and purple.

From the title page double-spread drawing that depicts 6 crows sitting in different poses on a tree branch, readers surmise that something exciting is about to happen to their knowledge about the people-wary crow. In the same way that a flock of crows communicate their urgency in "caw" sounds, so, too, are we ready to discover many interesting things about crows, such as, why do they "caw" several times?

The reader learns that there are many different types of crows ranging from the raven to the jackdaw; however, the rook is the most common. The intelligence of crows is apparent in the New Caledonian crow who uses a twig to root out bark beetles; the only bird known to use a tool, as did ancient man. A crow menu of beetles, mice, eggs, grasshoppers, apples, and worms, to name a few items in their diet, is listed and shown; 650 different kinds of food have been found in their stomachs.

Emphasized, however, is the crows' language ability. Some have been taught to imitate human sounds such as, "Hello," "Ha, ha," without having their tongues split. Dwight Chamberlain's recording equipment and his experimental work carried out in the 1960s show that in the wild they make a large number of different sounds ranging from cooing, rattling, and growling to screaming. The 6 muscles in the crow's syrinx enable it to do this. Chamberlain recorded different kinds of calls that he categorized as assembly (alert), mobbing (when they identify an enemy such as the great horned owl), scolding, threatening, courting, contentment, and more.

Nicholas Thompson, who has been studying the crow for more than 10 years, expresses the theory that the number of "caws" and the pauses between really express different degrees of emotion or feeling. For example, the closer the crow or the more urgent the situation, the more rapid or intense are the "caws." In his illustration, "I am angry," as the crow flies closer to the owl, the emotion becomes, "I am *very* angry," which is translated into short, rapid bursts of "caws."

Crows, who have always been regarded by farmers and hunters as being smart, can count. This has been shown in tests where they will not fly within shooting range of a hunting blind if 2 hunters go in and only one comes out. David G. Nicholas, another researcher, suggests that crows vocalize their "caws" in "bursts" or sets from one to 9, with a range of 6 the most frequent, interspersed as long or short caws. He theorizes that they are identifying themselves in their own code. Crow A says to Crow B, "I am a crow," Crow B responds by saying, "I am another crow," etc. This system would be useful for identifying the location and the flock. In a sense, the code is like a name. Meanwhile, Nicholas Thompson continues to investigate their "caws." In one of his recent experiments, he thinks he may have heard the young crows learning their sounds as human beings do their ABCs.

As the author says repeatedly throughout, "Listen to the crows." In 1973 a federal law protecting them followed the realization that they are neither bad because they eat corn nor good because they eat insect pests. "They are just crows, part of nature." "What are they saving to each other?"

Thematic Analysis

The demythifying of crows and removing them from the value judgments of good or bad are clearly stressed in this book. The main theme is an acknowledgment and respect for crows as a part of the natural order. As a corollary, some interesting studies that are part of the study of the language of the crows are mentioned. A reader will learn to appreciate this common species and be more aware of some of its idiosyncrasies.

Discussion Materials

Read or tell youngsters a little about this author and the artist from the sections on them in the back of the book. A jacket illustration of the colorful shiny black crow, if held close enough, will be effective in generating interest, especially if the topic of their language is mentioned. Several illustrations and some information can be used: members of crow family (picture p. 2); crow with twig (picture p. 4); crow's diet (picture pp. 6-7); words (picture p. 9); "mobbing" (picture p. 11); crow's enemy (picture p. 13); crow's syrinx (picture p. 14); "talking" (picture p. 17); "one to six" (picture p. 22); and "listen" (picture p. 28). Talk about the experiments by: Dwight Chamberlain (p. 15); Nicholas Thompson (p. 18); and David G. Nicholas (pp. 23-27).

Related Materials

Suggest the author's latest books, *Animals and Their Niches* (Morrow, 1977) and *The Controversial Coyote* (Harcourt, 1977). Keith Robertson's *In Search of a Sandhill Crane* (Viking, 1973), about a boy exploring the northern woods of Michigan, is for the same or older readers. Alison Morgan's *A Boy Called Fish* (Harper, 1973; pap., 1973) is also for the same readers. John Lonzo Anderson's *Izzard* (Scribner, 1973), about West Indian life, is suitable for younger readers. For owl fanciers try Mary Garelick's *About Owls* (Scholastic Bk. Service, 1975). Three films are suitable: *Birds: How We Identify Them* (Coronet, 11 min.); *Migration: Flight for Survival* (EBEC, 13 min., color); and *Flamingo: Variations on a Theme* (IFB, 30 min.). These films are for primary and middle graders, middle and junior high age, and junior high age up, respectively.

7

Understanding Social Problems

TODAY'S CHILDREN become aware of the urgent problems of the time at an increasingly earlier age. The developing values of the intermediate-age youngsters are partially shaped by the sometimes puzzling behavior of people toward a particular personal problem or social ill. Because youngsters are able to judge responses and make decisions for themselves, opportunities to examine, in stories, the central problems of our contemporary society will give them a better basis for evaluating their own attitudes and behaviors.

Current social concerns are treated in the books in this chapter. Half of them deal with some of the ethnic groups and problems that are of continuing importance. Some of these books deal with two or more issues in the kind of complex relationship that often is found in real life. The rest of the books emphasize problems with interpersonal social relations that youngsters must solve. Some of the problems have a long history; however, all have now been accepted as legitimate social concerns.

Betsy Byars, *The Pinballs*
    Harper, 1977, $5.95; lib. bdg., $5.79

This author expresses some of life's problems in a way that appeals to children. Her 1971 Newbery award title, *Summer of the Swans*, about a young girl's reactions to a retarded brother, is one example. Here in 26 short unsentimental chapters, she describes one summer when 3 foster children begin to care about themselves and each other. The placing of children in foster homes represents one of this society's continuing and, perhaps, increasing problems that often masks a history of abuse. Youngsters from age 9 to 13 will read this story.

The 3 young people are pictured on the jacket on 3 bowling alley pinballs emphasizing the "knocking about" that characterizes the lives of foster children. The picture relates directly to the heroine's final conclusion that ". . . pinballs is just a stage we're going through" (p. 135), but "we are not pinballs" (p. 136).

Carlie, a teenager whose main occupation is watching television, is generally at odds with her new stepfather, Russell. Although she tries to stay away from him, one of his blows eventually gives her a concussion. When the court places her with Mr. and Mrs. Mason, Carlie arrives to find Thomas J. and Harvey already there. They have been preceded by 17 foster children who have been placed in the Mason's home over the years. Mrs. Mason, a friendly soul, assures Carlie that things will be better and promises to teach her to sew, to Carlie's disgust. Carlie, who does not have much trust left, does not believe Mrs. Mason's opinion that she, too, can help others.

Eight-year-old Thomas J., who immediately helps Carlie find her misplaced earring, sometimes dreams up a picture of himself in diapers at the age of 2 toddling up to the Benson twin's farmhouse so he can see his mother at the end of the path. Thomas and Jefferson Benson, the maiden ladies who took the toddler in, are now 88 and in the hospital, each with a broken hip. Because the twins are deaf, Thomas J. (named after them in their birth order), basically a sweet-natured child, yells at people. He sleeps in the top bunk in a room with 13-year-old Harvey.

Harvey has not seen or heard from his mother—except for the time he spotted a group picture of her in the *New York Times*—since she left 4 years ago to live in a commune in Virginia. His father, who never gave him any mail from his mother, was drinking more than before and playing a lot of poker at night. Even when Harvey won the third prize for writing an essay his father did not change his mind about going out the night the prize was presented. His father's car ran over him and broke both legs. When he was ready to leave the hospital, the court placed him with the Masons.

The emotionally abandoned and physically assaulted children make an odd assortment. Carlie is hardened to her misery, Harvey suspicious, and Thomas J. bewildered. Harvey surprises Carlie with his quiet politeness when she brings him a tray. She tells him that she has never been able to find the sequel, *Appalachian Nurse*, to her favorite story of a nurse. They share some confidences, and Carlie suggests that he write down all the bad things that have happened to him. Knowing it is a futile effort, Carlie even starts to write a letter home promising to be good.

On the way home from visiting the Benson sisters, Mr. Mason and Thomas J. stop at the farmhouse because the boy is worried about the garden. Although they forget to pick up the Kentucky Fried Chicken, Mrs.

Mason cleverly arranges a picnic supper in the backyard. Carlie also helps by trying to cheer up the two dejected boys.

Later, Carlie pushes Harvey in his wheelchair to the library to try to locate his mother's picture so that he can write to her. He cannot find the picture; however, Carlie finds and reads avidly, *Appalachian Nurse*. Harvey's father takes him out to a Bonanza restaurant not long afterward as a means of apologizing. However, he tells the boy that his mother has never written to him and that she never will. Harvey is despondent.

Thomas J. also gets sad news: Jefferson Benson has died of heart failure. He goes to the funeral and cries out of pity and loneliness for the two old ladies who never kissed or even hugged him. Mr. Mason explains that some people find it difficult to express love as he did before he met the warm-hearted Mrs. Mason. At the hospital, Aunt Thomas tells the boy sadly that she and Jefferson had always planned a double funeral. At home, Carlie starts to enjoy sewing and to believe she has a special knack for helping people. When Carlie goes up to see the portable color television that Harvey's dad has given him for his birthday, she discovers that his toes are discolored. When he is put in the hospital with an infected leg, Carlie and Thomas J. visit and are distressed because Harvey is so depressed. Determined to help, they carefully choose a free puppy that is a good "licker." On their next visit, the puppy climbs all over Harvey and licks him. Harvey sobs with pent-up emotion. After he recovers, they have "cokes" and plan for the future cheerfully.

Aunt Thomas dies the following week. Thomas J., remembering how the Benson sisters used to trim his hair, gets a haircut. After the funeral, he and Carlie talk about his coming experiences as a new elementary school pupil. She explains thoughtfully that they are no longer like pinballs. Instead, they have all seen how an understanding parent or surrogate parent can help to instill confidence.

Thematic Analysis

The theme of this story about children who live, even temporarily, in foster homes illustrates the possibilities of love, trust, and understanding between the generations. It emphasizes the corrosiveness that self-pity can cause and the constructiveness that a hopeful attitude holds. While implying the full horror of child neglect and abuse, the story deals realistically with this social problem by developing the characters of the children and showing the unique ways in which they handle their grief.

Discussion Materials

Introduce the story and characters (pp. 3-7). For background use: Thomas J. and Harvey talk (pp. 23-26); Carlie can help (pp. 28-29); pinballs (pp. 29-30). Four other episodes are good for talks or reading aloud: sewing (pp. 45-47); Thomas J.'s arrival (pp. 52-53); youngsters' reminiscences (pp. 59-62); parents (pp. 64-66).

Related Materials

A filmstrip, *The Pinballs* (Walt Disney) can be used to illustrate the title and to aid poorer readers. Also suggest the author's story about 3 children who give an old man renewed vigor, *After the Goat Man* (Viking, 1974; pap., Avon, 1975). Marion Dane Bauer's *Foster Child* (Seabury, 1977) is about a 12-year-old girl who is placed in a foster home where children are abused emotionally and sexually. Richard Peck's *Are You in the House Alone?* (Viking, 1976; pap., Dell, 1977) deals with a teenage rape victim. Both of the two latter titles are for older or better readers. Family relations are dealt with in a series of 6 filmstrips, *Marriage, Separation and Divorce* (Current Affairs). Two of these are suggested for use with this title: *The Stranger in My House* and *Who Can I Trust?*

Barbara Cohen, *Benny*
Lothrop, 1977, $5.95; lib. bdg., $5.49

This author is known for her previous popular easy-to-read books for children. This one, set in the period just before World War II, treats one of her recurrent themes—the problems of an American-Jewish family. The hero in this book, Benny, has problems and adventures that are symptomatic of his heritage and the times. Eighteen chapters tell the story which anyone from age 9 to 12 will find enjoyable.

The jacket drawing by Richard Cuffari shows Benny in his baseball outfit, bat in hand, standing in front of his father's grocery store. Each symbol illustrates one of Benny's pressing problems.

Benny is in the sixth grade in Newark, New Jersey, in the spring of 1939. His greatest problem is his inability to arrange to play baseball, at which he excels, with the school team because he has to work in his father's grocery store after school. Benjamin—the youngest in a loving Russian-Jewish family—feels inferior in comparison to his studious older brother, Sheldon, and capable sister, Evelyn. Although everyone likes him, even Henry Silverberg, Evelyn's boyfriend, Benny feels that he is good only at playing baseball. His best friend, Morty Katz, agrees. Especially since his mother's operation in the fall, however, Benny has had to take charge in the store when his father is making the deliveries. As Benny knows, there is a depression and the few customers they have demand the home service in return for shopping at the corner store rather than the supermarket.

A bright side of Benny's life is his close friendship with uncle Moe and aunt Goldie. Aunt Goldie has always been one of his favorite people, and because she has two daughters and no son, he has been her favorite. She is a warmhearted person who has willingly made a place in her home for a German refugee boy, Arnulf. Arnulf, however, seems to be a difficult but smart youngster who argues too readily with Sheldon and others. Nevertheless, good-natured Benny manages to get along with him. He often travels on the street car to visit aunt Goldie and uncle Moe and joins them on a trip to the World's Fair in Flushing, New York.

Meanwhile, Benny has an opportunity to show the team—Carlo, Willy, Matthew, Double-Dip Cohen, and the Captain, Mac—his pitching "stuff" in the schoolyard. He watches the eighth-grade gang of girl bullies. His teacher, Mrs. Elfand, encourages his love of music and helps him with his difficulties in mathematics. She also is responsible for getting Mac to let Benny play baseball. Mac wants Benny to play after school in an important game and promises to ask his father when Benny explains why he cannot do so.

As the days pass, the family goes to the World's Fair much to Benny's delight. They have Sunday dinner at Goldie's who, unlike her usual self, has been complaining about Arnulf. Benny gets to know Arnulf much better. They eat and talk together in Arnulf's bedroom after he performs a chemistry experiment for Benny. Benny learns that Arnulf's parents in Germany are Aryan but his natural mother was Jewish. Benny knows that with Hitler in Germany, Arnulf would be in great danger because of having one Jewish parent. He also notices that Arnulf, who regularly reads the shipping news in the *Times*, is very unhappy.

Benny, who is studying Hebrew and looking forward to his Bar Mitzvah, and especially to reaching the age when he can wear long pants, is still tied to minding the store. Mac, however, persuades him to lock up the store and play for the game. Benny is punished by having to spend Sunday alone at home. When Goldie calls to say that Arnulf is missing, Benny, acting on a hunch, goes to the Hanseatic Line at Pier 59 on its final sailing to look for the missing boy. Benny's hunch proves correct and for finding Arnulf he becomes a "mensch" and a regular hero in both families. His father even goes to watch him play baseball with the team during a weekday game.

Benny remains humble in spite of his sudden elevation in the eyes of the family to whom he expresses admiration for the brave Arnulf.

Thematic Analysis

Understanding that prejudice against Jewish people is a problem of long-standing is one of the helpful themes in this story. Some background about Hitler and Germany may be important for youngsters who know World War II only through history. Another theme is youngsters' positive attitudes toward their own unique capabilities regardless of whether these correspond with their family's favored expectations. The story also highlights some of childhood's familiar patterns of development in a manner that will help build confidence.

Discussion Materials

To set the scene list the main characters, display the jacket drawing, and use the information in Chapters 1 and 2. The episode on the "movable bridge" is good for atmosphere (pp. 28-31). Several other good episodes are: Goldie (pp. 35-37); the World's Fair twice (pp. 41-43, 73-75); school (pp. 51-55); baseball (pp. 22-23, 58-65, 108-113); father comes (p. 119); Arnulf (pp. 80-87, 92-96); punishment (pp. 114-118).

Related Materials

Allegra Maud Goldman (Harper, 1976) by Edith Konecky is about a young Jewish girl in New York in the 1930s. *A Pocket Full of Seeds* (Doubleday, 1973) by Marilyn Sachs deals with the persecution suffered by a young French-Jewish girl during World War II. In Miriam Young's *A Witch's Garden* (Atheneum, 1973) a youngster is caught as a go-between in the prejudice of 2 families. Mankind's foolishness is well illustrated in the Jewish tales of Isaac Bashevis Singer, *The Fools of Chelm and Their History* (Farrar, 1973). An aspect of Jewish life is demonstrated by a family holding the Passover seder in the film *Preserving Roots: Passover* (Films, Inc.)

Evelyn Sibley Lampman, *The Potlatch Family*

(A Margaret K. McElderry Book) Atheneum, 1976, $5.95

This is a fine book from an author who writes about the Indians of North America. It is a moving description of one summer in the life of a young Chinook who discovers, with her older brother's help, both her Native American heritage and herself. Well written and interesting, it will appeal to both sexes of 10 to 14.

Each of the 11 unnumbered chapters carries Diane de Groat's ornamental Native American design. The uncluttered sand-beige jacket serves as a background for the heroine's profile. Several figures who arise from her memory listen to the compelling arguments of her brother, Simon, as he persuades them to recreate their Indian ways in a potlatch ceremony for the whites. The muted colors suggest earth tones.

Plum Longor, a freshman at Sunset Community High School, has two large problems: her father gets drunk and she has no friends. Inwardly Plum blames everything on being Indian. She lives along the Coast range of Oregon in the house grandma Longor bought when she moved away from the Grand Ronde Reservation to help her son Willie, whose first wife's death left him with 3 children. Lucy is now married to Hank Pierce, a Chinook fisherman; Simon, who is 25, is in a Veteran's Hospital; and 20-year-old Milo, crippled from childhood by polio, lives at home. Willie, a convincing talker, soon married Nancy Wing who produced Plum, now 13 years old, Chris, who is 11, and Andy, 9. Mom (Nancy) is the town launderette manager and pop (Willie) is a logger who has had increasing difficulty keeping his job because of his binges. Plum cowers as the school bus, stopping first at the prosperous Carl Schulz dairy farm to drop off fat Mildred, then pulls up to her ramshackle house and barn. Although all the kids on the Cooperville bus have been to elementary school with her, having them see her neglected home still hurts. The girls on the bus except Mildred, her usual seatmate, do not believe her when she says that she has been asked by a senior Rally Squad girl to try out for the Squad.

Today, in the spring rain, Plum finds her father lying drunk on the porch and she disgustedly helps put him to bed. Milo and grandma also help and wish that Simon, who has been back in the United States for 3 years after serving in Vietnam, were home so that things would be better.

When the broken porch step squeaks and grandma opens the door, Milo and Plum see her hugging Simon, who has come home on leave from the hospital. Simon is tall and thin for a Chinook. He looks at his snoring father, and cheers the family by complimenting Milo on his library job, his half-brother on his growth, and Chris on his resemblance to mom's family, the Lachances. Mom finally arrives, and Simon announces that he wants to have a welcome-home party the next weekend. To make it special for mom, he plans to put pop to work installing a shower while he is out of a job for the next few days. Things seem like the old days; however, Plum notices that Simon takes pills every few hours.

On their way to get the lumber on Sunday, Simon stops at the Schulz dairy farm to see his old high school chum, Perry, who is visiting his uncle.

Perry's father owns the logging company where pop works. Plum is horrified when they call each other derogatory names such as "Siwash" and "Dutch." She is further perplexed when Mildred says Plum is her best friend and that she wants to come to Simon's party.

For Plum, the anticipation worsens as Simon calls it a powwow and invites those who come from the Grand Ronde reservation. A look at the guest list of 14 grown-ups and 18 youngsters convinces her it will be a terrible flop. Simon's insistence on bringing mom's grandparents, the Lachances, down from an old shack a couple of miles walk away does not help. They comment that Plum looks like her grandmother who married a white man and bore Nancy, her mother. At first they—as Tututni—are awkward with grandma Longor, a Chinook. However, Simon's enthusiasm and Milo's information about their heritage succeed in bringing everyone to the day of the first potlatch.

Simon welcomes everyone by giving a brief history of their Native American background. He speaks about their being second-class citizens and suggests that they have a potlatch once every weekend during the summer to earn extra money and show their proud heritage. Ronnie Wachino, who is 16, is eager to do so, and Mildred gladly becomes an official blood sister. Simon, exhausted by the effort he has expended, goes to bed for 3 days while preparations are made for the next potlatch and Perry secures a suitable warehouse to hold it in.

During this period Mildred surprises Plum by asking how she can be popular, too. Plum gets Mildred to go on a diet in return for which she promises to stop scowling and to smile more. Plum goes for a motorcycle ride with Ronnie and talks about Indian heritage and pride. He suggests that the potlatch is really for themselves.

With the advent of summer the potlatch ceremony is held every weekend. Everyone contributes: pop narrates the history; Dave Beckett tells Chinook stories; Simon dances in a feather cape that grandma made; and Milo plays the drum. There is native food and there are baskets and arrowheads made by the Lachances. The project is a big success. Perry takes the reservations, and even the American wife of a Chinook changes her mind and wants to participate. Plum's schoolmates also ask her for tickets.

Early in August, however, Simon kisses them all good-bye and leaves with Perry for the Veteran's Hospital in Portland. Before the week is over, Perry returns with a letter from Simon saying that the Chinook Spirit, Kahnie, has taken him into the next world. The letter also tells them not to grieve and to carry on in the proud Indian way. They hold the Saturday night potlatch for the visitors. On Tuesday everyone goes to watch pop scatter Simon's ashes from Hank Pierce's fishing boat. After the last potlatch in September, Perry suggests that the summer earnings be used for a scholarship for Indian youngsters. Milo, a serious student, is pleased. Plum is also pleased because of her new interest in Ronnie, but especially because her two greatest problems have disappeared through the intervention of her loving older brother.

Thematic Analysis

The themes of heritage and friendship are closely interwoven. The customs and manners of the Oregon Coast Indians are reconstructed in this modern story that also shows their problems today. The characters are well developed and enhance the story to make it a moving one. Simon's short life and legacy of pride to his kin convey a poignant message.

Discussion Materials

Since the family information is scattered, use the first and second chapters (pp. 1-20) and information about the Lachances (pp. 21-28, 39) to introduce the story. A transparency of the jacket design will make a good background for describing talk about a powwow (pp. 41-54). Indian history of the region also bears retelling (pp. 17, 37-40, 47-54, 65-67, 73-77). Other subjects for talks are: Mildred and Plum (pp. 8-9, 34-37, 61, 78, 84-89, 113-114); the Indian Movement (pp. 77-78, 96-100, 102-106, 134); Simon and Perry (pp. 21-25, 30-36, 107, 121, 134-135); the Lachances (pp. 47-54); and potlatch (pp. 55-78, 115-119).

Related Materials

There are 3 films and a filmstrip that can be used: *Shelley Whitebird's First Pow-Wow* (EBEC, 8 min.); *The People Are Dancing Again* (Center for Urban Education, 28 min.), about Oregon's Siletz tribe; *My Hands Are the Tools of My Soul* (Texture, 54 min.); and *Stories Told by Native Americans* (EBEC, series of 4). Molly Cone's *Number Four* (Houghton, 1972) and Joyce Rockwood's *To Spoil the Sun* (Holt, 1976) are moving accounts of Indian heritage; the latter is about the Cherokees. *The Rain Dance People* (Pantheon, 1976) by Richard Erdoes and *The Apache Indians* (Scholastic Bk. Services, 1978) by Gordon C. Baldwin deal with the Pueblo and Apache tribes, respectively. *The Apache Indian* (Coronet, 10 min.) is another suitable film. A series of 4 films, *Who We Are* (Pyramid) can be used to spotlight prejudice.

Scott O'Dell, *Child of Fire*

Houghton, 1974, $6.95; lib. bdg., Hall, Large Print Books, 1976, $8.50

The prolific author of award-winning titles that are also popular treats Chicano gangs in this story. The lives of 2 juvenile offenders are shown through the eyes of a parole officer. The historical roots and current controversies are explored in 32 easy-to-read chapters by an author who is familiar with the subject and terrain. Both sexes from age 10 to 14 will enjoy it.

The jacket is striking. On a white background, it portrays the long-black-haired hero, Manuel, in jeans as he kneels with a red muleta in the pose of a matador. Superimposed on this scene are depicted the disembodied claw of a fighting gamecock, with its lethal spur attached, and also a small fishing boat. The red color of the muleta appears on the back jacket, too, which has a scene of Tijuana showing several hawks and early Spanish horsemen.

Officer Delaney of Mar Vista near San Diego, California, remembers Manuel from the previous year. Delaney, demoted from police detective after an old friend, whom he had trusted, escaped from his care, works well with his caseload of 42 boys. He goes on Sundays to the bullfights in Tijuana with Lieutenant Morales of the Mexican police to check on his boys—this time he is checking on Ernesto de la Sierra, 16 years old, and head of the Owls gang. Delaney sees a boy kneel with a red rag awaiting the entrance of the bull, Tiburón Negro (Black Shark), and wonders why Lieutenant Morales takes the "loco" boy in tow after a matador is gored by the angered bull. When the 16-year-old boy says he lives near Mar Vista, Delaney offers to drive him home. Morales's parting remark is to be on the lookout for drugs and for Ernie if he sees him with Paco Chacon in a green pickup truck.

After the interminable delay when crossing at the border, Manuel says that he and Ernie are dropouts who are the number one leaders of the Conquistadores and Owls gangs, both of which have been involved in illegal cockfighting and betting. Delaney, who notices that Manuel stutters, suggests stopping to eat at the El Sombrero Cafe where Yvonne waits on them. Manuel who is in love with the girl, who is older than he, is speechless with joy when she murmurs "Mucho Macho" after he tells her that he plans to dedicate the bull to her. Delaney silently wonders about this machismo strain that can be traced back to the Conquistadores. Ernie walks in flashing a diamond ring and a $1,000 roll that he tells Delaney his dead aunt in Mexico left him. Because it is late, Delaney takes Manuel home to his wife, Alice, a history teacher, who likes the boy because he reminds her of their son Mark. Manuel, who is a romantic who would have liked to travel with Coronado to find the Seven Cities of Cibola, leaves early the next morning. He honored an old Spanish custom followed by guests by taking $1.70 from the cookie jar.

Delaney has a busy day visiting the high school where he learns that Manuel was a good student, making inquiries and discovering Ernie recently was in Mexico selling chickens and pigeons, and going to look around Ernie's uncle's garage. Finally Delaney heads for Manuel's grandfather's Rancho de los Tres Gavilanes Rojos (Ranch of the Three Red Hawks). Formerly a large grant to a General of the Spanish King (Manuel's great-great grandfather), it now consists of a few acres and a crumbling adobe occupied by Saturnino de Lagos y Castillo, a goatherd, a fat stepmother, and the two pretty sisters of Manuel. Delaney finds Manuel and suggests he return to school. In response, Manuel shows him the gang's new fighting cock, Cortez. Delaney concludes his work day by going to the cafe to tell Yvonne that Manuel is only 16 and comes from a broken-down ranch, not like the one he has probably romanticized to her.

As Christmas approaches, Delaney encourages the gangs to accept the merchants' offer to be in the Annual Mar Vista parade. The Owls ride in new dealer cars and the Conquistadores ride their traditional horses up and down Main Street for 2 miles. Manuel wears seventeenth-century Spanish armor.

Soon afterward at the Sierra garage, Delaney witnesses Ernie's quarrel with his uncle for not opening the pen to let his homing pigeons in. When the police tell Delaney that Ernie's aunt died poor and could not have left him the money and jewelry, he abandons any hope he had for the boy.

Although Alice is against the violence and illegality of cockfighting, Delaney, who hopes he will be able to suppress trouble among the gangs, agrees to go to Las Palmas for a cockfight with the Conquistadores and to return with the Owls. The Owl cock "Lightning," who is handled in the last "hack" by Ernie, is beaten by the Conquistadores' "Cortez," handled by Manuel, as Yvonne watches. Ernie throws his dead bird on the trash heap, while Manuel puts the bleeding Cortez in his pen for the walk home after he finds the horses have been deliberately driven off a cliff and killed. Everyone is sure that the Owls are responsible.

Even Alice worries about gang trouble now. Delaney tries to avert it by arresting Ernie at the garage when he learns Paco Chacon is on his way to take the green pickup truck. Acting on Morales's advice, he drives Ernie to jail fully expecting to be knifed. Returning quickly, he intercepts Manuel, on his horse and armed with a musket, only to be confronted by Chacon. Luckily Delaney sees him coming and sends Manuel to call the police. When Manuel returns and sees that Chacon has knocked out Delaney, he kills him. Delaney and Manuel discover that Mexican heroin is being transported in the bands of Ernie's homing pigeons. While Manuel is hospitalized briefly, Delaney instructs Yvonne to return his $300 that she has taken fraudulently claiming that he is the father of her unborn baby. Manuel signs aboard a tuna boat headed for South America. In spite of his increased caseload, Delaney follows the shipping news closely to learn that the American, Manuel Castillo, has been imprisoned for leading a mutiny.

As grape harvesting time arrives at the La Cresta vineyards in May, the mechanical picker that the owner is bringing in occasions sounds of "huelga" (strike) among the families in the barrio. Manual appears after escaping from the prison. As Delaney takes him to the ranch, they pass the vineyards and he hears the story. Two days later as the huge machine arrives, Manuel, whose friend plays a guitar accompaniment, kneels at the end of a furrow. Delaney, who remembers the bullfight scene, runs desperately to save him as the machine arms gather in the grapes and the flesh of Manuel de la Castillo.

Thematic Analysis

This story dramatically recreates the conflict of cultures and past heritage. Manuel is a romantic figure out of tune with present reality. The story also illustrates the nature of good and evil in the persons of Manuel and Ernie. It states a position of humaneness and shows how progress without regard for the conflict of cultures can debase one. Included also is background information on the locale, gang problems, and our society's ineffectual remedies for those trapped.

Discussion Materials

The jacket drawing and Delaney's first sight of Manuel can be presented (pp. 15-19). Lieutenant Morales's presentation of the gored matador to Manuel can also be discussed (pp. 20-26). Background and a definition of "machismo" are given (pp. 34-42). Present the antagonist, Ernesto de la Sierra (pp. 5, 42-46, 57, 63-66, 96-105, 118-119, 148-150), and the protagonist, Manuel de Castillo (pp. 15-19, 27-32, 34-42, 47-48, 51-56, 105, 108-113, 120-125, 130-131). The following make exciting book talks: parade (pp. 99-105); cockfight (pp. 114-131); Ernie's arrest (pp. 151-158); the tuna boat (pp. 173-180); La Cresta (pp. 193-203). Also interesting is some of the historical information (pp. 51-56, 67-79, 108-113).

Related Materials

Terry Dunnahoo's titles *Who Needs Espy Sanchez?* (Dutton, 1977) and *This Is Espy Sanchez* (Dutton, 1976) deal with Mexican Americans. The film *Children of the Fields* (Xerox) also treats Chicanos. Relevant filmstrips are: *Contemporary Chicano Life* (Bilingual Educational Services); *Mexico, the Proud People* (Current Affairs); *Shaping the Future, the Sophisticated City and the Spanish-American Style* (Current Affairs); and *Juvenile Justice, Society's Dilemma* (Current Affairs). *Durango Street* (Dutton, 1965; pap., Dell, 1972) by Frank Bonham (see *Introducing Books* by John Gillespie and Diana Lembo, Bowker, 1970), on Black gangs in California, can also be seen as a filmstrip (Current Affairs). Suggest *A House on Liberty Street* (Atheneum, 1973) by Mary Hays Weik and *A Nation of Newcomers: Ethnic Minority Groups in American History* (pap., Dell, 1967) by J. Joseph Hutchmacher.

Robert Newton Peck, *Last Sunday*
Illus. by Ben Stahl. Doubleday, 1977, $5.95

In another of his long list of novels for youngsters, the author treats the ordinary and the exceptional in the life of a child as he did in *A Day No Pigs Would Die*. This time he adopts an easy colloquial style enlivened by many full-page back-and-white line drawings that highlight the tempo of the story, and add an interest of their own. Boys and girls from 10 to 13 will find this story gripping—boys for the baseball playing hints, girls for the pleasure of seeing one of their own sex in the game so long ago, and both sexes for the reality and understanding that accompany the alcoholic pitcher's death.

It was the custom in the 1930s in the small Vermont town of Canby, as it was in many other towns, to hold Sunday afternoon baseball games with the Canby Catfish defending the plate. There is one difference between the Canby team and others, however—12-year-old Babe serves as the bat girl and mascot. In spite of being a "gofer" for "hot dogs" and grape crush for the 300-pound coach, Hawg Hogarth (p. 81), Babe takes her job and the game seriously. She is part of the team and one of the main rooters for the pitcher, Sober McGinty, who is also the town drunk. Ruth "Babe" Babson lives happily with her papa, Alf, whose favorite pastime is tinkering with his Hudson car, which Babe rightly surmises is really a Babson by now. Mama is a fine upstanding woman who goes to Sunday service and sees that Ruth does also. Mama also sets a generous Sunday table.

On the fateful Sunday, aunt Hobart, Papa's sister, arrives in her pea-green Model A to attend the evening revival meeting scheduled for Durkee's lot. Aunt Hobart is a tall spinster who encourages her niece in many ways, and especially by helping to teach her how to play baseball. Both she and Babe chafe slightly at the prolonged Sunday dinner (p. 31) which threatens to cut into ball time. However, it is the more serious delay of trying to resuscitate Dan "Sober" McGinty from his Saturday night binge that makes them slightly late. Babe loves McGinty in spite of his alcoholism and always tries to help him get to the pitching mound on Durkee's lot where he once again becomes a hero (p. 12). McGinty went to school with her mother and works in the local pulp factory, but his life—as with any alcoholic—is one of total dedication to liquor.

Nevertheless, the two females get him up and dressed from among the garments in the piles of junk in his shack. However, Babe simply can't find one purple team stocking (p. 56). Just as they arrive, the Wiggins Warriors, Canby's perennial rivals, arrive in their yellow school buses. They are all named Gitbo, except for Sanchez, who, also, is no doubt related in some way to the manager, Injun Joe Gitbo, who dresses and looks like an Indian although some say his heritage is French.

The game progresses but with many interruptions: the appearance of a billy goat who eats everything in sight (p. 64); the display of the new screeching fire engine and volunteers from Hoover (p. 83); the arrival of the Sons of Italy Marching Band with papa Morelli who continue to celebrate Italian-American Day; the early appearance of the black horses and wagons of the revival meeting scheduled to take place next in the lot (p. 117). The game continues, however, until Hawg Hogarth realizes that Sober McGinty is dying. He starts to cry and tells Babe that Dan is pitching his last game. They cry together as McGinty kisses his baseball and stumbles off the mound into the coach's arms. Babe, feeling only sorrow for the good man and baseball hero she loves, kneels beside him as he dies.

Thematic Analysis

The confrontation by a youngster of the death of a beloved older friend as a result of alcoholism places this serious problem in our society in a poignant yet realistic perspective. It is treated without sensationalism and in human terms as children would view it. A secondary theme is the timelessness of women's struggle for equal opportunities: females playing on the baseball field in integrated teams is yet to be accomplished almost 50 years later.

Discussion Materials

There are many excellent choices for book talks. For baseball fans appropriate talks are: aunt Hobart teaches Babe how to prevent stolen bases (pp. 27-30) and "Sober" McGinty plays "hard" (pp. 126-132). For thematic emphasis discuss: McGinty is propped up (pp. 41-50) and McGinty dies on the mound (pp. 136-142). For humor and entertainment, choose various divertisements at Durkee's lot: Butler the goat (pp. 61-70): Canby's Silver Coronet Band (pp. 92-96); the Sons of Italy Parade (pp. 106-111); revival meeting convenes (pp. 114-120).

Related Materials

Another book by the author will interest the same readers: *A Day No Pigs Would Die* (Knopf, 1972; pap., Dell, 1974) has a male hero and treats the theme of familial love and devotion. For better or older readers, suggest *The Cheese Stands Alone* (Houghton, 1973; pap., Archway, 1975) by Marjorie M. Prince, about a girl entering the adult world. Lucy J. Sypher's *Cousins and Circuses* (Atheneum, 1974), about a girl growing up in an earlier era, and Carole Hart's *Delilah* (Harper, 1973), about 2 weeks in the life of an independent 10-year-old, are both suggested for the same or younger readers. Some nonprint materials also relate: a filmstrip, *American Women's Search for Equality* (Current Affairs); a film, *Tillie's Philodendron* (EBEC, 1977, 7 min., color); and 18 transparencies, *Alcohol and Alcohol Abuse* (Lansford Pub. Co.).

Doris Buchanan Smith, *Tough Chauncey*
Morrow, 1974, lib. bdg., $6.43

Known for her sympathetic exposition of youngsters' feelings and thoughts when they are caught in unusual circumstances, the author, in this story, writes about a boy who makes a difficult decision to ask to be placed in a foster home. Youngsters from the age of 9 to 14 will read it avidly. The frontispiece is by Michael Eagle.

Although 13-year-old thin and wiry Chauncey Childs looks only about 11, he is one of the two toughest kids in the seventh grade in Rambleton, Georgia. The other is Jack Levitt who tries to steal a bike from a 6-year-old and blames it on Chauncey. Chauncey desperately wants to get even. He spent the first part of his life being picked on for his small size and the last for being neglected and tough.

His grandpa especially blames him for everything, even for coming home 10 minutes late. God and grandpa are always right, and grandpa, with whom he lives, is determined to teach Chauncey a lesson by whipping him with his belt and locking him in his room for each offense. This last time, grandpa drops his skeleton key. Chauncey waits until both of his grandparents have gone to work before leaving for his mother's apartment. Both his mother's and his grandparents' homes are within 2 miles of his school. After his drunken father left, Chauncey remembers living with his mother and his first stepfather, Harry Daniels, and young Harry Jr., both of whom he liked. When they left there was another new stepfather who departed when the new baby died. Chauncey was sent to mama's parents while she looked for Harry Daniels and his son. Now she is back again with a new boyfriend, Ron. While he waits for his mother, he makes french fries and watches television; however, when his mother does not come home, he returns to his grandparents' house.

As he rounds the corner of the storage shed, he sees some kittens that he decides to keep there in spite of his grandfather's hatred of cats. He just hopes they will be safe. This fear and having his grandpa talk in front of him about his mother going around with tramps firms his resolve to run away. The year he got tough, he hopped freights and set false alarms, so running away is easy especially now with the key in his pocket. When he returns to his mother's apartment, he is furious because she is not there and he starts to wreck a neighbor's yard. When the lady next door stops him, he tries to get even with Jack Levitt, a tormentor, by claiming to be him. With time to kill, he steals some candy and gets into a movie for half of the regular price. Finally, he reaches his mother and tells her he wants to live with her.

When grandma telephones looking for him, he goes outside and throws a rock at a girl on a bike. The boys nearby reprimand him; however, the same fat lady next door intervenes and Chauncey goes back to the apartment and vomits from fear. Later, he takes some money from his sleeping mother and buys some popcorn and his first cigarettes which make him dizzy. He spends the rest of the morning walking around trying to think it all out. Finally, he returns to mama knowing that 4 years ago when she first left and he saw grandpa shoot some cats, he had started getting tough in retaliation for being neglected and abused.

When mama insists that she must take him back to his grandparents, Chauncey runs to their house and listens from under the porch. He hears them talk about something warping grandpa, perhaps the strappings he got as a boy. Grandma insists that mama sign Chauncey over to them. Chauncey runs to the railyard and in trying to hop a freight falls under the train. After an operation, he awakens to find everybody there. Aunt Ann, the fat lady, also visits and tells him good things come in small packages. Although he goes home to mama, his grandparents come for him.

There is a television in his room now and grandma brings him soup, but the extra attention does not change his feelings. He realizes his mother is a robot to permit him to be destroyed in this way. He also dreams about winning contests and things to do with a crutch. Everything comes to a head, however, when he hears grandpa's rifle and sees him shooting some kittens around the shed. Painfully, Chauncey brings the one that remains, Little Orange, to his bureau drawer. When he finds that his mother's telephone has been disconnected, he decides to return to school immediately in spite of his crutches. He puts Little Orange in the laundry closet and heads for school. He meets Jack who apologizes for tormenting him, in return for which Chauncey hits him with a crutch.

In his absence, grandma puts Little Orange in his room and continues to argue with grandpa about letting Chauncey keep the kitten. Chauncey cautiously takes the kitten to school where some boys toss the kitten around like a ball. Jack helps save him and Chauncey finally trusting him tells Jack that he is going to run away that night. He spends 2 nights in an empty garage with the kitten. Jack visits bringing him directions to the local children's shelter. Although Jack tries to talk him into going back, Chauncey goes to the authorities to ask to be placed in a foster home. He knows that it is the best solution for him.

Thematic Analysis

Child abuse and neglect are never pleasant. They are, however, among our most prominent social ills. This story deals honestly with a difficult theme by showing a youngster's recognition of being hopelessly trapped in a family situation that can only lead to more harassment. Finally, he courageously takes a step toward freeing himself by turning himself over to surrogate parents. The choice is difficult. The tough veneer that is built by the youngster as a defense against acts of emotional and physical cruelty is exposed for what it is.

Discussion Materials

Set the scene and introduce the young hero. Emphasize Chauncey's outer toughness and inner tenderness toward the cats, and memories of grandpa killing them (p. 40). Chauncey's thinking through the situation is important (ch. 6). Two episodes about falling under the train (pp. 93-98) and recuperating in the hospital (pp. 104-111) can be used. Also highlight the story of Little Orange: saving the kitten (pp. 142-144); grandma puts it in his room (pp. 172-173); Chauncey's feeling (p. 182); conversation with Jack (pp. 184-191); and Jack's visit (pp. 197-199, 202-205).

Related Materials

Foster Family Services Selected Reading List, 1976, 78 pp., $1.90 (HF1.452F81/4, S/NO17-090-00030-5) is available from U.S. Superintendent of Documents, Washington, D.C. 20402. The filmstrip *Violence in the Home: An American Tragedy* (Current Affairs, 1978) and the film *Child Abuse: Cradle of Violence* (Bonanza/Mitchell-Gebhardt, 20 min.) are appropriate. Florence Parry Heide's *Growing Anyway Up* (Lippincott, 1976) deals with the disturbing feelings generated by having a widowed mother and a stepfather. Wilma Wolitzer's *Out of Love* (Farrar, 1976) describes the not uncommon efforts of a youngster to bring divorced parents back together. Two more titles that deal with a youngster's attachment to a cat and pups are good for younger readers: Nola Langner's *Dusty* (Coward, 1976) and Charlotte Baker's *Cockleburr Quarters* (Prentice-Hall, 1972; pap., Avon, 1973).

Anne Snyder, *My Name Is Davy: I'm an Alcoholic*
   Holt, 1977, $5.95; pap., New Am. Lib., 1978, $1.25

In a fast-paced 11-chapter narrative, the author writes about a youngster who cannot believe he is an alcoholic until he suffers the death of a loved one. The author, who has many magazine articles, television scripts, and books for juveniles to her credit, has also raised 3 girls in Van Nuys, California. She knows the scene and temper of childhood alcoholism of which she writes. Her book, *First Step*, which highlights Alateen and a teenager with an alcoholic parent, won the 1972 Friends of American Writers Award. This title which deals with a prevalent contemporary problem will be read eagerly by youngsters from 11 to 16.

Diane de Groat has created a jacket that commands attention. In shades of blue with a rising orange moon in the background, it shows the hero sitting on the beach pensively thinking about his girl friend's death.

Dave Kimble, an only child from Van Nuys, California, spends his fifteenth year reading compulsively, daydreaming about having sex with beautiful Linda Harper, and drinking. Alienated, Davy who has been drinking in solitude for a long time has it down to a pattern. After he wakes and showers each morning before school, he fortifies himself with a couple of drinks from a cough medicine bottle that contains scotch from the family wet bar. He now carries the "cough syrup" to school to sustain him through the English class that bores him, the typing clatter that gives him a headache, and the physical education that he cuts more often than not. Since his 50-year-old mother, Martha, has started school to keep busy, and his white-haired father, Frank, is not home very often, his increasingly obvious "shakes" are not observed, especially because he is so young. One day Davy spills some scotch on Linda's boyfriend, Mike, while the three of them are at the lockers. Davy is surprised when Mike calls the odor the "nectar of the Gods" and invites him to lunch with the gang. Davy is thrilled and mildly amused at some of the gang for injecting oranges with vodka. Later he joins the gang on their usual Wednesday night cruise of the Boulevard. They give him his first experience with "mooning" (displaying a naked bottom out of a car window). Discovering that he is a virgin, they then try to fix him up with Maxi. He passes out drunk in her camper and wakes to see her dressing. As Maxi drives him home, he cannot remember whether he really had intercourse with her or not. Both his mother and father are home, and his mother exclaims, "My God, you're drunk." After his father upbraids him for stealing the liquor and indicates that it is manly to take a few drinks, Davy sleeps.

Maxi, however, receives a swollen lip and other bruises from her father who has been drinking heavily since her mother died 2 years earlier. When Davy calls on her, Maxi, a year older than he and also lonely, takes him to her special hideout on the concrete wash behind the park. They talk and drink. Over the weeks as they become absorbed in their daydreams and drinking, they become friends. Whem Maxi's father goes off fishing, she decides to have a big party for everyone, BYOB style (Bring Your Own Bottle). When Davy tries to get someone to buy his liquor, he is told "run along sonny." He finally steals the booze from a chain drugstore. At midnight all the partygoers except Maxi and the gang leave. They play chug-a-lug and stripping games. Davy wins chug-a-lug but Maxi, whose cards have been fixed, looses the stripping game. She refuses to strip and the others forcibly take off her clothes. Davy finally covers her with his jacket. After everyone leaves, Maxi tells Davy that she is crazy about him. They become lovers. They go to the movies, the skating rink, the beach, and her camper to share the booze. Although Davy is aware of his symptoms of alcoholism—diarrhea, vomiting, hangovers, and loss of appetite—they both continue to drink. When they try to get someone to buy their liquor and are beaten, Maxi insists that they quit and start going to Alcoholics Anonymous (AA). Davy tells his parents who protest that all he really needs is a "good kick in the ass" or a visit to a psychiatrist. He sees the psychiatrist who tells him to come back when he has quit. Davy becomes cool to Maxi's idea. Meanwhile, Maxi who has quit starts to have hallucinations and convulsions. Davy, who continues to drink secretly, agrees to take her to AA.

At their first meeting, the AA greeting (see title) is given by a young man. They listen to the Twelve Steps (code of behavior), Twelve Traditions or Principles, and stories of other young people who are alcoholics. Maxi feels great relief; Davy, however, resents AA's influence. They separate until Maxi telephones and asks him to come and celebrate their first dry month. Restless, he goes and persuades Maxi to go with him to Vista Beach. The gang is there and Linda pours Davy a drink, while Mike spikes Maxi's coke with alcohol. Maxi despairs when she sees Davy drinking and the beach party ends in a drunken skinny-dipping brawl. Before he passes out, Davy hears them all run into the surf. A nightmare that someone has drowned, pierced by a scream, briefly disturbs his drunken stupor.

Davy comes to in the morning only to hear the counterman at the beach shack comment on the girl's drowning last night. Davy knows now that Maxi really is the victim. He contemplates suicide for forcing her to come to the beach and crashes the family car. He arrives at the concrete wash and cries. He does not go to Maxi's funeral for he is still too busy sinking in his own alcoholism. Mike pushes him to the ground, his father hits him, and a young boy pleads with Davy to buy him some wine. Davy finally surrenders to the knowledge that he is an alcoholic. He goes hopefully to AA where he can finally say, "my name is Davy, I'm an alcoholic."

Thematic Analysis

Childhood alcoholism, one of our society's serious problems, is the theme. It has long been known that 14 is the age at which many youngsters become addicted to drugs such as alcohol. Lately, the age has declined to 12 and even younger. The theme shows clearly a young alcoholic's needs, societal acceptance of drinking, and family obtuseness about the symptoms. The pressures that are placed on our alcoholic children, both permissive and restrictive, are well expressed. The tragedy of wasted well-meaning measures and the hopefulness of the treatment as outlined in AA are clearly shown.

Discussion Materials

This story tells itself. A mention of the plot and the main characters, together with a display of the cover art, will stimulate readers. Use the picture on page 12 of the locker-room episode to illustrate the acceptance of drinking by the gang. Refer to a review of Davy's earliest memories of drinking: (pp. 18-19). Other book-talk episodes are: "Mooning" (pp. 24-25); Davy meets Maxi (pp. 26-31); Davy's drinking pattern (pp. 34-36); the wash (pp. 39-43); the party (pp. 74-153; picture p. 50); the fight (pp. 57-59); the psychiatrist (pp. 74-75). Introduce book talks on the symptoms of alcoholism: (pp. 68-69, 77-79, 118-119, 121-123, 126-127). Discuss AA as pictured in the book: (pp. 61-62, 67, 80-89, 90-92, 95-97, 126, 128).

Related Materials

A film, *Francesca Baby* (Walt Disney, 1977, 2 reels, 46 min., color), about the effects of alcoholism on a family, and 2 filmstrips, *Understanding Alcoholism* (Eye Gate, 2 strips) and *Stress, Sanity and Survival* (Current Affairs, 1978), are useful with this title. Another filmstrip, *Teenage Nutrition: The Picture of Health* (Current Affairs, 1977, 2 strips) is also helpful. Two books that deal with youngsters and addictive drugs are *That Was Then, This Is Now* (pap., Dell, 1972) by S. E. Hinton and *Go Ask Alice* (Prentice-Hall, 1971; pap., Avon, 1972), anonymous. The latter is also available as a filmstrip from Current Affairs. Several other books are suggested: Isabelle Holland's *Heads You Win, Tails I Lose* (Lippincott, 1973; pap., Dell, 1977); Peggy Mann's *My Dad Lives in a Downtown Hotel* (Doubleday, 1973; pap., Avon, 1974); Adrienne Richard's *Into the Road* (Little-Atlantic, 1976); and Robert Cormier's *I Am the Cheese* (Pantheon, 1977). Also suggested is Barbara Corcoran's *The Winds of Time* (Atheneum, 1974), which emphasizes a youngster's need and search for love.

Laurence Yep, *Child of the Owl*
Harper, 1977, $5.95; lib. bdg., $5.79

The author has other critically acclaimed books to his credit. This one treats a young Chinese girl's first experience of living with her grandmother in San Francisco's Chinatown and learning something of her ethnic heritage. The story, told in 7 chapters, takes place, as the author states in an afterword, between August 1964 and April 1965. The convincing story has an easy reading style that flows from the author's familiarity with the setting. Youngsters from 9 to 13 years old will find it absorbing.

Cheun Meik (Taste of Spring) has drawn an arresting twilight scene of Grant Street in San Francisco for the jacket. It portrays the girl and her grandmother in the shimmering rain in front of one of the tourist shop attractions in the Chinese section of San Francisco.

Twelve-year-old Casey Young (nicknamed because her father had a lucky year betting on Casey Stengel's team) has spent 10 years, since the death of Jeanie (her mother), with Barney, her father. They have traveled up and down California while Barney worked as a short-order cook or a fruit picker and spent his slender earnings gambling. Nevertheless, Casey loves him. Morey, a musician friend, gives Barney some money whenever they are stranded. Casey knows no other life, and has become independent through her experiences. However, she is hurt once again when Barney who has had a winning streak is mugged and lands in the hospital with a broken leg.

Casey stoically accepts living in the interim with her maternal uncle, Philip Low. Phil the Pill, as he is dubbed by Casey, is a successful lawyer in San Francisco. However, his sense of superiority and that of his family, wife Ethel and daughters, Annette, a junior at Berkeley, and Pamela, who is 12, make them uncomfortable with Casey around. Casey who sees through their airs is only thankful that she was not sent to her other uncle in Los Angeles. Casey, however, is summarily bundled off to her maternal grandmother, Ah Paw (Paw-Paw) who lives in San Francisco's Chinatown far removed from her successful American children.

Casey knows little about her Chinese heritage. She is surprised by the tiny crowded upstairs room that Paw-Paw occupies in a tenement in this crowded section, as well as by the buzzer code her grandmother requires to protect her from any unwanted visitors. Casey begins to learn about old Chinese customs and stories. One of the first is the owl story, a beautiful legend of filial devotion. Paw-Paw reveres her antique owl charm which is given to the youngest member of the family. Another is the story of the "Eight Immortals" whose statues Paw-Paw points out in the shop windows.

Casey goes to the nearby Chinese school where she is an adept learner whose ability is doubted, especially by the strict teacher of traditional Chinese. Schoolwork, which is important to Paw-Paw who still works as a seamstress in a neighborhood factory, becomes oppressive for the young nomad. However, her friendship with a girl her own age, Booger Chew, whose great-aunt owns the tenement in which they both live, is a bright spot in Casey's life. Booger, a budding fashion artist, who would prefer to be Tallulah Bankhead, makes a good companion and friend. Paw-Paw's venerable old friend and Portsmouth Square game opponent, Mr. Jeh, and his nephew, Gilbert Pachinko, who drives a purple Cadillac for a big gambler, are also friends. Including Sheridan, Barney's old alcoholic friend who works at a local Orange Julius shop, this mixture of old and new people in Casey's life begins to shed light on some of the problems in her former life with Barney and in Chinatown. Although Casey has trouble trying to stay warm while cooking the rice for supper in the small room, she nevertheless enjoys living there and learning about being Chinese. Paw-Paw takes her shopping for groceries and teaches her to eat with chopsticks. Since Barney calls collect once and sends a few postcards after he is discharged, Casey only momentarily feels abandoned.

She is soon caught up in an exciting adventure. A thief steals the antique owl charm and sends Paw-Paw to the Chinese hospital with a broken leg. Casey goes about her daily chores with some comfort from the Chews. Together with Mr. Jeh, she searches for the charm, without success, at Mr. Fong's (he is a fence), and at the souvenir shop on Grant Street. She continues to search with Booger at Jack's Pool Hall, still without success. However, when she visits Paw-Paw in the hospital, the old lady tells Casey she knows who the burglar is. Suspecting correctly that it is Barney, Casey goes to some of their old familiar haunts and gets the charm back. Paw-Paw decides to sell the recovered antique charm to the museum where it can be enjoyed by all and to use the money to pay the hospital bills. She reminds Casey that she, too, is a child of the owl and that she should forgive Barney.

Thematic Analysis

There are several secondary themes that deal with love and family relationships. The main theme, however, that is developed is the value of knowing and appreciating one's heritage. It emphasizes the need for a sense of history to help identify oneself and an awareness of the present strengths and weaknesses of one's culture group. The inner freedom that results is highlighted. The charming portrayal of Chinatown and its inhabitants adds fascinating information.

Discussion Materials

While illustrating the heroine and her grandmother from the jacket portraits—by book jacket or transparency or slide—introduce the story and main characters (pp. 1-37). The owl legend bears retelling (pp. 38-114). For the flavor of Chinatown, describe the Chinese school (pp. 40-43); Jasmine (pp. 59-81); "Eight Immortals" (pp. 90, 164-165); Portsmouth Square (pp. 94-99); groceries (pp. 131-139); chopsticks (pp. 141-142); Mr.

Fong (pp. 159-163); Grant Street (pp. 164-169). Other anecdotes that emphasize the theme are: Paw-Paw in the hospital (pp. 193-199); I am a child of the owl (pp. 203-205); forgiving (pp. 213-215).

Related Materials

The author's other titles—*Dragonwings* and *Sweetwater*—can be suggested. Also recommend *Dragonsong* (Atheneum, 1976; pap., Bantam, 1977) by Anne McCaffrey, about a girl who overcomes a cultural bias. *Zero Makes Me Hungry* (Lothrop, 1976), edited by Edward Lueders and Primus St. John, is a collection of twentieth-century poems on ethnic and cultural traditions. Michael Dorman's review of political events during the 1960s, *Confrontation: Politics and Protest* (Delacorte, 1974), can be used. The films *Pamela Wong's Birthday for Grandma* (EBEC) and *Family Business* (Crown Intl. Productions) both treat Chinese-American girls and their families in urban settings. The filmstrip *Gambling: A National Pastime* (Current Affairs, 1978) relates well with this story.

8

Identifying Adult Roles

ALTHOUGH AN APPROPRIATE sex role is usually determined in infancy, children generally learn appropriate social roles throughout childhood and adolescence. They spend a great deal of time during their middle years learning to recognize and appreciate the behavior of mature adults. This identification or socialization process gives youngsters both satisfaction and the desire to emulate. By assuming these social roles, children exhibit increasingly independent actions and adult behavior as they mature. Exposure to responsible adults is of inestimable benefit. Reading, viewing, or listening, however, is an alternative way to provide youngsters with vicarious exposure to the varying patterns of adult behavior.

Many different adult role models from volunteer child-care worker to house-husband to teacher to old homesteader woman to an elderly great uncle are shown in some of the books described in this chapter. Each book contains an adult whose mature sense helps sustain and give insight to a youngster. The young person's responses lead toward a healthy personal and societal role.

Marion Dane Bauer, *Shelter from the Wind*
> (A Clarion Book) Seabury Press, 1976, $6.95

The author has a firsthand knowledge of the panhandle area of Oklahoma of which she writes, having retraced her steps there before writing this book. A graduate of the University of Oklahoma, like the adult heroine in this book, the author expresses herself well in this story that is evocative of place and feelings. In addition to teaching creative writing, Mrs. Bauer cares for her children, 4 dogs, and numerous other pets in her Minnesota home. Her knowledge of both is apparent.

Mike Eagle's jacket drawing of the sandstone house set against a blossoming mimosa tree and guarded by a shepherd dog will appeal to 9- to 13-year-olds, especially girls, who will enjoy the 11 chapters of good reading.

Twelve-year-old Stacy lives over her father's grocery store in a small country town near Cimarron City, Oklahoma, where the wind never stops blowing. Stacy sometimes thinks that the constant wind is one reason why her mother left them some years ago. She can remember that her mother was from Colorado and her daddy had been a sailor. She also recalls her own younger tomboy pleasures. Now her stepmother, Barbara, is expecting a baby. Stacy feels awkward in her own developing body. The banging screen door of the grocery store continuously reminds Stacy of her frustrations. Finally she runs away.

Stacy, an Okie by birth, knows that in this hot, dry country she should have brought water to quench the thirst that finally overtakes her. By this time, however, she has left the dusty town and sad memories far behind as she leaves the main road heading unconsciously west toward Colorado. Lost and exhausted from running, Stacy collapses only to awaken as a dog licks her. Two shepherd dogs lead her several miles to a small sandstone house set in a dry gulch area (shown on the jacket).

Old Ella, the doughty owner, takes her in. Stacy likes the independent old woman who accepts her and lets her stay without asking probing questions. Stacy learns many things, about both Old Ella and herself. She learns that things are not always what they seem. For example, Ella went to the University of Oklahoma and was a city girl who came to this desolate place as a bride. Ben, a sheepherder, had built this desert homestead as a wedding gift to Ella. When Ella arrived and saw the place, however, she almost changed her mind and left. Nevertheless, she loved Ben so she stayed and planted the mimosa, or wedding tree, where it would be sheltered from the wind behind their home. Ella at first bore stillborn babies and later none. As time passed Ben, who had always been a hard worker, changed, and one day he just walked away. Old Ella, however, stayed to watch the mimosa tree bloom, sustained by the sale of each shepherd dog litter, her own hunting and cooking skills, and an occasional visit from a concerned Black Mesa neighbor, Mr. Henderson.

Black Mesa is 5 miles from the old Santa Fe cattle trail which is still recognizable because it is 6 wagons wide. Mr. Henderson also lives only 5 miles northwest of Ella's home. Now that she is older and alone he visits occasionally to check on her. When he brings Ella a bottle of Early Times liquor and they sit down to share a drink and talk, Stacy goes outside. There, stimulated by Ella's previous conversations and independence, Stacy admits to herself that her mother left because she was an alcoholic. Stacy wonders if she is like her and later proves she is not by taking a drink and getting sick.

Old Ella's tales of her respect for and understanding of the departed Ben make a deep impression on Stacy. Stacy also admires Old Ella's skill in bagging a jackrabbit and turning it into a delicious stew for supper. However, it is the shepherd dogs who command all her young love. Merlin and the bitch, Nimue, named after the white fairy, who provide the puppies that are Old Ella's chief livelihood, are also her companions. Stacy, who reads the book about King Arthur that Old Ella brought with her, approves of the romantic names. She never suspects that she will be alone with Nimue when the litter arrives.

Since Old Ella is out and overdue when Nimue's pups begin to arrive, Stacy does her best to make Nimue a comfortable corner in which to deliver them. She also helps as much as she can with the difficult and protracted birth of the first puppy, a male for whom she immediately feels a strong attachment. She names him Lancelot, and helps tend the other puppies, 7 males and 2 females. Afterward Merlin leads Stacy to Ella who has stumbled and hurt her ankle. When Stacy gets Ella home, the old woman is in great pain, but, nonetheless, examines the puppies. She tells Stacy to drown Lancelot because he has a harelip and will soon die in agony.

Stacy is stunned as she takes this final step into accepting and coping with reality. Only her love and admiration for Old Ella force her to accept the easier death for Lancelot at her own hands. She buries him under the mimosa tree and hacks off branches in anger to put on his grave. Then she goes with Merlin to get Mr. Henderson to come and help Old Ella. When Stacy decides to return to her father, stepmother, and new baby, Old Ella gives her the other bitch puppy for herself.

Thematic Analysis

A strong, compassionate adult who can help befuddled youngsters sort out the frustrations of their young lives is very important. Here an independent old woman who understands both freedom and responsibility is a beacon light to the heroine. The theme of running away from home, which knows no one common denominator or theme, is expressed together with a true ideal of choice, feminism, and liberation. The animal (or dog) theme is also useful for this audience.

Discussion Materials

The jacket drawing may be displayed while the runaway theme of the story (pp. 9-13) and the main characters are introduced: Old Ella (pp. 26-30); Ben (pp. 32-33); Mr. Henderson (pp. 63-69). The episode of running away tells well (pp. 20-25). The problem, the mimosa, and Stacy's thoughts can also be told (pp. 35-43). For life with Old Ella use the following episodes: Ella's books (pp. 49-51); jackrabbit stew (pp. 54-62); visitor (pp. 63-69). All youngsters will enjoy the whelping scene (pp. 73-89) and Old Ella's rescue (pp. 81-85). Save the conflict and resolution for the reader by hinting only: Lancelot (pp. 86-91); the gift (p. 107).

Related Materials

Three books will appeal to the same readers: *The Boyhood of Grace Jones* (Harper, 1973; pap., 1975) by Jane Langton; *The Liberation of Clementine Tipton* (Houghton, 1974) by Jane Flory; and *Dear Bill, Remember Me?* (Delacorte, 1976; pap., Dell, 1978) by Norma Fox Mazer. The National Book Award winner, Walter D. Edmond's *Bert Breen's Barn* (Little, 1975) is a fine evocation of Tom Dolan's progress to manhood and should be suggested to all. Two filmstrips can also be related: *Adolescent Conflict: Parent vs. Teens* (Sunburst, 1977, 2 strips) and *A Life Apart: A Modern Day Frontier Family* (Current Affairs, 1976). For younger children, the informational title *Discovering What Puppies Do* (McGraw-Hill, 1977) by Seymour Simon provides good illustrations by Susan Bonners on the birth of pups.

Beverly Cleary, *Ramona and Her Father*

Illus. by Alan Tiegreen. Morrow, 1977, $6.50; lib. bdg., $6.01

This author of 22 books beloved by youngsters has had a distinguished career as a children's librarian, and she is also a wife and the mother of twins. She has an unsurpassed talent for writing stories for children and has received the Pacific Northwest Young Reader's Choice award many times, a particular treat for a native Oregonian now living in California. In this story, the heroine, Ramona, fully realizes that even through adversity she is a proud part of a happy family. Readers from age 7 or earlier to age 10 or older will enjoy this title.

The jacket drawing portrays the characters in the distinctive pen sketches that readers have come to associate with these stories. Ramona and her father are sketched kneeling on the floor against a bright orange background. Eighteen line drawings and the frontispiece sketch of Ramona and her father are included.

Cleary fans everywhere know that Ramona Quimby is 7 now and in Mrs. Rogers's second-grade class. Beatrice, her older sister better known as Beezus, also goes to the Glenwood School and is in the seventh grade. Beezus's friend Henry is in the high school spending most of his spare time practicing track for the Olympics to be held in about 8 years. Things have definitely changed this fall.

As Ramona colors with her crayons, sings Ye-e-ep (making a "Joyful Noise to the Lord," as instructed in Sunday School), and makes a long Christmas list, Beezus comes home from school worrying about doing Mrs. Mester's promised creative writing unit. Although Mrs. Quimby says it is just a "difficult age" Beezus will outgrow, she has no answer except "don't bother your father, now" when he comes home and says he just lost his job. However, Mr. Quimby did not forget to bring the girls a present of gummy bears. Ramona is worried and crosses out her entire Christmas list. She wants only "One happy family" now.

Ramona wishes she had a million dollars as she watches her father cleaning, smoking nervously, and waiting for a phone call while their mother goes to work for a doctor full time instead of half-time. She even imagines that she might become a television commercial star and practices making loud crunching noises like those heard in some commercials. She tells her teacher, Mrs. Rogers, forthrightly that her pantyhose is wrinkled. However, she reacts with injured feelings when her father tells her that the teacher, in addition to saying many good things about Ramona in their parent–teacher conference, also says that Ramona sometimes shows off and forgets her manners. Her father eventually has to cut the burs out of her hair from the crown she made for herself while she waited for him at school. When he tells her he would not trade her for a million dollars, she is happy once again.

However, the rest of the family is depressed by Mr. Quimby's unemployment and their increasing shortages. Picky-picky Beezus's cat refuses to eat the cheaper food. Another worry is that the car starts to sound funny. Only Ramona manages to stay cheerful, but when her friend Howie's grandma sends them a huge pumpkin everyone soon catches the spirit as Mr. Quimby whistles and carves a scary jack-o'-lantern. Later the same night Ramona hears a noise and they all find that Picky-picky who likes melon has eaten part of the pumpkin. Mrs. Quimby cleans it up and puts the good parts away in the refrigerator while Beezus, whose cat has been banished to the celler, yells at her father to stop smoking and killing himself. Ramona worries anew wondering why adults do not know that children worry about them (p. 85).

Partly because the review work at school bores Ramona, she finds diversion in deluging her father with "Quit Smoking" signs. When he says, "stop," and they have leftover pumpkin for every meal, it takes only his failure to come home when expected one day to bring tears to her eyes. The tears turn to anger when he finally arrives, until he starts drawing the "largest picture in the world" (state of Oregon) with her. Enjoying this and noticing that he is not smoking make her happy again.

For the creative writing unit, Ramona helps Beezus interview old Mrs. Swink about what she did as a child. When Mrs. Swink explains how she made stilts out of tin cans and string, Ramona and Howie make some. They stay up walking on them and singing "99 Bottles of Beer on the Wall" until dark.

By early December, the Sunday school starts casting for the Christmas program: Henry as Joseph; Beezus as Mary; and Davy, Howie, and Ramona as the three shepherd's sheep. Mrs. Quimby is too tired at night to do more than fasten a head and tail to pink-rabbit pajamas. The parents argue because Mr. Quimby wants Ramona to learn she cannot have everything. Ramona is outraged when she overhears this. She thinks her father is around too much and accuses him of smoking again. When he tells her he is trying to stop they exchange mutual words of love. However, she still would like a full sheep costume like Howie's.

A few days before Christmas, Mr. Quimby gets a job and everything seems almost right again. On the night of the pageant, Ramona slinks around so no one will see her. She discovers that the 3 female replacements for the shepherds are willing to blacken her nose with mascara so that she looks like a lamb. From the stage, she looks out at the audience and sees her father wink at her. She knows he is proud of her. Filled with joy, Ramona wiggles her tail.

Thematic Analysis

A warm family story on the surface, this title deeply reinforces the early school age youngster's need for harmony and repeated exposure to the love and affection of an adult. The approval that is bestowed consistently upon Ramona, in spite of real problems, is something that all children seek. To find it given, in this story, by a father to a young daughter belies myths to the contrary. The nonsexist style is commendable.

Discussion Materials

Ramona is well known among youngsters. A novel approach would be to ask some of them to book talk this story. Other children will be stimulated by hearing their friends talk about a book friend, and adults can listen and learn a great deal about the perception of a child. The jacket and name will "sell" the book.

Related Materials

A treat for all viewers is *Janko* (Bosustow, 7 min., color), a film about something small enlarging itself. For current information about the family, try the filmstrip *Today's Family: A Changing Concept* (Current Affairs, 1978). Also in filmstrip is the *Best of Encyclopedia Brown* series (Miller-Brody) for young viewers. Three books for the same readers are: Carolyn Haywood's *Away Went the Balloons* (Morrow, 1973); Sid Fleischman's *The Ghost on Saturday Night* (Little-Atlantic, 1974); and Ellen Raskin's *The Tattooed Potato and Other Clues* (Dutton, 1975). Two fantasies are also suggested: *The Lost Farm* (Atheneum, 1974) by Jane L. Curry and *A Stitch in Time* (Dutton, 1976) by Penelope Lively.

Eleanor Clymer, *Luke Was There*

Illus. by Diane de Groat. Holt, 1973, $4.95; pap., Archway, 1976, 95¢

A well-known author of easy-to-read popular stories for children remains faithful to her reputation in this 6-chapter story about a young boy. Ms. Clymer, born in New York City, has more than 46 books to her credit. This one about young fatherless Julius who has great responsibility suddenly thrust upon him will appeal to 9- to 12-year-old youngsters.

Diane de Groat, an artist who won the 1972 annual prize of the Society of Illustrators, generally works from live models. In this title, she has translated her vision of the main characters onto the pages in vibrant pencil strokes. The 12 drawings are crisp and beautiful.

Every time Julius remembers the scary events of last year he thinks of Luke. It all started when his mother had to go to the hospital and he and Danny went to the Children's Home. However, Julius also knows it really started 3 years ago when he was 5 or 6 and used to roller-skate with his father. That was probably just before his father left and they moved in with an uncle. Not long afterward, his mother married José. Julius was happy because José played ball in the street with him. When his younger brother Danny was born things changed. José left them and mama took sick.

Julius does not like the Home and he returns to his apartment. Luke, a tall athletic young Black man comes for him. They make friends and Luke gives Julius his magnifying glass to look through. Reassured by Luke's quiet authority, Julius settles into the Children's Home. Luke who comes to the Home fairly regularly to be with the youngsters takes some of them to his apartment. Julius sees the Indian rug on Luke's wall, one of his treasures from his recent days among the Indian people.

When they return to the Home, Luke and Mrs. Kronkite, the Head, talk before Luke leaves. Julius, who sees them, thinks Luke has gone forever. He breaks down, accusing the departed Luke of deserting him after all his fine talk and affection just the way his father, his uncle, and José did. Finally calm, he silently steals out of the Home leaving Danny there.

Julius meets Max, another youngster, who befriends him and teaches him how to beg quarters. When Max snatches a purse, is caught, and blames Julius, the bitter youngster decides to run even further. The desperate boy has one misadventure after another. He runs from an old bum and tries to join a bunch of hippies at a lake picnic until they try to take his magnifying glass. Tired and hungry, Julius meets Fernando and Louie who give him food and take him to a vacant apartment to eat it. Julius, however, filled with disgust by a mouse he sees in the apartment, and wary of the two, leaves. In desperation he asks a lady on the street for help and receives a dollar bill and the advice to trust someone once in a while. She also tells him to go home. Unfortunately, Louie has brought his father to the vacant apartment too late to help—Julius is already on his way home.

Everything is fine in the empty home until the phone rings and he hears footsteps in the hall. Julius runs all the way to Grand Central Railroad Station where he carries bags and earns about a dollar. While he is there little Ricardo, who is all alone, attaches himself to Julius. This is the last straw. Julius decides to take him to the Children's Home.

When they arrive, Luke greets Julius and tells him he came the minute he heard that Julius was missing. He explains that everyone is upset. Julius hurriedly explains that Max made up the story about the purse-snatching to protect himself. Finally settled and reassured about Danny and Ricardo, Julius glows with renewed hope when Luke gives him the magnifying glass for good and tells him he will come to see him when he can but that he must work the visit in around his regular job. Secure for the first time, Julius can look after Danny, go to the hospital to see their mother, and plan on going back to mama and the apartment. Luke will be there when he is needed.

Thematic Analysis

Buffeted about without a male person on whom to count, a child needs and longs for such a figure—this is the main theme. Luke, a caring individual, is important to this boy. His affection and steadfastness as an adult point the way for the youngster. A youngster's difficulty in reacting with either caution or acceptance toward the many situations one meets is also highlighted. The multiracial and urban character of the story will be familiar to many and useful for others to know about.

Discussion Materials

Display the title-page drawing of a magnifying glass and close-up of Luke and Julius (p. 71), and explain briefly how Julius met Luke. More views of Luke's room (p. 12), the street scene (pp. 6-7), and the magnifying glass can be used (pp. 17, 20). The street misadventures can be traced: purse-snatching (pp. 30-31); the old bum (p. 34); hippies (pp. 40-41); vacant apartment (p. 47); running (p. 52-53); Grand Central Station (pp. 56-57). For a happy ending show Luke hugging Julius (pp. 66-67).

Related Materials

Ivan Southall's *Benson Boy* (Macmillan, 1973) concerns a boy's ability to deal with adult emergencies. *It's Not What You Expect* (Pantheon, 1973; pap., Avon, 1974) by Norma Klein and *The Winter of the Birds* (Macmillan, 1976) by Helen Cresswell are also suggested. *The Hidden World: Life Under a Rock* (Macmillan, 1977) by Laurence Pringle is illustrated with photographs that point out natural ecosystems under common rocks. Two filmstrips can also be shown: *The Stranger in My Home* (Current Affairs), about a new adult in a broken home, and *Values: Right or Wrong* (EBEC, 6 strips), about such values as responsibility, honesty, and appreciation of others. The title *Luke Was There* (LCA, 1978), a 16mm film, is also suggested.

James Lincoln Collier, *Give Dad My Best*
Scholastic Bk. Services, 1976, $6.95

Written by an author of exciting fiction for young people, this title is a sharply observed reminiscence of a young boy growing up in the Great Depression. Popular music of the era and a keen awareness of the young are both highlighted by an author who has teenage children and an interest in music.

The 10 chapters trace the life of a boy during one long summer of 1937. Youngsters from 9 to 14 will appreciate the easy writing style, as well as the attractive jacket, that shows the hero puzzling over his problems.

Jack Lundquist, who was born in the golden year of 1924, before there was even any thought of the 1929 crash, lives in Stevenstown, Massachusetts, close to Boston, with his sister, Sally, his 8-year-old baby brother, Henry, and his dad. Warren Lundquist has played trombone for some famous names: Paul Whiteman, Mal Hallet, Bix Beiderbecke, and Tommy Dorsey. Even when things got bad in 1931–1932, he and his friend, Dave Johnson, had a club date with Dave Warren's Jolly Lads. Now, however, Dave has long since taken a regular job in the local mill, but dad refuses. He manages to get an average of about 9 night jobs a month at $5.00 a night at the Elks Club, while cheerfully promising anything to everyone and singing, "Happy Days are here again." Jack, however, remembers his Mt. Holyoke-educated mother going crazy, being evicted when he was in the second grade, and living in a continuous state of worry. Easygoing dad calls him "an old worrywart."

Meanwhile Jack spends his time trying to take care of the family and living with the fear that the family will be split up by having Sally sent to the old grandparents in New Orleans and Baby (Henry) to an uncle and aunt in Chicago. His own daydreams include making money and being a baseball diamond hero. With Charlie Franks, his best friend who is also a baseball fan, he plays team ball and they both talk about going to Fenway Park. For personal fun, Jack occasionally has a drink of Moxie (the cola of the day), uses "in" words such as "beeswax," and plays the 12-inch Victor Red Seal recordings that his father buys in profusion despite their pitifully small income. Jack finally secures his dad's word that Sally will get a dress for school that she desperately needs. He is not sure that this promise will be kept, and rails at his father to get a regular job. Dad answers that he is still "making it."

Through his grocery delivery job for Mr. Conklin at 25¢ an hour, Jack gets a job as general helper and second bartender with Mr. Slater at the Lakeside Boat Club (Nipmuch Boating Association). In the quiet May of club business, Jack finds and returns Hobart Price Waterman's wallet with $154 for which the wealthy estate owner calls him an "honest kid" and gives him a $10 reward. This windfall causes mixed feelings and thoughts. Henry, who does not want to be called Baby, questions him about the possibility of the family's being split up. After calming his brother's fears, Jack listens to the records and thinks more about money and baseball.

Eventually, he muses, "How can you be the father of your own father," and talks to Charlie about going to see the Red Sox and Yankees.

As he waits for the big day, the pressures build: he overhears Slater taking kickback money from vendors, sees the secret money bag where it is kept, and stands by at home as dad goes again to New York City to look for band work. In disgust Jack decides that since Charlie Franks's family agrees to it, they will go to Boston with his reward money. Jack and Charlie see Jimmy Fox and Lou Gehrig, and Jack buys himself a mitt for $6.95. However, when they return, both are kicked off the team for cutting practice.

Jack works at an alfresco party at the Waterman's and gets his first taste of living like a millionaire. He is so excited after describing it to Sally that he tells her he will steal, if necessary, to get her the dress she needs. By his fifth weekend at the club, he has $31.50 with which to pay bills and buy food. With only $12.00 left, he gives Sally $8.00 for an outfit. He has decided that they will have to make it on their own. When he discovers that they are seriously in arrears for the rent, Jack recalls years ago standing on the sidewalk beside their records and other poor possessions and demands that dad do something. Dad who had had no luck in the city hits him.

Jack runs all the way to the lake where he plunges into the cold water. Still furious, he steals the bag with more than $300.00 in it and returns home. He tells the aghast Sally and gives his apologetic father $50.00 toward the rent. After he buys a jackknife to replace the one he inadvertently left near the stolen money, Jack and Sally talk about how to spend the $300.00. However, when Jack overhears Dave's plans not to play any more he suddenly realizes that it is no use to keep on bailing dad out.

Jack puts the money back, and is confronted by Slater who demands that he repay the missing part. Jack, equally angry because the money was obtained unethically by Slater, says he will not and he quits his job. Fortunately he gets work 2 days a week at the Waterman's and by the end of the summer is living happily at Frankie's secure in knowing that Sally and Henry are also well cared for by relatives. Dave Johnson tells Jack what an excellent musician his dad is, and that there is really no point in trying to change him.

Thematic Analysis

The main theme is the acceptance of adults for what they are. Woven into the story are many subsidiary themes that treat responsibility, honesty, and ethical behavior. The primary theme is perhaps one of the most important for youngsters to learn. To accept parents as they are and form one's own ideal adult roles, rather than to try and to fail in efforts to manipulate people, is a valuable lesson that hopefully can be resolved in childhood. A sense of living history pervades the story since the writing captures the flavor and tempo of the 1930s through presentation of the economic pressures against a background that depicts glimpses of the musical life and style of the period.

Discussion Materials

The jacket drawing with the hero's picture and the symbol of dad (trombone) makes a suitable introduction to the story, together with the main characters (pp. 1–40). Dad and Dave reminiscing (pp. 45–47) and Sally's dress (pp. 48–50) illustrate the fundamental conflict. Other episodes worth telling are: playing baseball (pp. 70–76, 109–112, 113–117); the boat club job (pp. 50–52, 80–84, 85–88, 99–104); stealing (pp. 168–180); returning money (pp. 208–215); Hobart Price Waterman (pp. 54–59, 130–140); worries (pp. 60–63, 64–66, 96–98, 154–156, 192–193); dad (pp. 91–94, 157–163, 186–187, 197–202). A group discussion about ethical behavior or the value of honesty is useful under an able moderator.

Related Materials

Four books that treat youngsters' problems can be suggested: Peter Dickinson's *The Gift* (Little-Atlantic, 1974); Geoffrey Household's *Escape into Daylight* (Little-Atlantic, 1976; pap., Archway, 1977); Patricia Windsor's *Diving for Roses* (Harper, 1976); and Marilyn Sachs's *A Pocket Full of Seeds* (Doubleday, 1973). The first two have heroes and deal with courage and survival; the latter two have heroines and also concern courage in the face of adversity. The first title is recommended for better readers. Two filmstrips that treat the Great Depression are: *Changing American Values: The Dust Bowl Legacy* (Multi-Media Productions, 1977, 2 strips) and *To Kill a Mockingbird* (Current Affairs). The latter is from a Pulitzer Prize-winning novel about a young girl growing up in the South during the Depression. Another Current Affairs filmstrip, *Who Can I Trust* (1977), and the Center for Humanities slide set, *Becoming an Adult: The Psychological Task of Adolescence* (3 units), may be related to the theme. An old-time radio program tape, *The Great Gildersleeve/Hal Perry Looking Back* (Audio Forum, 57 min., cassette) will set the scene. For another appealing scene-setter, use the all-ages film, videocassette, or S-8 *All About Music* (Pyramid, 1978, 10 min.), an animated tale of the caveman's discovery of music.

Jean Merrill, *The Toothpaste Millionaire*
Illus. by Jan Palmer. Houghton, 1972, $6.95

This author of numerous juvenile books is especially known for *The Pushcart War*. She has also been interested in the disadvantaged and has served as an associate editor of the Bank Street Readers. Both interests are evident in this book, prepared by the Bank Street College, that shows the inventive and mathematical ability of a Black boy and the pragmatic organizational skills of a white girl who bring together an integrated group of friends and with their help launch a successful business venture. All youngsters from 8 to 13 will be stimulated by the 22 brief chapters and the ideas that the readers will find there.

The attractive chocolate brown jacket shows the hero riding his bicycle, complete with saddlebags, surrounded by a field of large, shiny aluminum toothpaste tubes. There are 8½ pages of full-color pictures done in tempera that are as appealing as this success story.

When the story opens Kathryn (Kate) MacKinstrey had been living in East Cleveland for 2 years after moving from suburban Fairhaven, Connecticut. She liked the big older houses in the integrated community; however, she was lonely in the midst of the many children in her area. Her brother, 9-year-old James who was interested only in gears and cams, was no help. He either worked with his precious parts or had his nose in the Auction News to see where he could get a good buy. However, one day, in the middle of busy traffic, Kate acquires a good friend, Rufus, who gets off his bike to help her pick up her scattered schoolbooks. He puts them in his nylon saddlebags and promises to make her some bags for her books.

Twelve-year-old Rufus Mayflower is also in the sixth grade and in the same math class as Kate. He passes her a note explaining how much nylon she should buy at Vince's Army and Navy Store. Mr. Conti, their math teacher, asks her to read the note and he has the class try to work out the problem. Only Rufus's answer is correct. Nevertheless, Mr. Conti is pleased because the class likes the problem. After school Kate makes her purchases and goes to Rufus's home to have him cut and make the saddlebags. They become friends.

One day as they are shopping for toothpaste, Rufus decides not to buy it for 79¢ because he figures he can make a gallon for that price. He tells Kate about his grandma May Flower in North Carolina, who split her own name rather than take a slave-owner's family name, and who uses plain old bicarbonate of soda for cleaning teeth. Rufus decides to experiment by adding various flavors to the soda. Kate is the taster. Soon they have a bicarb, vanilla, and sugar mixture that is fine.

During the course of this experimenting, Kate and Rufus supply the math class with interesting practical problems such as how many tubes are needed to contain the amount in each bowl of paste (weigh paste and divide by 3.25 oz. per tube) and, on the basis of the estimated population, how much profit can Rufus expect to make if he sells it for 3¢ a tube and makes 1¢ profit per tube (200,000,000 people using one tube a month or 2.5 billion tubes a year at 1¢ profit = $2,500,000 profit a year). About half of the class and some neighborhood friends help pack the toothpaste in sterilized baby-food jars which Rufus sells at 3¢ a jar. Kate suggests that he go on the "Joe Smiley TV Show" where he talks as much about his grandma as about the toothpaste. Nevertheless, they get 689 orders. The price is unbeatable.

Soon, however, the kids start to wonder how much their work is worth. Rufus, an entrepreneur, who really only likes the inventiveness part, gives out stock in his new company. Kate receives 2 shares worth $5,000. Mr. Conti advises Rufus to keep 499 shares in order to maintain voting control of the company. Rufus is now officially in the toothpaste business.

Meanwhile, Kate, who possesses advertising and marketing acumen, buys Rufus 50 gross of aluminum tubes for his birthday. Even though Kate does not expect to spend $5.00 at the bankruptcy auction, because she thinks a gross is a dozen, she does think that they should put the toothpaste in tubes. When she receives 144 dozen she calls Rufus who brings friends and 4 grocery bikes to carry the tubes back to her laundry room because Rufus's mother wants the assembly line out of her kitchen. Next Kate looks for a machine to fill the tubes, while Rufus draws what it should look like. Kate traces the tubes to the closed Happy Lips plant and meets Hector, a mechanic who used to work there and now guards it. Together Kate and Hector figure that by paying $300 a month for rent and $9,000 to Hector, Rufus's company could have the plant and do the work. But when Rufus goes to the bank for a $15,000 loan, he is told that the bank does not lend money to youngsters. Quickly he convinces Hector, by giving him 15% or 150 shares in the business, that he should take out the loan. Later Hector appears on the "Joe Smiley TV Show" and tells how Kate found him.

Meanwhile, the school year ends with the 2 youngsters making up the Toothpaste I Math class exam with Mr. Conti. They work through the summer turning a tiny home industry into a regular small business. They learn first that their product costs more with the increased overhead and soon have to charge 15¢ for a tube. Kate works hard on the advertising, radio, and television where they are known for the absolutely honest commercial because Rufus promises and sends the recipe to people who cannot pay.

Soon a toothpaste price war breaks out among the 3 leading companies. Rufus, who is named the Business Man of the Year, receives a telegram to meet with the other 3 presidents to save the toothpaste industry. He also has his company investigated for fraud. Kate writes a movie script about their experiences and decides to write another about the toothpaste war. There is a brush with organized crime which is also in the toothpaste business. In spite of their problems, they make a 49% profit and Rufus makes more than a million dollars. He tells Kate before he bicycles to North Carolina during the following summer that he wants to retire and do something new. Although the new toothpaste factory is almost finished, making the original paste was the most fun. So he sells the business to Hector and leaves. Kate stays in East Cleveland to rest, catch up on her reading, and wait for Rufus's next brainstorm. A note asking her to price inflatable life rafts augurs well for the future.

Thematic Analysis

The straightforward theme of trying out the adult roles in business, realistically encouraged by all sectors of the community from home and school to bank and worker, is well developed. The range of abilities needed in any successful enterprise is also well portrayed. The emphasis on an integrated and harmonious community is an added benefit.

Discussion Materials

The book can be introduced by displaying the jacket and describing the main characters (pp. 7–11). The story can be told in outline from illustrations: Rufus helps Kate pick up the schoolbooks (p. 10); Kate reads the note to Mr. Conti in math class (p. 13); a homemade toothpaste mix (p. 20); an assembly line (p. 33); Kate bids for tubes (p. 42); Kate and Hector talk (p. 52); the loan denied (p. 59); The Absolutely Honest Commercial (p. 70); and the investigation (p. 85). Youngsters may also be interested in these anecdotes: making saddlebags (pp. 11–15); math or business problems (pp. 22–24, 24–26, 32–35, 39–49); grandma (pp. 26–29); Hector and the machine (pp. 47–51, 51–55); a movie script (pp. 77–82); the toothpaste war (pp. 74–76).

Related Materials

Several related audiovisual titles are suggested: the series *A Business of Your Own* (Classroom World Products, 15 cassettes) deals with such different areas as herb growing, earthworm breeding, etc.; *Charlie Needs a Cloak* (Weston Woods, 8 min., color) is an animated film about making a garment from sheepshearing to the finished product; *Who We Are* series (Pyramid, 1978, 4 films) explains racial differences; *A-M-E-R-I-C-A-N-S* (Churchill, 12 min., color) explores intercultural and racial bias. *Thank You, Jackie Robinson* (Lothrop, 1974), a book by Barbara Cohen, deals with young Sam who finds a baseball friend in an elderly Black man. For boys and girls who are interested in sports, use Martin Greenberg's *Run to Starlight: Sports through Science Fiction* (Delacorte, 1975). *The Great Brain* stories (Dial; pap., Dell) by John D. Fitzgerald will appeal to younger or slower readers, as well as to readers of this title. Three other titles are suggested: Naomi Mitchison's *Sunrise Tomorrow: A Story of Botswana* (Farrar, 1973); Edward Ormondroyd's *Castaways On Long Ago* (Parnassus, 1973); and Patricia A. McKillip's *The Riddle-Master of Hed* (Atheneum, 1976).

Katherine Paterson, *The Great Gilly Hopkins*
T. Y. Crowell, 1978, $6.95; lib. bdg., $6.79

This well-traveled author and winner of the 1977 National Book Award (See also Chapter 5, *The Master Puppeteer*) is fast becoming recognized as one of our best and most prolific writers for children. Her experience with raising 4 children of her own in Maryland adds a dimension that makes her stories shine. This one treats an 11-year-old foster child who, in trying to cope with her own longings and fears, mistrusts and schemes against anyone who is friendly toward her. The story covers an eventful fall in which the heroine finally meets an adult she loves. Youngsters from 9 to 13 will find its 14 chapters easy reading, as well as emotionally powerful.

The jacket art by Fred Marcellion sets the right note both realistically and symbolically. Against a neutral, yet warm, beige color, the front portrait shows the short-haired heroine behind the not quite transparent bubble gum that she had just blown to a superlative size and that obliterates her features. The portrait on the back jacket shows the burst bubble plastered on her now somewhat obvious features. Young readers will be attracted by the portrayal of this common occurrence.

Gilly (Galadriel) Hopkins brings a reputation as an intelligent brat to her latest foster home in Thompson Park, Maryland. Miss Ellis, who has been her social caseworker for nearly 5 years, practically begs Gilly to behave herself in this new foster home. Gilly, however, longs for her natural mother, Courtney Rutherford Hopkins, to come and get her. Meanwhile, she manipulates and schemes to keep everyone at a distance.

Gilly is nonplussed at her newest foster mother and home. Mamie Trotter, Melvin's widow, is very fat and practically illiterate and obviously protective and loving toward 7-year-old William Ernest Teague, another foster child who has been with her for 2 years. Trotter kisses Gilly and welcomes her warmly, while Gilly thinks to herself that she is with a gross guardian and a freaky kid in an old dark house crammed with junk.

In her narrow room, Gilly becomes even more upset as she looks again at her photograph of a beautiful young woman with a dazzling smile and reads the message on the picture: "For my beautiful Galadriel, I will always love you, Courtney Rutherford Hopkins." In the kitchen she is snippy to W.E., and Trotter tells her that she has no right to look down on him because he may not be as smart as she is. To make some amends she goes, at Maisie's request, to get old blind Mr. Randolph, a Black man who lives next door and who comes over and eats with them. Mr. Randolph tells her that W.E. is like a grandson to him. Later that night, Gilly writes to her mother imploring her to come and get her out of this terrible situation.

The next day Trotter takes Gilly to school where her records have already arrived. Mr. Evans, the principal, tells her he will not tolerate any nonsense and assigns her to Miss Harris's sixth grade. Miss Harris tells Gilly that the name Galadriel comes from Tolkien. She thanks Gilly for the malicious card Gilly sent to annoy her because it made Harris express her anger. She adds that they are alike, "both smart and know it." Gilly has never had such a cool teacher. Gilly fights the boys at recess and meets some of the girls. One outcast whose parents abandoned her, Agnes Stokes, attaches herself much to Gilly's annoyance. Everything is wrong: Agnes scares her, Trotter and W.E. make her sick, and Harris does not react to her schemes. Gilly finds her mother's address in San Francisco and mails the letter.

Later, at Trotter's request, she goes to Mr. Randolph's house to get a book to read aloud to him and finds $25.00 behind the "Sarsaparilla to Sorcery" volume of his encyclopedia. She is almost caught by Trotter who comes to help. Trotter reads to Mr. Randolph from his favorite book of poetry and Gilly reads him Wordsworth's "Cuckoo Song," savoring the line "Trailing clouds of glory do we come." Although she discovers from Mr. Randolph that "the meanest flower" really suggests humility, Gilly still goes up to her bedroom to hide the money and plans how to get the rest of the amount needed to get to San Francisco by bus.

Gilly begins to marshall her forces. She caters to Trotter by being nice to W.E. and helps him with his reading. She even watches television and plays with him. Trotter's obvious love for her, the thing she has longed for from an adult, almost unnerves Gilly. She uses Agnes as a decoy and W.E. as an accomplice to return to Mr. Randolph's for more money. She gets $40 and gives Agnes $5 vowing to return to find more. She starts a dusting campaign in both houses, but finds nothing more. Fighting her feelings of wanting to stay with Trotter, yet being nobody's real kid, Gilly packs her bag and writes to her mother for money. In desperation, because she thinks Mr. Randolph's lawyer son who is soon coming to visit will discover her theft, Gilly steals $100 from Trotter's purse and leaves. W.E. begs her not to go.

Gilly doesn't get beyond the bus station because the suspicious agent calls the police who call Trotter. Trotter will not let them lock Gilly up and takes her home. Trotter sees that Gilly returns the money and gives her a work schedule allowance to help pay back the sum she gave away. Gilly responds to this loving treatment and tries to help W.E. toughen up for life by teaching him to read and fight. Trotter is overjoyed and kisses Gilly. Just before Thanksgiving they all get the flu, except Gilly who nurses them. In the midst of all this, Mrs. Rutherford Hopkins, a small, old-fashioned plump woman arrives to announce that she is Gilly's grandmother. Horrified by the appearances of the bed-wet W.E. and the disheveled, sick Trotter who comes downstairs to remind Gilly about cooking the turkey, Mrs. Hopkins leaves promising to get Gilly out of there.

After Gilly cooked the Thanksgiving dinner on which everyone compliments her, Miss Ellis arrives to send her to her maternal grandmother in Londoun County, Virginia. Gilly protests while Miss Ellis laments for the "children of the flower children." Trotter, who genuinely loves her, finally says "You got to go." Her fairy tale finished, Gilly drives with her gentle grandmother to Jackson, an hour away. She reads and sleeps in her deceased uncle Chadwell's room and wonders why her mother left her. She also writes to all her good friends in Thompson Park.

Gilly's mother arrives to spend 2 short days over Christmas with her daughter and the mother she has not seen in 13 years. Except for her smile Courtney is not the girl in the photograph any longer. It is obvious that if it were not for the airfare sent by the lonely widow whose husband is dead and whose son was killed in Vietnam, Gilly's mother would not even be there. Gilly wants to vomit. Instead, she calls Trotter and asks to go back where she finally found love and acceptance. Trotter tells her that life is tough with few happy endings, that the home of her lonely grandma is Gilly's home, and that she loves Gilly. Gilly accepts this new awareness, secure in her knowledge that Trotter would be proud of her.

Thematic Analysis

The theme is a child's need to face reality rather than to submit to wish fulfillment in order to resolve the many conflicts of life. The story treats other themes, such as the vagaries of being a foster child, the burden of intelligence without understanding, and the social consequences of the most recent war. It touches briefly on the plight of the aging who may be alone, although they have close relatives. Primarily, however, it stresses how the love and caring of one adult for a youngster can give that growing person the sense of real security everyone needs to function well.

Discussion Materials

Provide some background on Gilly (pp. 1–4, 9) as you display the jacket, front (before) and back (after). Introduce the main characters: Miss Ellis (pp. 1–3); Trotter (p. 7); W.E. (p. 5); Mr. Randolph (pp. 11–14); Agnes Stokes (pp. 26–27); Miss Harris (pp. 54–55); Courtney Rutherford Hopkins (p. 9); Mrs. Rutherford Hopkins (pp. 106–108). Several episodes can be told: school and Miss Harris (pp. 6, 17–25, 53–59); stealing the money (pp. 33–35, 41, 61–65, 67–69, 71–75, 82); buying a bus ticket (pp. 86–92); making amends (pp. 93–103); the flu and the visitor (pp. 104–113); fried chicken supper and tears (pp. 123–128); in Virginia (pp. 132–135); letters (pp. 136–138). Suggest but do not specify: mother arrives around Christmas and Gilly learns something important.

Related Materials

For those who are or would be interested in Tolkien, use the filmstrip *The Hobbit* (Xerox, 1977), or the disc or cassette of *The Silmarillion* (Caldomon, 60 min.), a story that precedes the trilogy, first published after Tolkien's death. Read aloud from *The Father Christmas Letters* (Houghton, 1976) by J. R. Tolkien. Betsy Gould Hearne's *South Star* (Atheneum, 1977) is about the last daughter of a race of giants. Penelope Farmer's *A Castle of Bone* (Atheneum, 1972) combines fantasy and mystery in an adventure tale. Readers will also enjoy *Greeks Bearing Gifts* (Scholastic Bk. Services, 1976) by Bernard Evslin and *Flying to the Moon and Other Strange Places* (Farrar, 1976), poems by Michael Collins. All will learn from and enjoy the slide sets *Photography — The Creative Eye* (Center for the Humanities), which includes *How to Develop Film* and *How to Print and Enlarge.*

Richard Peck, *The Ghost Belonged to Me*
Viking, 1975, $6.95; pap., Avon, 1976, $1.25

The author of this exciting story that will delight readers from 10 to 14 is responsible for other popular titles. His background and interests are wide, ranging from his Illinois home to an English university and from architecture and poetry to creative writing. He writes a fast-paced tale of adventure that can be enjoyed by youngsters and others.

The jacket painting portrays, in eerie moonlight shades, the hero in silhouette staring at the attic and the ghostlike figure of a girl holding a tiny dog. It is an appealing invitation to read this title.

Alexander Armsworth's fifth-grade teacher at the Horace Mann School, Miss Winkler, often says that he possesses a glib tongue. However, his newest classmate, Blossom Culp, whose mother has gypsy blood, tells him that he has "the gift" to see the unseen. Alexander says simply that Blossom has skinny legs and that there are many ways to say that he is receptive (p. 3). Meanwhile, he simply tries to please his father by being practical and working on autos and pleases himself by learning about girls.

He has always lived with his family in Bluff City, a midwest town near St. Louis close to the Mississippi River, where people still talk, in this year of 1913, about the Louisiana Purchase Exposition and the World's Fair in St. Louis. The latest developments, however, are the electrified street cars and the new-fangled automobile. Alexander's father has an automobile, a 58-horsepower, Model C Mercer, that cost $2,600. Mr. Armsworth gives up hope that his son will develop any practical ability when Alexander packs the auto brakes with cotton wading. Bub Timmons takes over and fixes the car with ease. His father, Amory, continues to drink heavily because he lost a hand laying track for the new trolleys. Mr. Armsworth's generosity to the Timmons does not seem to help.

Alexander lives in the third largest house (23 rooms), in town as befits Joe Armsworth who is a successful building contractor. The rococo house was built in 1861 by a Captain Campbell who hanged himself in the parlor. Alexander has a back bedroom with a window that overlooks both Blossom's poorer quarters down a nearby lane and the Armsworth brick barn. It is here that Alexander sees his ghost (p. 6) and the pale halo around the barn that Blossom's mother says tells that it is haunted. Alexander goes to the barn only to hear a whine and scatching in the loft. He finds a bedraggled lap dog with a pink ribbon and a sore paw. He helps it and leaves, marking the wet stain spot in his mind. Later as he drifts off to sleep, he hears his older sister Lucille and her boyfriend, Tom Hackett, talking and petting on the porch.

Alexander's trips to the barn loft, once dragging Blossom along to try to make her confess that she is responsible for the goings on, are masked by his school days and Luella Armsworth's feverish plans for a May "coming-out" party for her daughter. A social climber, Mrs. Armsworth is anxious to help Lucille "catch" Tom, the scion of a wealthy family. She even tolerates 85-year-old uncle Miles, an erratic but excellent carpenter, who knows the town's affairs and people well, including Tom Hackett's father when he was a pharmacist.

Uncle Miles waits until the morning of the party before taking some of the scrollwork off the porch as he had been asked to do in order to make a pavilion in the yard. While he works he tells Alexander that the scrollwork was added to make the house look like a steamboat. He also tells him about ghosts and the old fear of being buried alive. Shortly before the guests arrive, Alexander leaves a note in the barn loft for Blossom whom he still thinks is trying to fool him.

While cousin Elvira Schumate ladles the punch, Alexander serves. He sees the rich Van Deeter's limousine arrive with regret, watches the Hacketts come in their Coey Flyer without Tom, observes Bub and Blossom watching from the bushes, sees Lowell Seaforth, the new young newspaper reporter approach, and witnesses the spectacle of drunken Tom Hackett driving into the flower beds and putting more liquor in the punch. Luckily Lowell heads him off.

Things happen quickly. Awakened that night by a blazing light, Alexander goes to the barn loft where a young girl wearing a damp green dress and glass brooch with flowers made of human hair shrieks a warning about a train and a man with one hand. Remembering Bub, Alexander, in his nightshirt, takes the streetcar and convinces the conductor that Amory Timmons is setting fire to the wooden trestle. Everyone, except Amory, is saved.

The next day after church when Lowell, who wrote a nice piece about Lucille's party, arrives, Alexander tells him about the ghost. That evening the ghost appears again and tells Alexander that she wants to be at rest above ground with her people. She also says that only her brooch remains nearby (p. 112). When the word about the ghost gets out, Mrs. Van Deeter calls and wants to see the barn. Uncle Miles tells more about Captain Campbell who transported the Dumaines's daughter from New Orleans on his steamboat which sank 12 miles from Bluff City. Captain Thibodoux (the real name of Captain Campbell) buried the dead child and then bought the land and erected the house with the family fortune that had been hidden in her hoops.

They quickly find Inez Dumaine's hitching-post grave marker between the house and barn. As Mrs. Van Deeter watches, they unearth Inez's brooch. Uncle Miles and Alexander (and secretly Blossom) take the remains by train to be buried in the family plot in New Orleans. Although a New Orleans newspaper man tries to steal the casket, the three, together with the help of uncle Miles's old friend, red-headed Sophie (Mrs. Pomarad), manage to place it in Cemetery number one, the oldest in New Orleans. Blossom receives Inez's brooch.

Some months later, Lowell and Lucille become engaged. Uncle Miles dies, but only after he has shared some of his worldly wisdom with Alexander.

Thematic Analysis

This multilevel adventure tale is a quixotic mix. On the surface, it is an exciting ghost story. Fundamentally, however, it is about a youngster's growing sense of his own adequacy because of the increasing unity between his imagination and his perception of reality. There are historical strands from the Civil War, geographical, of the Mississippi and the old quarters of New Orleans, social, of a Midwest town at the turn of the century, as well as deftly presented observations about human nature. The vivid touches that describe a boy's and girl's awareness of each other are human (p. 154). Even the generation span between uncle Miles and Alexander accounts for a large measure of the growing awareness of a boy.

Discussion Materials

There are many vivid episodes to tell. Introduce the story (pp. 5-8) and display the jacket drawing. Use the following: the everyday Alexander and the newfangled fire-escape drill (pp. 10-13); Blossom says he has "the gift" (pp. 15-17, 64-65); daddy's Mercer (pp. 22-23); the barn loft (pp. 23-26); warnings (pp. 77-80); rescue (pp. 81-88); another visit (pp. 110-112); the house's history (p. 27), Captain Campbell (pp. 99-110, 103-104, 122-123); funeral trip to New Orleans (pp. 150-157); and Cemetery number one on Basin Street and voodoo (pp. 171-176).

Related Materials

A recording of this title is available (Viking, VK III, or cassette, VK IIIC), as well as the sequel, *Ghosts I Have Been* (Viking, 1977), which has more about Blossom. Also use the author's mystery-adventure, *Dreamland Lake* (Holt, 1973; pap., Avon, 1974). More tales and poems of fright: *The Ghost in the Far Garden* (Lothrop, 1977) by Sean Manley and *The Skin Spinners: Poems* (Viking, 1976) by Joan Aiken. Frank Bonham's *A Dream of Ghosts* (Dutton, 1973) and Lucy M. Montgomery's *Magic for Marigold* (McClelland & Stewart, 1929, 1977) feature for reluctant and young readers a female sleuth, an imaginative little girl, and her great-grandmother. The latter preceded the sentimental favorite *Anne of Green Gables*. For younger readers, suggest Betsy Byars's *The TV Kid* (Viking, 1976), and for adolescents, suggest Paul Zindel's *Pardon Me, You're Stepping on My Eyeball* (Harper, 1976; pap., Bantam, 1977); both of these deal with facing reality. *Is There a Loch Ness Monster? The Search for a Legend* (Simon & Schuster/Messner, 1977) by Gerald S. Snyder is illustrated with photographs and is a suspenseful nonfiction book for the same readers.

Anne-Cath Vestly, *Aurora and Socrates*

Trans. from the Norwegian by Eileen Amos. Illus. by Leonard Kessler. T. Y. Crowell, [1969] 1977, $6.95

The Norwegian author of *Hello, Aurora,* who introduced readers to one little girl's reaction to her father as a house-husband, expands the story here with more about the Tege family. This title portrays the extended family from the little girl's perspective as they go through the adventures that arise as the house-husband begins to venture forth again as he finishes his Ph.D. degree. The translator has done a competent job with this episodic story that could be from any Western European land.

Illustrated on practically every other page, with pen and ink caricature-type line drawings that capture the humor and warmth, this story (consisting of 11 short chapters) will be enjoyed by youngsters from 5 up. The younger ones will enjoy having it read to them; it will appeal to older ones up to age 10, who can read it themselves.

Aurora Tege, who is of school age, lives with her parents and baby brother, Socrates, on the tenth floor of Building Z in Tiriltoppen. Her mother, Marie, is an attorney who goes to work, while her father, Edward, stays home to finish his dissertation. Socrates is both his son's name and the subject of his research, since he is a serious student of ancient history. Tiriltoppen is a new town with high-rise buildings and shopping malls, all a bus ride from the big town where the university is and Marie works. But for Aurora the best things are the new red sled that Socrates sits on in the apartment and the forest and little house to which Aurora pulls him on the sled when they go outside.

Aurora's friend, gran, lives beyond the fir trees on a little farm with her daughter, son-in-law, and 8 grandchildren, whose names all begin with "M" and a dog, Stovepipe.

Gran, who had been a dairymaid, is glad to let Aurora enjoy the freedom of the farm. When her father takes a temporary job teaching 3 days a week, Aurora and Socrates are pleased that gran will take them for one day a week. Uncle Brande, who lives in town, comes for the other 2 days. One Tuesday gran has to come to the apartment because Socrates is slightly ill. She has never taken an elevator or been on a high balcony so Aurora has great fun showing her around. Uncle Brande's days are exciting and gran's cozy, but the best are daddy's.

On one of daddy's days, he whistles through his housework, while Socrates washes spoons while sitting on the floor and Aurora dries. Something new is added when Nusse's mother gives them an old vacuum cleaner (Bala) in exchange for piano lessons from Mr. Tege for her daughter. The vacuum cleaner scares Socrates and sucks up Mrs. Tege's earrings when Aurora tries to vacuum them clean. Fortunately, daddy retrieves them. Aurora has a disappointment when she meets her two girl friends, Brit-Karen and Nusse, in the grocery store and discovers that Brit-Karen is moving to the top floor apartment in a new building in Tiriltoppen. It seems so far away.

Aurora forgets this distress when Nusse arrives all dressed up for her first lesson. Aurora is jealous and interrupts every 5 minutes until her father tells her to stop. Finally, she takes her 4 kroner received for Christmas and goes shopping. She can buy only a dishwashing brush (she reallys wants the dishwasher) for Daddy. When he sees her gift, he delights Aurora by sitting her at the piano. However, she goes to put on her best dress before her first lesson with daddy.

Uncle Brande on his day tries to calm Socrates who keeps looking for daddy. When they all go out, Aurora stops at the moving van to say good-bye to Brit-Karen. Aurora and Nusse, now her best friend, plan to rescue Brit-Karen and hide her in the closet. While Aurora goes to the supermarket for uncle Brande, Brit-Karen's mother comes looking for her. Although Nusse does not say anything, Socrates keeps chanting "little girl in closet." Aurora finally comes home and lets Brit-Karen out.

Father's day to read, defend, and celebrate his doctorate approaches.

Mother cajoles him into having his picture taken along with a family group portrait. Socrates cries until the photographer plays peek-a-boo with him. Then daddy moves to uncle Brande's for the last 2 weeks before the degree is to be received. Gran cannot take the children because she is busy taking driving lessons and uncle Brande has gone to his summer cottage early. So Aurora's real granny and her friend, Putten, come on the train from Bessby. Their arrival provokes another adventure in which Putten and Socrates are inadvertently locked in a cattle car while granny and Aurora go for a cab. Putten exclaims, "We're not cows," and Socrates says, "Moo," after they are released.

Daddy comes home and whispers at the door for Aurora to get him his bow tie and a book secretly because he does not want to make his mother more nervous about him just before the day when they are all to go to see him defend his thesis. Meanwhile, gran, who has won her driving license, inveigles her son-in-law into letting Morten, one of her grandchildren, and her sit in the truck. She starts to drive it away and pick up the other 7 grandchildren to drive once around Tiriltoppen. Her amazed son-in-law follows. When granny and her son-in-law meet Edward Tege, he invites them to visit the university the next day.

The big day dawns with everyone dressed up for the occasion. Aurora's hair is braided and she wears her coat and carries her handbag and sits between mother and granny. She fumes at one of the men in tailcoats who criticizes her father's work. Even after her mother explains the procedure to her and she sees her daddy receive many congratulations, including those of the critical man, Aurora will not shake his extended hand and says to him, "Can you look after babies?" Aurora finds her father sleeping in the flower-filled living room the next morning, and quietly goes out to play with Nusse.

Thematic Analysis

There are at least two themes. One is a little girl's need for love and reassurance from her father. The other, which is equally significant, is the importance of positive adult role models. Aurora is surrounded by these: a father who works at home and outside chores and a mother who does the same, both of whom adapt their life-styles and career choices to the family; and older relatives and friends who function in other life-styles while remaining active and providing an extended family. All are essential. Throughout, a child's instinctive drives, for example, jealousy and the need for security, receive attention.

Discussion Materials

Introduce Aurora, perhaps by reading *Hello, Aurora* and showing the setting (title page). Any of the illustrations, alone or separately, will introduce many incidents, for example: the Sled (opposite p. 7; pp. 14–15, 62); Aurora (pp. 10, 37, 56, 61, 109, 126); gran (pp. 22, 24, 28, 30, 33, 35, 117, 119, 122, 126, 129, 133); Socrates (pp. 39, 43, 67, 94, 101, 106); dad (pp. 16, 43, and Nusse p. 53, and Aurora pp. 64, 82, 87, 89); and Aurora (pp. 111, 140). Several excerpts and illustrations can be discussed: nursery school (picture p. 18); piano lessons (pp. 33, 53, 64); throwing a tantrum or being "fussy" (pp. 89, 94); or friends (pp. 16, 47, 70, 75, 144). The problem can be explained using Chapter 1; Chapter 2 will describe gran's confusion in Building Z. Each episodic chapter lends itself to book talks.

Related Materials

Philippa Pearce's *What the Neighbors Did and Other Stories* (T. Y. Crowell, 1973); Jonathan Gathorne-Hardy's *Operation Peeg* (Lippincott, 1974); and Yoshiko Uchida's *Samurai of Gold Hill* (Scribner, 1973) are all useful adventure stories for the same or older readers. For a story about an active older person, try *Fish for Supper* (Dial, 1976) by M. D. Goffstein, about grandma going fishing. Also try *There, Far Beyond the River* (O'Hara, 1973) by Yuri Korinetz, about a boy and a grandfather, and a film, *My Dad's a Cop* (Wm. Brose Productions, 18 min., color). A picture book about a boy and ballet lessons, *Max* (Macmillian, 1976) by Rachel Isadora, and *Flashlight and Other Poems* (Atheneum, 1976) by Judith Thurman, poems for early childhood, are also suggested. Use the film *The Time Has Come* (Third Eye Films, 1977, 22 min., color) for nonsexist education for parents and teachers.

9

Appreciating Books

Since children usually read a wide range of materials, they can be introduced to books of superior literary quality that also encourage abstract thinking. Many fine children's books are available to help youngsters recognize good writing and form some standards for selecting their reading material. It is important to expose them as early as possible to the pleasures of good literature.

It is also important to help youngsters to think abstractly. The ability to use concepts in abstract logical thinking is gained in a rhythmical pattern. A mastery of language expression and reading comprehension is one indication of the level of a child's success in this process. Encouraging a youngster to develop the ability to think abstractly by dealing with hypothetical propositions and variables in a situation is intimately connected with reading, understanding, and appreciating books.

This chapter discusses books that exhibit literary quality and require abstract thinking on the part of the reader. Each book stands on its own stylistic means of expression and its own level(s) of abstract thought. Yet, each can also be enjoyed as a rousing good story. Together, they represent a variety of fine books. The person who introduces them to children will ultimately initiate the level of the child's appreciation.

Natalie Babbitt, *Tuck Everlasting*
    Farrar, 1975, $5.95; pap., Bantam, large format, $1.75

One recognizes in the Prologue the elegant and rich writing style of Natalie Babbitt. The literary quality and sureness in treating universal themes that she shows are never more evident than here in a young girl's acceptance of mortality as a part of life. The story is timeless and destined to be a classic, appreciated by readers of all ages, and especially young people from 10 to 14.

A native of Ohio, who grew up with an interest in fairy tales and drawing, Mrs. Babbitt raised 3 children before she started to write her splendid books. Her first were in verse—*Dick Foote and the Shark* and *Phoebe's Revolt*. She has gone on to write well-known prose titles; the one before this, *The Devil's Storybook,* was illustrated by her as well.

The soft yellow jacket drawing by the author shows a small barn-red house on a lake with 2 figures in a rowboat in the foreground. The picture represents Winnie and Mr. Tuck (Tuck) on the lake as he tries to explain life and death.

Although the story covers only a few short days in the first part of August and distances of only a few miles from the Fosters' house near the woods and the town of Treegap to the small red house on the lake, it spans 70 years and incorporates 87 years before that. The quality of agelessness is gently suggested, although only 3 events occur on the fateful day in 1881. First, Mae Tuck dresses carefully pushing her gray-brown hair under a broad-brimmed hat to go on horseback to the woods at the edge of the village of Treegap to meet her sons, Miles, 22, and Jesse, 17, who come home every 10 years (Angus Tuck, their father, waits at home for fear of being recognized). Second, Winifred (Winnie) Foster, an almost 11-year-old only child, whose family owns the woods, thinks seriously about running away. Finally, a thin bearded stranger in a yellow suit appears at the Foster gate looking for someone.

Winnie feels put upon by her loving family, as a stranger approaches and asks if she knows everyone nearby. Her grandmother interrupts asking if Winnie hears the elf music from the woods. Winnie hears for the first time the tinkling melody that sounds as if it comes from a music box. The stranger hears it too and leaves.

Winnie plays on the lawn with a frog, wishing she had it for a pet. Finally she decides to go to the woods and maybe run away. There in the center of the woods sitting at the base of an enormous ash tree she sees handsome 17-year-old Jesse Tuck drinking spring water. They speak, and Winnie asks for a drink. He stalls her until his ma and Miles arrive shortly. Mae Tuck exclaims that the worst has happened and hoists Winnie onto her own horse. They start off, telling Winnie not to be frightened and the stranger they pass on the road that their little girl is learning to ride. As they continue, Mae's music box tinkles the elf music while Jesse pleads with Winnie to help them.

Winnie then hears the story of how the Tucks traveled West through the woods 87 years earlier, and drank from the spring. All except the cat. Tuck carved a T in the tree to identify the spot in case they needed more water.

Ten years passed without any of them changing, except the cat who died. Eventually Tuck shot himself without ill effects. They knew then that they were immortal and had better move on to a new place. So began their hopeless pattern. The boys went their way, the parents lived from day to day and every 10 years they visited together and resettled. Tuck was cheerless, Mae resigned, the boys sad and happy by turns. As Winnie willingly agrees to go home to Tuck, the yellow-suited stranger who has overheard everything, silently creeps away.

Although Tuck is pleased to see a new face after almost 80 years, Winnie is oppressed by the casual disorder of their house and asks to go home. Instead, Tuck takes her rowing to explain their predicament, Jesse proposes a drink of spring water in 6 years and marriage to the young girl who finds him attractive, and Miles takes her fishing and thinks aloud about his daughter, Anna, who would now be 80. Winnie is confused. The Tucks care for and love her, but she finally yields to her desire to go home which is stronger than her wish to stay. As they are preparing to take her home, the stranger bursts in and claims her, having already traded Winnie's return to the Fosters for their woods. The stranger plans to sell the water and offers the Tucks a share to display themselves and their immortality. When they refuse, he grabs Winnie. Mae, however, shoots him to prevent Winnie from being a child forever. The constable puts Mae in jail and takes Winnie home.

Jesse comes to the Foster's iron gate to tell Winnie that Miles and he are going to release Mae from jail through a window at midnight and also to give Winnie a bottle of spring water. Winnie offers to take Mae's place and fool the constable until the Tucks are well away. Two weeks after Mae's escape, Winnie, whose family understands her action, is playing again with her toad. When she sees it being eyed by a dog, she hesitates briefly and then runs for the bottle. She pours the liquid on the frog and says "You're safe, forever."

Many years later, Mae and Tuck return on a black-topped road to the bustling city of Treegap. The woods are gone as well as Winnie's house. They discover that 3 years earlier lightning destroyed the old ash tree whose remains were bulldozed away. Tuck also visits the Foster family cemetery to read the loving memorial that tells him Winifred Foster Jackson, wife and mother, died 2 years before at the age of 78. Mae nods as Tuck says, "good girl."

Thematic Analysis

The statement ". . . fixed points, best left undisturbed for without them, nothing holds together," expresses the theme. Tuck's rowboat discourse is an eloquent affirmation of the acceptance of death, just as Winnie's statement that she does not want to die is an expression of any child facing the reality. A slight secondary theme of sexual attraction is used in Winnie's awakening sexuality and reaction to Jesse.

Discussion Materials

Show the cover and read aloud the Prologue. Then introduce: Mae and Tuck (pp. 7-9); Winnie and her grandmother (pp. 10-12); the stranger and elf music (pp. 13-17); Jesse and Winnie (pp. 18-25); the Tucks at home (pp. 44-49). Some adventures serve well for book talks: the rough ride (pp. 26-39); the rowing incidents with Tuck and Miles (pp. 50-58, 77-79); confusion and attraction to Jesse (pp. 60-65); the stranger makes a trade (pp. 66-68); the stranger's own story (pp. 83-89); and the escape (pp. 104-112). The background story of the Tucks (pp. 31-35) and the Epilogue can be held for private reading or told depending on the book-talker's story approach.

Related Materials

There are several books for this audience that deal with dying and the death of loved ones: Robin Brancato's *Winning* (Knopf, 1977); Carol J. Farley's *The Garden Is Doing Fine* (Atheneum, 1975); Jane Gardam's *The Summer after the Funeral* (Macmillan, 1973); and Betty K. Erwin's *Who Is Victoria* (Little, 1973; pap., Archway, 1976). A film, *Death of a Grandy Dancer* (LCA, 1978, 26 min., color), treats this theme in a story about a boy and his grandfather. Stephen Chance's *Septimus and the Danedyke Mystery* (Nelson, 1971) is a suspenseful mystery story. H. M. Hoover's *Children of Morrow* (Scholastic Bk. Services, 1973) is a science fiction tale about nonconformity and survival.

Eleanor Cameron, *Julia and the Hand of God*
Illus. by Gail Owens. Dutton, 1977, $6.95

The ability to write many different types of books is the forte of this well-known author. From the popular *Mushroom Planet* series, popular with younger readers, to the adult essays, such as *The Green and Burning Tree*, to the National Book Award winner, *The Court of the Stone Children*, Eleanor Cameron writes superbly on ideas that stimulate readers. In this book, the heroine is younger than she is in the previously published, *A Room Made of Windows*. Indeed, it treats Julia's earlier life right up to her move to her own room with windows that overlook Berkeley and the Bay. It will appeal to both boys and girls between 9 and 13 because of the prominence of Greg, her older brother, in the story.

Gail Owen's jacket design, done in pale watercolor tones that suggest the spiritual nature of Julia's encounter with a bird caught in the underbrush, portrays this scene on the front and Julia standing on a hill on the back. The quaint clothing reminiscent of "the flapper era" is used on the jacket and in the 16 pen and pencil illustrations throughout the 15 chapters. The old-fashioned look is further enhanced by the decorative borders and soft images that perfectly complement the story.

Ebullient and imaginative, 11-year-old Julia Carolina Redfern spends the summer of 1923 growing up and learning to harness her intuitions and observations into a constructive force. As is the custom, her brother, 13-year-old Greg, and her mother, Celia Redfern, take the ferry to San Francisco to celebrate Julia's birthday lunch at the Green Door with uncle Hugh. He presents his niece with a blank journal bound in green leather to encourage her to write. Julia, who is very imaginative—she exaggerates says gramma with whom she and her mother and brother have lived in a crowded house in Berkeley since her father died in World War I—adores uncle Hugh and always asks him to tell about his experience in the San Francisco earthquake.

He recounts the catastrophe that lasted only 80 seconds yet demolished the city and concludes by saying that is how he first met aunt Alex. Julia often wonders privately why her rich uncle ever married the voluptuous and bossy Alex. She also continues to believe that she feels and suspects another earthquake as she walks on the sidewalk cracks and rolls down the grassy hill outside the museum where they go in the afternoon. Quiet and serious Greg, an aspiring Egyptologist, patiently explains to her, over a museum display case of Egyptian artifacts, that her feelings are due to natural causes. He also tells her that he is going to write his own illustrated history of Egypt. Julia knows that he has great drawing ability; however, she does not realize that they are also the talented children of a would-be professional writer.

They have dinner at their aunt and uncle's palatial home near Nob Hill. Afterward when Julia suddenly hears the dog, Jennie, prancing in the kitchen, she runs to embrace both Hulda, the cook, and Jennie. However, Hulda tells her that Jennie died the week before. Stunned Julia demands that everyone who heard the dog's nail on the kitchen floor speak up. They all say they did except aunt Alex who is commonsensical and will not tolerate anything supernatural or "medieval." After this Julia finds it even more difficult to tolerate her aunt.

On the ferry ride back to Berkeley, Greg tells Julia that aunt Alex is the rich one and that they live with gramma because their mother has to work in the music store to pay off some debts their dad left. Julia still finds it difficult to accept her aunt and gramma until Celia tells her that she is just like gramma who always sides with Greg, while Julia does the same with uncle Hugh. She begins to see aunt Alex and gramma, who insists that there are no animals in heaven, in a different light.

One day Julia convinces her friend Maisie that they should cremate the dead mouse Julia has brought along with her. Maisie uses one of her mother's good saucepans which is burned beyond recognition while the girls look out the window. Mrs. Woollard opens the apartment door to a thick and very pungent smoke. She orders Julia out and tells her never to come back. Later she spanks Maisie and tells gramma that Julia deserves the same. Celia tells Julia that she must repay her for replacing the saucepan. Gramma expresses disbelief that Julia will repay her and tells Julia that she is as bad as her father who left so many bills. Celia Redfern cannot repair the damage both suffer, the older one with guilt and sorrow for hurting Julia, the younger one with shattered illusions.

Julia, determined that she will repay her mother, tries unsuccessfully to get a library job. She finally gets a job weeding for Dr. Maurice Jacklin whose gardener, Old Barty, cannot abide this chore. Just before Julia meets the retired scholar in his cantilevered house in the Berkeley Hills, she frees a small bird with a tinkling song from some brush, feeling that it is some kind of omen. She tells the doctor who thinks it must be a house finch. He introduces her to his 3 Siamese cats and agrees to pay her 30¢ an hour. Over the summer, she tells Dr. Jacklin all her problems. He responds by listening, sharing lemonade and cookies, and giving Julia a plain gray ledger to start writing in because she cannot bear to spoil her birthday journal. He also shows her his outstanding collection of paintings. Julia develops a "Mung-gow language" that the cats seem to use.

At home Greg continues to illustrate his long Egyptian history scroll, while Julia reads, until one terrible night when Celia, who has gotten a raise, tells her mother that they are moving. Gramma begs to have Greg stay and promises him the bedroom and the desk Mr. Redfern made for Julia. When Julia protests, the lonely older woman reaches out suddenly and inadvertently knocks ink all over Greg's work.

Another catastrophe intervenes suddenly in this crisis. On September 18, Mrs. Gray lets Julia's class out early because of a threatening forest fire in the hills. In spite of the high wind and the sight of people standing in front of the downtown stores watching for signs of fire, Julia goes up to Grizzly

Peak beyond Dr. Jacklin's empty house. There, in a delightful glen, she falls asleep until some tinkling sounds awaken her to the danger of the flames that are almost on top of her. Running down to Dr. Jacklin's, Julia helps him carry several paintings down to his sister's safer dwelling. By evening when the winds finally have died down, Berkeley has suffered greatly. While gramma thinks that the fire is "the hand of God," Julia remembers that it was actually a bird's song that had saved her. For her, the omen is fulfilled.

When gramma goes to England to visit relatives and the Redferns move, with aunt Alex's help, to a lovely cottage of their own, Julia realizes that everything has changed. She is ready now to record, in her bound journal, all that has happened. She calls it *The Book of Strangenesses*.

Thematic Analysis

The rich, complex plot provides an opportunity for the youngster to appreciate a fine writing style and explore in an abstract way the many possibilities that exist here. The story can also be read easily as an adventure in growing up, with many episodes familiar to childhood regardless of place or time. Love of animals is one and curiosity about the supernatural another. The theme is the supreme harmony of the natural order, and man's intuitive ability to use it wisely and be helped by it.

Discussion Materials

Many episodes can be presented based on the central character and the theme illustrated on the jacket; Julia finds the bird (p. 86); Julia hears bright notes (p. 127); Julia's desire to write (pp. 14-17; picture p. 64; pp. 95-97, 100, 167-168). Other adventures that children will enjoy are: Jennie (pp. 35-38); the cremation (pp. 60-70); the "Mung-gows" (pp. 87-92); a birthday party (pp. 11-26; picture p. 14); the San Francisco earthquake (pp. 18-23); the Berkeley fire (the back cover; picture p. 128; pp. 119-126, 127-139); letters to the newspaper (pp. 142-147; picture p. 144). Transparencies of the illustrations of the ferry ride (p. 8), the library (p. 80), and the Music Store on Shattuck Street (p. 120) will help establish the locale. A talk on Greg and his interests and talents (pp. 27-34; picture p. 30; pp. 106-118) and Dr. Jacklin (pp. 87-97; picture p. 92) will entertain budding Egyptologists and scholars.

Related Materials

A filmstrip set, *To Be a Woman and a Writer* (Guidance Associates, 2 strips), and a film, *Dear Lovey Hart, I Am Desperate* (Walt Disney, color), can be used for the career-minded. *Earthquake!* (Simon & Schuster/ Messner, 1977) by Gloria D. Miklowitz is also applicable. The same readers will appreciate the following books: M. E. Kerr's *Is That You, Miss Blue?* (Harper, 1975; pap., Dell, 1976); Constance B. Hieatt's *The Castle of Ladies* (T. Y. Crowell, 1972); and George Selden's *The Genie of Sutton Place* (Farrar, 1973; pap., Dell, 1974). For readers who are more practiced in abstraction of thought, suggest *A Pattern of Roses* (T. Y. Crowell, 1973) by K. M. Peyton and *The Visitors* (Lippincott, 1977) by John Rowe Townsend. Both are time fantasies; the latter deals with the future. Harold Lloyd's film classic, *Girl Shy* (Time-Life, 1976, 60 min.) can be shown in two sittings.

Vera Cleaver and Bill Cleaver, *Trial Valley*
Lippincott, 1977, $7.95

An earlier Cleaver title, *Ellen Grace* (condensed in *Introducing Books*, p. 56), foretold the ability of these authors to capture the imagination of the young. This title is a sequel to *Where the Lilies Bloom* and will appeal to youngsters from 11 to 16, especially girls. The Cleavers write of the Luthers 2 years after they buried their father. The story covers a summer in the life of the Luther family in the Blue Ridge country of North Carolina. The heroine, Mary Call Luther, is as strong and steadfast in her growing up years as ever. The authors, noted for their characterizations of people and place, prove this ability once again. This story is not dependent on the book to which it is a sequel.

The jacket painting by Wendell Minor portrays Mary Call in a thoughtful pose sitting on Old Joshua and gazing over the lower mountain and clouds. She could be any contemporary girl with her long corn-color hair and her jeans and sandals. The pale colors emphasize the poetic quality in the girl and the story, reminiscent of a pastoral symphony.

Mary Call Luther now 16 continues to lead her brother, 12-year-old Romey, and her sister, Ima Dean, wildcrafting on Sugar Boy or Old Joshua, as her mother Cosby did before her death. The proud girl sells the medicinal plants and roots to Mr. Connell who sells them to laboratories. The three Luthers do not take a penny from their brother-in-law and neighbor, Kiser Pease, who married their 20-year-old sister, Devola, right after Roy Luther's burial.

Kiser has turned out to be better than Mary Call first thought he would. Although he is the minors' legal guardian, he turned over all their property rights to Devola and has been generous and helpful. Mary Call, however, has a stern sense of responsibility and independence, although lately she has felt some conflict about the 2 rebellious youngsters who call her a "slave-driver" and question her about her insistence on teaching them to read, widening their horizons, and trying to make something of them. She begins to question her own dedication to them and her ideals at the sacrifice of her own personal life. Life in Trial Valley, however, leaves precious little room for such romantic thoughts, even if Kiser and others think Mary Call should pay more attention to herself as a woman. The practical everyday chores have to be done, and are second nature to this girl of the wilderness.

One day when they are out with Kiser and Devola picking flowers, they find a little boy in a wooden cage by the creek. He says his name is Jack Parsons and that the Widder Man left him there. Five-year-old Jack tells a rambling story about his various first names and Babe, his mama, who ran away from their holler (hollow). Kiser, who labels himself uncle Ugly for Jack, is overjoyed at finding the boy and sets about immediately to spoil him.

As the Luthers go wildcrafting, Romey and Ima Dean take turns telling Mary Call that she invites the boy's stares by wearing her clothes too tight and asking what "in love" means. They tell her that both 18-year-old Gaither Graybeal and 21-year-old Thad Yancey are in love with her. The talk is cut short, however, when Kiser and Devola arrive at Mary Call's house and ask her to keep Jack until they can convince him they want to adopt him. Jack who wants to stay with Mary Call happily calls "Bye brother" to Kiser.

Mary Call loves her little charge, but can't help thinking that only a short 9 years from now, she will be 25 and still shackled to "her kids." When Jack insists on sleeping in her bed, she knows that she has a real conflict. The next day she also finds that the other children do not accept Jack and want to know if Kiser is going to pay her for keeping him. She finally sends them all to Kiser and Devola who are delighted to have them. While they are gone, she mops the floor and is helped by Gaither who often joins her in this chore as he talks about the big house he is going to build. When Kiser returns the youngsters, he tries to tell Mary Call something about being womanly. He says to Mary Call that he thinks she will marry Gaither, but Devola thinks it will be the new social worker, Thad Yancey.

Romey and Ima Dean flatly refuse to work the following day because they are going to town with Kiser to the carnival. So Mary Call takes Jack out walking in the Valley. Thad arrives and tries to talk, but instead stalks away. Jack asks Mary Call if Thad was mad, and adds, "he likes you." The other two children return home sullen and disappointed about the freaks they saw at the carnival. Ima Dean cannot even keep her supper down. Later when Kiser brings a wagon to make it easier for Mary Call to bring Jack wildcrafting, he insists on waking him. Jack screams thinking he is being taken away. Mary Call meanwhile thinks about Thad's abrupt visit. She also thinks that she has no personal freedom because of the children, and now it is even worse. She takes Jack to Devola's while she climbs Old Joshua and sits looking toward Virginia, Thad's home (see cover painting).

Mary Call's favorite daydream has everything just the way she would like it: the children reading instead of complaining about not having a television set and having no sewing machine or a ready-made excuse for her not to sew Ima Dean's school clothes. She loves the children, but can hardly stand them. As they straggle back to the house one afternoon they see Gaither's horse and Thad's car at the gate. The two young men vie for Mary Call's attention as she thinks about what to do with Jack. Kiser and Devola want him back, but Jack carries on and will not go. Mary Call tells Kiser to take him to Constable Henry Cheek; however, Kiser tells her to keep him a while longer. He finally threatens. Mary Call is stung by this and decides to show Kiser about responsibility by packing up and moving to his house. They are all welcomed with open arms, and Kiser even pulls out Ima Dean's loose tooth.

The following day Thad, Jack, and Constable Cheek go to Chilly Hollow looking for Babe without success. When they return, Mary Call tells Jack that he cannot live with her anymore, and besides Kiser wants to adopt him and buy him a pony. The three Luthers say goodbye to him and walk home. Mary Call continues to lecture the younger two. Ima Dean responds that they are not idiots, and Romey adds that they want to hear about her and any marriage·plans she has. When they see 2 horses tied up, they know Gaither is there. He has brought Mary Call a present, "Dan," and has also cooked their supper.

Before daylight, Mary Call is awakened with the news that Jack is gone. They all search in the pouring rain. Constable Cheek joins them and tells Mary Call that Thad told him he was going to marry her and take her to Virginia. She is forced to confront her own reality and romantic attraction. Gaither and Thad join the searchers. As the 3 young people comb the swollen creek banks, Mary Call discovers Jack in the wooden cage. As he comes out, she loses her balance and is carried into the water. Jack falls in too. Gaither rescues Jack, Thad saves Mary Call. Getting his courage up,

Thad asks her to marry him, and leaves when she says she cannot. She knows she will not have anymore daydreams about him.

Mary Call willingly keeps Jack now until he is old enough to make other arrangements. Gaither, whom the little boy likes, helps her and Kiser does not interfere as much. It is a positive solution for her, full of life's compensations in Trial Valley.

Thematic Analysis

There are several themes: developing sexuality, responsibility, and concern for the environment; and learning to look positively on the factor of compensation in life. All are well developed; however, the last one is at a deep level of abstraction and can best be appreciated at this age by the most thoughtful.

Discussion Materials

Some background music, a pastoral symphony, for example any of the movements in Beethoven's sixth symphony, will provide a subtle background for a display of the jacket. Encourage youngsters to read *Where the Lilies Bloom* either before or after this title. Introduce the Luthers and Peases and Mary Call's two suitors. Also describe Jack, the crux of the problem (pp. 21-28). Some good book-talk episodes are: the carnival (pp. 62-78); Indian lore (pp. 84-85, 124-126); wildcrafting (pp. 11-16, 85); courting (pp. 46-61, 89-92, 128-132, 152, 153); responsibility (pp. 96-111); and Chilly Hollow (pp. 115-120).

Related Materials

Home before Dark (Knopf, 1976; pap., Bantam, 1977) by Sue Ellen Bridgers is about a 14-year-old who has to assume many adult responsibilities; it can be suggested for older readers. The story of a 19-year-old growing up in New York City, M. B. Goffstein's *Daisy Summerfield's Style* (Delacorte, 1975) is also a good choice. Eth Clifford's *Search for the Crescent Moon* (Houghton, 1973) presents a picture of Indiana in the 1840s, and Joan Clarke's *Early Rising* (Lippincott, 1976) depicts England in the 1880s. A clever pixilation film, *Taxi* (NFBC) will entertain this audience.

Mollie Hunter, *The Wicked One: A Story of Suspense*
Harper, 1977, $5.95; lib. bdg., $5.79

The winner of the 1975 Carnegie Medal for *The Stronghold*, Maureen Mollie Hunter McIlwraith, a native of Scotland, has produced another suspenseful tale based on her country's lore to add to her distinguished record. *The Kelpie's Pearls* and *The Walking Stones* are 2 more of her books in which she writes with style and verve about superstition and imagination. The lyricism of her colloquial manner of expression is best appreciated when the story is read aloud. Children from age 10 to 13 will appreciate the special excitement.

The jacket drawing by Stephen Gammill is both stimulating and attractive. The letters on the back and front of the jacket are in a bright green which stand out against the misty grayish brown background. On the front top half behind a protective mist is a prominent set of teeth letting out an angry yowl, purportedly by the Grollican or monster, while the bottom half shows the main characters—the Grant family—standing in a solemn straight line.

The story is not a new one, at least to those whose roots are in the Highlands of Scotland. It deals with the monster, the Grollican, who takes perverse pleasure out of bedeviling some people, especially someone like hardworking Colin Grant, who has a quick and fierce temper. It is said that once a victim is chosen, the Grollican annoys that person for life. Anna, Colin's good wife, knows this firsthand because a relative had this problem. When Colin comes home to his small croft (farm) after a day's work in the woods as a forester, he decides to tell what has happened to him to Anna and their boys, Hugh and Hector the twins, and young Ian with the crooked shoulder. It is the second time he has had an encounter with the invisible beast, but now he is sure that the Grollican has marked him because his bonnet (hat) has a hole rubbed in it. As all Scots know, that is how the Grollican marks its victim.

Colin tells his family that he tried to hit the Grollican and heard him scream, but that a fallen branch also hit Colin. The steady and strong twins want to catch the Grollican, until Colin explains its invisibility. Ian, however, asks if they can tempt the monster to show himself. Colin replies that the monster is too ugly to do that. Compassionate Ian mutters, "poor thing," as Anna adds that the Grollican is sometimes sorry for its mischief. Knowing they are in for trouble the crofters sadly go to bed.

In the morning they look out on their ravaged farm. Everything has been smashed. Ian finds the footprints of the large, hairy, big-footed Grollican. In a rage, Colin takes his 3 dogs, Fios, Luath, and Trom (Gaelic for knowledge, swift, and weighty) to hunt the monster. Fios gets its scent and a battle rages until, as the Grollican loses its power and starts to become visible, Colin calls the dogs off. At that minute Colin is knocked out. When he recovers, Colin sees the dogs losing the battle to the Voght, a greenish animal with huge red eyes, a long green mane of horsehair, hooves for hands, a long tail, and dressed in woman's clothing, who has come to protect her offspring. Meanwhile, the Grollican repairs the damage at the croft. Ian observes that it has a conscience. Colin, however, keeps justifying himself instead of mastering his quick temper. Finally, in disgust, Anna tells him to take the cattle to the hill. There he meets a beautiful woman in green with a golden chain who kisses him and puts him under her power. He knows she is of the fairy people, but his senses flee and he continues to slip away to meet her. One day he comments that the cattle are sickly looking and not his, while she tells him that the Grollican told her to go to the hill to meet Colin. Once more enraged, he drives the cattle down the hill and finds his hand magically and firmly attached to one of the cows throughout the stampede over hill and vale to a large cave.

Inside he sees the green-clad fairy people who tell him his cattle are back on the hill. To keep peace they also promise never to lend themselves to the Grollican's tricks again. They offer Colin anything to leave. Just before he is tempted to say he wants gold, the fairy woman gives him a rhyme with which to get a small brown filly who never tires.

The filly proves tireless and plows night and day. As long as she is never yolked to anything but a plough she will bring him good money when he rents her to neighbors. Colin finally starts to face up to his fault and consequently begins to cure it. He also tells Anna about the fairy woman and begs her to help him stay away from her. It is not long before Anna has to have the twins tie Colin up and sing psalms loudly to get him through until dawn when the fairy woman's spell is broken. This time the Grollican fails, and doubly so when it cannot get past the charm over the door.

Ian, who has taken care of the filly with great affection, sees the Grollican briefly when the monster enters the barn to do mischief. Feeling sorry for the sadness behind the wild look in its eyes, Ian talks to it. Almost visible, it has a flat nose, thick lips, fangs, furry gray head, 4 hairy arms, and 6 fingers on each hand. It says, "Do you like me?" As Ian begins to believe it is trying to be friendly the Grollican pleads with him to hitch the filly to a cart to save an injured sheep. Torn by his compassion for animals, Ian hitches up the filly, "Ian's Lass," and loses her. Only the harness remains. Colin returns only to vow he will emigrate to the United States to escape the Grollican. The twins decide to stay on the croft.

Just before they sail, the local minister asks Colin to take young Flora

MacKenzie, whom he found wandering in the meadow near her father's burned-out cabin the same day the filly disappeared. When they see the brown-eyed, brown-haired lass and Ian's love for her, they all know that she is truly "Ian's Lass."

The trip to America is uneventful until they dock and hear the Grollican call to Colin from the pier. Colin and Ian dump flour on the monster to keep it visible while the police and firemen trap it in a warehouse. There Colin, in return for washing it down, gets the Grollican's promise to work for the Grants for as long as there is one alive.

The bargain works and the Grants prosper. However, as any Scot knows the Grollican has the last laugh because it is a creature of the "other world" and will live forever.

Thematic Analysis

This exciting tale, successful in the genre of the supernatural, also has several levels of meaning. Because of this, it is ideal for promoting abstract thought. The truism of a grown man's failure to curb his too-ready temper leading to irksome trouble is generally accepted. The common sense of folktales that treat many of man's ills in disguise helps youngsters to stretch their imagination and test their sense of reality. The elements of both imagination and reality are present for the youngster to deal with.

Discussion Materials

After giving a description of the main characters and problems, choose among the various episodes to give the flavor of suspense: meeting the Grollican (pp. 7-15); hunting the monster (pp. 19-25); stampeding cattle (pp. 39-48); the filly, "Ian's Lass" (pp. 51-55); fairy magic (pp. 61-70); the Grollican and Ian talk (pp. 74-88); the ruse (pp. 89-101); Flora (pp. 104-116); dockside (pp. 120-128).

Related Materials

Suggest 3 books for the same readers: Mollie Hunter's *A Stranger Came Ashore* (Harper, 1975; pap., 1977); Elizabeth Coatsworth's *The Wanderers* (Scholastic Bk. Services, 1972); and Joan Lingard's *Across the Barricades* (Nelson, 1973; pap., Grosset, 1975). The first two deal with fantasy; the latter deals with the contemporary troubles in Northern Ireland and is a sequel to *The Twelfth Day of July* (Nelson, 1972). Younger or slower readers will enjoy the Scottish tale *Janet Reachfar and the Kelpie* (Seabury, 1976) by Jane Duncan. An animated film, *Why Not* (CFS, 6 min., color), about a family's flight into fantasy, is also suggested.

Penelope Lively, *The Whispering Knights*
Illus. by Gareth Floyd. Dutton [1971] 1976, $5.95

In a time-displacement fantasy—a particularly successful genre in British juveniles—that is easy reading but requires some thought, Penelope Lively has written another fast-paced children's adventure, related in 10 lively chapters. The British expressions, such as telly and motorway, seem so clear and familiar because of the author's flowing style and command of dialogue that children will quickly grasp the meanings. Boys and girls from 9 to 13, as well as younger readers, will appreciate it.

The numerous pen-and-ink live drawings by Gareth Floyd and the foreboding illustration on the jacket add definition and interest to this story about 3 fifth-grade school chums who become involved in the town struggle to keep out the motorway. In the course of this effort, they meet an old lady, Miss Hepplewhite, evil Morgan le Fay, and whispering knights that have emerged from the locale's monument stones.

In high summer (August) in the Sharnbrook Valley which runs along the river of the same name, the talk is all about the motorway that is coming through. In the largest town, Steeple Hampden, which is near Oxford, the business community is upset. Farmers and shopkeepers alike are banding together to fight this latest invasion that threatens the peace and livelihood of this somnolent Cotswold area. Mr. Harris, a schoolmaster, has spent the summer at the newspaper office writing and collecting signatures for a petition. His son, William a fifth-grader, who like his father has a need to find out about things and also possesses an active imagination, has been spending the summer reading about Morgan le Fay and legends and exploring the countryside.

His friend, Martha Timms, who lives on a farm in the valley, has been doing her usual chores and also suffering from more than her normal number of nightmares. Martha is a timid child who scares easily, much to her sturdy family's dismay. This time, however, her dreams seem to foretell future events.

Susie Poulter, another schoolmate, is the practical "doer" of the trio. Her mother owns a village shop in which she works. Susie's ability to cope with her real world is an asset. The 3 chums seem to fit well together in their play hours.

In his explorations, William comes upon an old abandoned house and barn that has acquired a tenant. A friendly old woman Miss Hepplewhite serves him tea and tells him about the ritual of Walpurgis which she remembers from her girlhood. He also goes once again to the ancient hillside site where the legendary Stones lie scattered. He never tires of looking at this place that is reminiscent of the Salisbury plain or Stongehenge and imagining the ancient road that led to the Stones.

In the midst of all the talk about the motorway, William and his friends find time to visit Miss Hepplewhite who serves refreshments and tells more of the local legends. Walpurgis and Morgan le Fay live in her tales, and especially the Stones which according to legend were once knights that did battle defending good against evil.

Susie continues to work in the real world of the shop, while Martha sinks into her disturbed dreams. William, however, with his strong urge to find out about everything combines the practical work of helping his father circulate a petition against the incoming motorway even while he becomes fascinated with the lore, the magical occurrences of cake disappearance and telly disturbances, and the eerie atmosphere of the churchyard gravestones. William sees Morgan le Fay near Miss Hepplewhite's barn and tries to ward off her approach by throwing a rock. She instantly turns into a stone statue. He remembers that Miss Hepplewhite has told them that Morgan is especially fond of working her evil through children. Miss Hepplewhite cautions that the "bad side of things" is always with us and that Morgan always looks for weaknesses. William notes that Morgan bears a remarkable resemblance to Mrs. Steele whose elderly husband owns a factory in nearby Bauton. He also recalls from recent memory that Sharnbrook River Valley people say that it would be more logical to put the motorway through industrial Bauton.

Meanwhile, Martha, who continues to be afraid of her dreams, accepts a ride in Mrs. Steele's chauffered Rolls Royce. William and Susie go to the Steele's residence, Clipsham Manor, to rescue their friend whom they believe to have been kidnapped by Morgan or Mrs. Steele. The three of them dash into the nearby church where William, remembering more of Miss Hepplewhite's advice that Morgan "can't abide reason," fashions a straw cross to hold her off. Frantic and injured in the skirmish, they run to the hospital in Chipping Ledbury when Martha tells them that she saw the Stones moving from her window in the Manor. Their respite is short-lived as Mrs. Steele arrives at the hospital to collect Martha. Quickly they get on the Steeple Hampden bus bound for home. When William notices the apparently driverless Rolls following them, he stops the bus and they run across the fields looking for help. The car follows and plunges into the river as they hang on to a ledge. They hurry up the nearby hill to the Stones, while a horseback rider follows calling "Martha." To William's astonishment, the apparition is riding behind him on a wide road that has just appeared, while ahead, mounted in battle formation, are the knights led by a younger Miss Hepplewhite. The noise of battle is obliterated in the peals of thunder from the sky. The Stones are victorious. The children hear Miss Hepplewhite exclaim before she disappears that their task—the first in 200 years—was completed magnificently. As she departs they can still hear her saying that children are vulnerable.

The following day the newspaper announces that the Steeles' abandoned Rolls has been found in the Sharnbrook River and that Mr. Steele is closing his factory and will soon join his wife to live in Jamaica. Although this item is important to William, his father and others find the announcement that the motorway is not going through more cause for celebration.

Thematic Analysis

Being able to identify easily the abstract theme of good versus evil is satisfying to many readers as they confront their own moral development (p. 19). Further, an equally important theme, but one requiring the more difficult step of thought abstraction, is the author's portrayal of what may be the 3 elements in any individual in the character of 3 young children: Susie, outgoing and practical; Martha, sensitive and dreamy; and William, actively curious about the real and the imaginary. The plot's resolution parallels the hero's resolving of the two other elements into a transcendent, harmonious whole in a healthy personality. This level of abstraction at this age is possible for only a few. For everyone, however, it is a rousing tale of adventure among the commonplace.

Discussion Materials

This title lends itself to a discussion about the nature of good and evil. A person knowledgeable about the moral development of children should be able to moderate (Kohlberg, *Moral Development*). For book talking, introduce the story by displaying the jacket and giving some background on Morgan le Fay, explaining that she represents evil. Follow this with an introduction to Miss Hepplewhite who tells William tales about Morgan (pp. 14–17). Other episodes of magic can follow: (pp. 28–29, 30–34); Walpurgis night (pp. 35–37, 38–39); strange occurrences (p. 44; picture p. 49). William, Susie, and Martha should be introduced briefly, and the motorway explained (pp. 55–59, 62–66). Describe: the petition (pp. 74–77); whispering knights (picture p. 75); and the Stones and Morgan's reincarnation (pp. 67–70, 72–73).

Related Materials

Four books that treat the theme of good versus evil can be suggested to the same readers: Madeleine L'Engle's *A Wind in the Door* (Farrar, 1973; pap., Dell, 1976); Ruth M. Arthur's *The Autumn People* (Atheneum, 1973); Susan Cooper's *Greenwitch* (Atheneum, 1974); and Patricia Wrightson's *The Nargun and the Stars* (Atheneum, 1976). They are all superb examples of the fantasy genre. The first title is for older readers; the last title is a 1976 Hans Christian Andersen Honor book and has an Australian boy hero. Everyone will enjoy the 1977 award-winning film for children, *The Cosmic Awareness of Duffy Moon* (Time-Life, 1977) which shows in live action a boy's realization of his dependence on magic rather than on his own resources.

David Macauley, *Castle*
Illus. by the author. Houghton, 1977, $8.95

In a format similar to his 4 previous books—*Cathedral, City, Pyramid,* and *Underground*—this author now adds the construction of a castle and walled town. *Harper's Bulletin* rightly called him "the Lewis Carroll of architecture" because of his singular ability to recreate in detailed pen drawings that cover practically every page that medieval spirit that permeates the illustrations and text.

The white jacket for the large-sized book bears the recognizable signature of this author-illustrator—a brilliant rendition of the front view of an architectural concept. Youngsters from 9 to 14 will savor the line drawings that illuminate the explanatory text.

The author-illustrator presents the planning and construction of a "typical" castle and town in the thirteenth century in Wales. Lord Kevin's castle is imaginary. However, the building processes and appearance are similar to those used by the English from 1277 to 1305 in their conquest of Wales. The town—Aberwyvern—is also imaginary, as are the characters—all except King Edward I of England, whose plan was to conquer Wales. The characters of Kevin the Strange and James of Babbington are based on historical figures. The construction of Lord Kevin's castle was one tangible facet in King Edward's superior strategic skill and ability to foresee that many installations would be needed to conquer the wild and rebellious Welsh. Like any program whose very success is its downfall, the construction of the castles and walled towns had to be carefully located to withstand siege, and to encourage settlement ultimately by the Welsh. The plan for peaceful assimilation would take longer than Edward's life span. In the early spring of 1283, Kevin le Strange was rewarded for loyal service by King Edward I of England by being named Lord of Aberwyvern and given title to land in northwest Wales. With Kevin's land holdings in England and his personal fortune, the King had a ready-made partner for the costly conquest. Lord Kevin hired James of Babbington, an experienced construction engineer, to choose a site and build his castle and town. From shipboard, James selected a site on a hill at the mouth of a river overlooking the sea. The high limestone outcrop had natural defenses since it faced the water on the bluff side and the land at the foot of the hill.

Soon diggers and carpenters arrived, along with boatloads of lumber and hardware, to put up barracks for the English soldiers, who would secure the area, as well as large temporary quarters for Master James and his staff and Lord Kevin and his family. The workers made smaller dwellings for themselves at the foot of the hill. They also began digging a ditch that would enclose the castle and town. They erected a palisade (fence) along the inside of the ditch which would later be replaced by a wall.

Except for the winters when the majority of the workers went back to England, they worked for 3 years before the castle and wall were almost finished. The castle was planned around a water well surrounded by an inner ward that would contain a large chapel, barns, sheds, and a private greenhouse and garden for Lady Kevin. This area was surrounded by an inner curtain wall and an elaborate system of bridges, barriers, and gates. The outside curtain wall that surrounded the entire castle was thick, and it had walks, battlements, and high towers.

By this time, Master James had brought over 3,000 people: quarrymen, mortar makers, and carpenters to construct both castle and walled-town houses. Lord Kevin had started to collect money through his bailiff, Walter of Ipswich, from his tenants outside the wall. Together with the money from his English lands and personal funds the total helped King Edward I pay the heavy costs of conquest. The houses within the wall, rented to only English at first, were inexpensive in order to encourage occupancy. The number of houses increased. The townspeople eventually pooled their money and labor to erect a church—the only stone building in the town.

An arched Great Hall and living spaces for the noble family, Robert the Chaplain, and Lionel the barber and doctor were finally provided in the castle. In October of 1288, 5 years after the building began, the entire outside of the wall was whitewashed to stand both as home and as symbol. Lady Catherine and her entourage arrived that spring. Two years later Lord Kevin granted Aberwyvern a charter relieving them of taxation. By

1294 the castle town was a thriving community which received King Edward I with a feast and celebration.

King Edward told Lord Kevin to prepare for a siege because several Welsh princes had been leading rebellions. In the spring of 1295 Prince Daffyd of Gwnnedd surrounded the castle with hundreds of ships and besieged them by land with catapults, battering rams, a siege tower, and sappers to tunnel under and collapse the wall. The castle, however, was well prepared with provisions and countermeasures. Daffyd finally left in defeat when none of his measures succeeded in breaking the spirits of the people or the walls of the castle.

Slowly the time came when both English and Welsh passed freely through the gates of Aberwyvern. Two hundred years after Edward's death a peaceful accommodation had been made. More than 400 years later, the castle stands roofless and neglected, a monument to former glory and the wall which had once been impressive is now bothersome to the inhabitants who must move around it.

Thematic Analysis

The underlying theme is the ability of human beings to plan and work toward freedom knowing that the fulfillment of this goal may come, if at all, slowly over a long period of time. Externally, the title deals practically with the construction techniques and life-styles that existed in Western Europe during this period of conquest and consolidation. These will fascinate youngsters; this glimpse of a way of life far different from that of today will intrigue them.

Discussion Materials

Since this is essentially a picture book for older children and adults, an introduction of the illustrations to small groups or of transparencies of them to larger audiences will be valuable. Accompanying the visuals should be a brief description taken or read from the text. Begin by reading the author's introduction and pointing out that the glossary will explain strange words that appear. A game can be played with two small teams. Ask one to locate a picture that illustrates 18 of the words in the glossary (assign alternate words to each team). The team that can satisfactorily identify the words with the corresponding picture in the shortest time wins.

Stress the cleverness of England's King Edward I's plan for the conquest of Wales that combined military engineering with farsighted hopes. For a shorter presentation you could show only the illustrations that show the gradual development, those marked with an asterisk (*). The following illustrations can be used in any sequence: Master James chooses the location (p. 6); an early view (*pp. 8-9); the castle plan (p. 10); cross sections of the outer wall (pp. 12-13); the front of the castle from Aberwyvern (p. 15); occupations (pp. 16-17); tools (p. 18); overall progress (*pp. 20-21); Master James at his desk (p. 22); the walls (pp. 24-25); the construction under snow (*pp. 26-27); internal tower construction begins again in spring (pp. 28-29); openings and inside details (pp. 30, 31); summer, 1284 (*pp. 32-33); the following spring and work in the towers (pp. 34-35, 36-37); October 1285, outer curtain finished (*pp. 38-39); dungeon and Chapel (pp. 40-41); garderobe (toilet) (pp. 42-43); view from castle to town (p. 44); almost finished, 1286 (*pp. 46-47); houses and the town (pp. 48-49, 50-51); finished (*pp. 52-53); weapons (p. 55); Great Hall and kitchen (pp. 56-57, 58-59); more buildings for Lady Catherine's arrival (*pp. 60-61, 62-63); aerial view, Aberwyvern has a charter (*pp. 64-65); King Edward's visit (pp. 66-67); prepare for rebellion! (pp. 68-69); weapons of siege (*pp. 70-71, 72-73, 74-75); a growing village, Aberwyvern (*pp. 76-77); the castle today by moonlight (pp. 78-79).

Related Materials

Four books set in medieval times can be suggested: Elizabeth Marie Pope's *The Perilous Gard* (Houghton, 1974), a tale of magic and romance; Niels Jensen's *Days of Courage* (Harcourt, 1973), an exciting adventure story which won the Danish children's book prize in 1972; Joe Lasker's *Merry Ever After: The Story of Two Medieval Weddings* (Viking, 1976), a story of noble and serf weddings in the Middle Ages; and Isaac Bashevis Singer's *The Fools of Chelm and Their History* (Farrar, 1973), a satirical look at the foolishness exhibited by certain "wise" men of an earlier age. For those who appreciate the elements of design, use the film *Bass on Titles* (Pyramid, 1978).

Norma Fox Mazer, *A Figure of Speech*

Delacorte, 1973, $5.95; pap., Dell, 1975, 95¢

This is the story of a 13-year-old girl whose compassion for her aged grandfather places her in opposition to her family. Norma Fox Mazer continues to give juvenile readers stories that treat the universal problems of childhood and adolescence in an easy reading style. Reading her novels helps to expand a youngster's thoughts about these problems. Youngsters from 9 to 14 will identify with the heroine in this story and appreciate her dilemma.

Jenny Pennoyer, the fourth child in a hardworking family of 5 children, 2 parents, and a paternal grandparent, feels unwanted. Baby Ethel whom she takes care of is the only one who is younger than she. Vince, Frankie, and Gail are all grown. Jenny, however, is close to her grandfather who practically raised her because Jenny's mother was very busy. As this young girl who looks like a Modigliani portrait reaches the age of puberty, she has 2 close friends, Rhoda, to whom she confides her feelings in a stay-over visit, and grandpa, Carl Pennoyer, who at 83 is sometimes irritable and calls himself an "old codger."

Jenny, who regularly visits with grandpa in his basement apartment, silently lists her liabilities—ugly and unloved by family—and her assets—strong legs and grandpa. Although reminiscences about grandma and grandpa when they lived on the farm cheer her, the loss in a traffic accident of the retarded neighbor boy, Micky, causes grief. However, worst of all is being told by her mother that grandpa is going to have to move. Jenny knows that his arthritis would be better if he lived upstairs; however, she also knows that she is the only reason he even gets out of bed. The situation deteriorates gradually until Vince, who has been attending college for only a month, unexpectedly brings his bride Valerie home. Frankie, who has been sleeping in the living room, is dislodged.

Grandpa is asked to live upstairs with Frankie so that Valerie and Vince can have the basement apartment. He refuses. Grandpa remains hurt and shaken as Gail throws a party upstairs, Mrs. Pennoyer talks about paying the rent on grandpa's plot, and Valerie cooks a meal. Grandpa will not eat with the family, preferring to cook downstairs. Inadvertently he starts a small fire which seals his fate. While grandpa is sick from the shattering experience, Vince and Valerie fix up their new apartment and Mrs. Pennoyer sorts through grandpa's furniture and clothes.

The Pennoyers visit a home for the elderly—Castle Haven on Snooks Hill—and tell everyone how nice it is. To Jenny they are using "pretty words for ugly things," where everything is just a figure of speech. Jenny also visits the home knowing full well grandpa is going, whether he likes it or not. Grandpa, who is better, accuses himself of being a nuisance and decides to go away when Jenny tells him about the home. To Jenny's delight he seems to be his old self again. One day she finds that he has gone walking for 3 hours to satisfy himself about his physical stamina. She also notices a road map in his pocket.

Soon afterward both he and Jenny leave for his old farm where they plan to live. They take a bus to Alliance and change there for New Sayre. On the long ride each has different memories of the farm, common only because they were younger and remember it with affection. From New Sayre they still have 8 miles to go to the place on Turkey Hill Road. Fortunately, a 12-year-old boy driving a truck gives them a ride to the bottom of the hill road. After a hot, dusty walk, they are confronted by the farmhouse that has deteriorated over the years and been broken into by vandals. It is a disaster area. Grandpa protests that he will soon fix it up. There is fresh water from the well and there is an outhouse, but there is little else. They eat apples from the trees and drink well water. The nights are cold and damp and the rain comes in through the many holes. Grandpa often acts bewildered in the middle of the night and begins to cough. Later, Jenny senses that he is missing and goes outside to look for him. She finds him lying dead under a tree on the frosty ground. Jenny says good-bye painfully and goes home.

The body is collected by the State Police. The family learns that death was due to overexposure, but that the old man also had bronchitis and cancer of the throat. Living on the farm had been a beautiful, but impossible dream, Jenny now realizes. However, she also knows that her parents' words of consolation that grandpa didn't suffer much are their own protective illusions, simply figures of speech.

Thematic Analysis

Several themes appear in this story: aging, preadolescence, and family relationships. Each gives the reader food for thought; however, the intergenerational orchestration will help the reader to think more deeply about different points of view, even in the most distressing emotional situations. The themes are both contemporary in their emphasis and ageless in their quality.

Discussion Materials

This story is delicate and should be presented briefly for the readers to gain their own insights. Jenny, her grandpa, and her family can be introduced (ch. 1-11). The turkey lice story about the grandparents will lend a gentle humorous touch (p. 27); mother and Jenny discussing grandpa (end of ch. 4) and Mrs. Pennoyer's grumblings about old age and dying (pp. 86-87), introduce a somber note about the problem in their home. Jenny's visit to the home for old people (pp. 124-129) and grandpa's decision to leave (p. 137) may provoke a lively discussion among a group of young readers about this topic. The title as first stated (p. 113) and finally explicated by Jenny (p. 197) helps to specify the youngster's gain and the parents' loss in insight into the situation.

Related Materials

Elizabeth Winthrop's *Walking Away* (Harper, 1973; pap., Dell, 1974) also concerns a girl and her grandfather and learning about death. Three other books about old age are useful: *Changes* (Harper, 1973) by Gil Rabin; *Cinnamon Cane* (Harper, 1977) by Melinda Pollowitz; and *Dodo Every Day* (Harper, 1977) by Ilse M. Vogel. Eda LeShan's helpful title, *Learning to Say Goodbye* (Macmillan, 1976) is suggested together with the filmstrip *America's Aged: The Forgotton Many* (Current Affairs, 1976). Norma Fox Mazer's *Saturday, the Twelfth of October* (Delacorte, 1975; pap., Dell, 1976) is about a girl overwhelmed by the difficulties of adolescence who copes by escaping into a world of fantasy. This science fiction fantasy won the 1975 Lewis Carroll Shelf Award.

D. Manus Pinkwater, *Lizard Music*

Illus. by the author. Dodd, 1976, $4.95

This author of several juvenile titles—*Wizard Crystal, Magic Camera, Wingman,* and *Blue Moose*—has a clear recollection of childhood and its effect on the imagination. Both the author and his wife write for children and also run a school, Superpuppy, for canines, in Hoboken, New Jersey. Youngsters from 8 to 12 will enjoy this story of a young boy on his own for 2 weeks who tracks down the origin of the lizard musicians he sees on television late at night. Youngsters will also be intrigued by the black-and-white drawings that illustrate the text. The bright raspberry colored jacket that also bears a black-and-white drawing of lizards is guaranteed to attract.

It has been a long summer in McDonaldsville for sixth-grader, Victor, because his parents are irritable and need a vacation. They finally depart to spend 2 weeks in Colorado, leaving 17-year-old Leslie in charge of her 11-year-old brother. When Leslie immediately joins a bunch of her "creepy" friends for a 2-week camping excursion to the Cape, Victor is delighted. He thinks his sister is weird anyway and prefers to be alone. She leaves money and frozen TV dinners for him. The first thing he does is to forge Leslie's name on 10 sheets of her blue note paper. Each note supposedly from Leslie says the same reassuring things, and even at the height of his adventure he never forgets to mail one a day to his parents. In case they call, Victor plans to say Leslie is out bowling or on a date. His inventive mind thinks of everything.

Finally free of the pedestrian, he can watch television and work on his model DC-10 at night. Victor adores Walter Cronkite and his summer replacement, Roger Mudd. He even tried to start a Cronkite fan club among his schoolmates until they began to label him "crazy." He watches the game shows (which he thinks inane), commercials (which he studies closely), and the late news. Victor also likes the local late news broadcaster Bob Barney, whose show comes from the city of Hogsboro a few miles south of McDonaldsville. Finally, his special treat—the late movie— appears, and Victor watches it critically, being a connoisseur of the fantasy-science-fiction genre. Nevertheless, he almost falls asleep until he sees 5 or 6 real lizards playing regular instruments on the screen. He falls asleep as they play and sway to the strange music and wakes in the morning to a hissing television.

That morning he eats breakfast, smokes a cigarette for the first time, and vomits. Victor then decides to take the bus to Hogsboro because he goes infrequently. During the ride, an elderly Black man in a raincoat and rumpled hat with a string of toys and dolls and bottles around his neck boards to cries of "Hey, Chicken Man give us a show." The old man obliges by taking off his hat and producing a big, fat chicken who performs tricks with the toys. Victor claps with the others.

Victor gets off at the bus depot and starts walking through the city. He eventually comes to an old run-down neighborhood where there are few people and many vacant stores. In one vacant store window he notices an old faded record album cover that has a faint picture of 5 lizard musicians entitled "The Modern Lizard Quartet Plays Mozart." It starts to rain as he walks on and he turns into the nearest doorway where he bumps into the Chicken Man. Up close Victor sees that Claudia, the chicken, is very old and its owner is both old and scary. The Chicken Man suggests that Victor is looking for something. He talks as if he knows about the lizards. When he tells Victor to look in his palm, he shows him a tiny green lizard. Victor runs. When he finally gets home, he changes his clothes and finds in his pocket a pink card lettered "Herr Doctor, Prof. Horace Kupeckie, Plt.D. dreams expl., saws sharpened, etc., by appt. City Bus Terminal, Hogsboro."

Victor thinks about this as he eats and watches television and thinks he sees a lizard on Roger Mudd's shoulder. He watches the late movie about the Pod people who probably populate the earth. Victor figures that since Leslie is unreal the invasion has already taken place. He knows he walked among many Pods in the city. His attention returns fully when Lucas Cranach, Jr., who is being interviewed on the street by Bob Barney, waves and says "Hello" to Victor. Cranach and the Chicken Man and Professor Kupeckie are the same person.

After breakfast the next morning, Victor writes his observations about lizards in his notebook and thinks his science teacher would be proud of him. He returns to the old neighborhood only to see a realistic lizard poster advertising the zoo bus. He meets Shane Fergusson, the owner of a little corner store, who is a friend of Matthias Grunewald (the Chicken Man). Trying hard to understand what is happening to him, Victor goes on successive days to explore the zoo and reptile house with the man of many aliases who tells the boy to pick his favorite and so becomes Charlie, while at night Victor now also sees lizard game shows. Over hot dogs and root beer Charlie tries to explain real and pod-like people. Finally, he arranges to take Victor on a rubber raft to the middle of Lake Mishagoo (Indian for Lake-so-big-you-can't-see-other-side) adjacent to Hogsboro where Victor, he, and Claudia, the guide, arrive on Diamond Hard, the invisible, floating island inhabited by 5-foot lizards who walk upright and speak English. They are treated royally, especially Claudia, because Reynold the First deified an unhatched egg from which their new leader will hatch when an unexpected visitor comes ashore. Victor observes that many share the same name without confusion and that they serve a delicious food that tastes like everything. He is taken inside the volcano crater in which they live in a friendly unhurried manner to see their 4 monuments: The House of Plants (with a Truth Tree that goes Brrrh at lies); The House of Ideas (where for an Agama dollar you can shout your idea and thus preserve it); The House of the Egg (where Claudia who acts like she has been on the island before hatches the egg); and the House of Memory (where Victor finds his old stuffed pet squirrel). Charlie stays on Diamond Hard, as it starts to float away, to take care of Claudia who is taking care of the baby chick. Victor, however, is sent home on a surfboard pulled 20 miles to shore by a turtle.

A couple of days after this fantastic adventure, Leslie comes home followed by mom and dad who bring him a belt with a turquoise lizard on the silver buckle. When Victor checks to find that Shane Fergusson has not heard yet from Charlie and he is not picking up any lizard television shows either because the island has not started to float back, he waits patiently. Meanwhile, he saves his money to buy an inflatable raft and an intelligent chicken.

Thematic Analysis

This humorous story of a boy's fantastic adventure has a theme that augments its value as an exciting story. Its abstract concerns with simplicity of life-style, genuineness of human beings, and awareness of the environment are woven into the fabric of the story by a masterful plotter. It speaks directly to children who will absorb and appreciate the deep underlying message.

Discussion Materials

Introduce the setting, story, and Victor (pp. 9-18) and his first thoughts of lizards (pp. 18-22; picture p. 19). Also describe the first appearance of the Chicken Man, Charlie (pp. 25-27), and Shane Fergusson (pp. 55-59). Relate the notebook list of lizard observations (pp. 47-50). For television monster movie buffs tell about a couple of the movies that Victor sees that youngsters also may know: "The Island of Dr. Morbo," (pp. 16-17); "The Invasion of the Pod People," (pp. 38-40). Others may enjoy: visiting the zoo (pp. 63-64); the reptile house (pp. 78-83); story about eating (pp. 95-97); and the boat trip to Diamond Hard (pp. 99-107). Briefly tell that the island has lizard inhabitants and 4 museums, the House of Ideas, Memory, Plants, and the Egg that the visitors explore. The reader will do the rest.

Related Materials

A film or videocassette for individual use, *Universe* (IFB, 5 min., color) takes the human spirit traveling into other realms of space. *There Will Come Soft Rains* (Listening Library, 1977) presents a reading of a science fiction tale by Ray Bradbury; the title also appears as a filmstrip. For the nonfiction fans suggest the kit, *The Everglades: Exploring the Unknown* (Troll Associates, 1977). Two novels for the same readers are *The House in Norham Gardens* (Dutton, 1974) by Penelope Lively and *The House with a Clock in Its Walls* (Dial, 1973; pap., Dell, 1974) by John Bellairs. Both are time fantasies; the former is about a girl and a sacred New Guinea shield, the latter is about a boy and his uncle who is a wizard.

Biographical Index

Biographical information about authors may be found by consulting one of the sources listed here. The abbreviated form preceding the source is used in the index entries. For some authors, information was not available at time of publication. The following title was used as a preliminary check for all authors listed here: *Children's Authors and Illustrators: An Index to Biographical Dictionaries*, ed. by Dennis La Beau (Gale Research Co., 1976).

ABYP   *Authors of Books for Young People*, 2nd ed. Martha E. Ward and Dorothy A. Marquardt, eds. Metuchen, N.J.: Scarecrow Press, 1971.

AICB   *Authors and Illustrators of Children's Books: Writings on Their Lives and Works*. Miriam Hoffman and Eva Samuels, eds. New York: Bowker, 1972.

CA   *Contemporary Authors*, vols. 1-76. Detroit: Gale Research Co., 1962.

CB   *Children and Books*. Zena Sutherland and Mary Hill Arbuthnot, eds. Glenview, Ill.: Scott, Foresman, 1972.

CLR   *Children's Literature Review*, 2 vols. Ann Block and Carolyn Riley, eds. Detroit: Gale Research Co., 1976.

IBYP   *Illustrators of Books for Young People*. Martha E. Ward and Dorothy A. Marquardt, eds. Metuchen, N.J.: Scarecrow Press, 1975.

JBA   *The Junior Book of Authors*. Stanley J. Kunitz and Howard Haycraft, eds. New York: H. W. Wilson, 1951.

MJA   *More Junior Authors*. Muriel Fuller, ed. New York: H. W. Wilson, 1963.

SA   *Something about the Author: Facts and Pictures about Contemporary Authors and Illustrators of Books for Young People*, 10 vols. Anne Commire, ed. Detroit: Gale Research Co., 1971-1976.

TBJA   *Third Book of Junior Authors*. Doris De Montreville and Donna Hill, eds. New York: H. W. Wilson, 1972.

Title-Author-Illustrator Index

Titles fully discussed and summarized in *Introducing More Books* as well as those listed in "Related Materials" are cited in this index. An asterisk (*) precedes all fully discussed titles. Authors and illustrators are cited for fully discussed and summarized titles only. A dagger (†) precedes names of illustrators.

Subject Index

This index is intended to expand the possibilities for reading guidance by providing additional themes and topics for the titles that are discussed fully in this book. Other titles that fit in these categories can be found in the "Related Materials" section that appears in the treatment of the books listed below.